THE WORLD'S CLASSICS

603
EIGHTEENTH CENTURY
TRAGEDY

Oxford University Press, Amen House, London E.C.4

GLASGOW NEW YORK TORONTO MELBOURNE WELLINGTON
BOMBAY CALCUTTA MADRAS KARACHI LAHORE DACCA
CAPE TOWN SALISBURY NAIROBI IBADAN ACCRA
KUALA LUMPUR HONG KONG

EIGHTEENTH CENTURY TRAGEDY

Edited
with an Introduction
by
MICHAEL R. BOOTH

LONDON
OXFORD UNIVERSITY PRESS
NEW YORK   TORONTO
1965

This volume of
Eighteenth Century Tragedy
was first published in
The World's Classics
in 1965

Selection and Introduction
© Oxford University Press *1965*

PRINTED IN GREAT BRITAIN

CONTENTS

192030

CONTENTS

INTRODUCTION

THE eighteenth century is more noted for its comedy than its tragedy. The tragic writers did not really know what to do with their art; there was no general agreement as to what tragedy should be or what it should try to achieve. The reasons for its weakness are mainly two: the influence of Shakespeare and Elizabethan tragedy generally, and the conflict between current ideas in tragic writing which were opposed to each other on basic questions of treatment and emphasis. It is paradoxical that Shakespeare, whose frequency in the repertory and popularity among critics and editors were increasing steadily, should be like a dead hand across contemporary tragedy. But this is the case. Playwrights tried to copy his style and grandeur with disastrous results, an attempt which culminated in the fraudulent *Vortigern* at Drury Lane in 1796, a play by William Ireland which actually was performed as a previously undiscovered Shakespeare tragedy. The effort to be Elizabethan was, of course, at variance with the effort to be classical. In *Cato*, Addison had advanced as an ideal, not only in the form and verse of his tragedy, but also in his main character, an all-powerful and controlling Reason which exercised restraint and decorum and a civilizing morality utterly typical of the intellectual mode of the Queen Anne period. Following Addison, some authors tried to make the stuff of tragedy out of abstract ideals of morality and rationality; in effect, to present in dramatic form essentially non-dramatic matter, to discourse intellectually in a medium intended for the expression of deep human emotions and passions. The classical style naturally clashed with the legacy of Restoration heroic tragedy and its tempests of love, its passion-swept hero of abnormal martial prowess. Abdalla, in *Irene*, is a survival of the type, and his presence in a classical tragedy, like the prolonged and largely irrelevant love interest in *Cato*, is symptomatic of the uneasy compromise between old and new ideas that made a patchwork of many eighteenth-century tragedies. New ideas of the nature of man—his basic goodness, the importance of benevolence and good-heartedness, the evils of a corrupting society—quickly found their way into both comedy and tragedy, and are exemplified in *The London Merchant* and *The Gamester*. These two plays represent a different kind of tragedy in another respect also, a tragedy written entirely in prose with a domestic setting. Such concepts of man were capable of treatment in moral blacks and whites, and the underlying melodrama of the sentimental approach is merely continued and enlarged in later tragedies like *The Iron Chest*, where the ultimate absurdity of the moralistic and humanitarian robber chief is a comment on the awkwardness of the general adaptation of benevolent sentimentalism to dramatic form. Thus it can be seen that eighteenth-century tragedy is neither uniform nor coherent; nor are the styles briefly described here kept separate from each other, for two or three of them are often combined—with varying degrees of clumsiness, depending on the skill of the dramatist—into one play.

There is no need, however, to apologize for presenting a selection of eighteenth-century tragedies. Except for *Irene*, all the plays here were immensely popular, and remained stock pieces until at least the second half of the nineteenth century. The great actors of their time—Kemble, Mrs. Siddons, Kean, Macready, Irving—all played in them. Lady Randolph and Mrs. Beverley were two of Mrs. Siddons's great parts; Kean's performance of Sir Edward Mortimer was one of the theatrical sensations of his day. The four plays that did remain in the repertory offered a variety of excellent parts, and, in an age when the actor was generally more important than the play, the survival of these tragedies indicates that they possessed notable theatrical values. Collectively, they represent the most significant achievements of eighteenth-century tragic dramatists.

George Lillo's *The London Merchant*, or *The History of George Barnwell* (1731), was one of the first tragedies of the period with a domestic, middle-class setting. It was also the first tragedy of the century that deliberately appropriated the lofty moral aims of comedy which the comic writers had been loudly proclaiming since the Restoration, although their sincerity can be questioned. But Lillo was very serious indeed. For him, 'the more extensively useful the Moral of any Tragedy is, the more excellent that piece must be of its kind'. The purpose of tragedy is 'the exciting of the Passions, in order to the correcting such of them as are criminal, either in their nature, or through their excess'. The Prologue describes his play as a 'moral Tale'; it becomes the stage (in this case, tragedy) 'thoughtless Youth to warn, and shame the Age / From Vice destructive'. Characters in the play make moral points directly to the audience. So instructive was *The London Merchant* held to be that for years it was regularly acted on holidays for the edification of apprentices. Lillo felt that his moral aim could be attained within a framework of middle-class vice and virtue, and much of the Dedication and Prologue are given over to the justification of a tragedy of 'private woe'. He thus became one of the earliest advocates of the suitability of private and domestic life for tragic themes, and in a very real sense anticipated the work of Ibsen by more than a century. Unlike Ibsen, however, Lillo is hopelessly sentimental, and his play is steeped in the ethical benevolism of his time. The fifth act is a sermon on repentance and salvation, as well as a highly emotional treatment of friendship and love. The wise and virtuous Thorowgood is a stock sentimental figure, full of moral platitudes (though other characters are certainly not without them). Lillo's City background—he was a jeweller—is interestingly reflected in Thorowgood, who is the apotheosis of the English merchant, rather like Addison's Sir Andrew Freeport. The type had appeared before, in Steele's *The Conscious Lovers*, but *The London Merchant* has much more in it of the glories of commerce and the beneficence of the trading class. The rigidly enforced morality, and the emotional over-indulgence (the trademark of the sentimental dramatist) appear to us as faults, but they did not seem such to contemporary audiences. *The London Merchant* represented a new kind of play for the eighteenth century, a calculated attempt to change the direction of tragedy. Its value for us lies in this attempt rather than in its merit as a tragedy.

Edward Moore's *The Gamester* (1753) is greatly indebted to *The London Merchant*, and conceived in the same spirit of morality and sentimentality. Both men were working in the same area of domestic prose tragedy, and both plays have in common such stock sentimental devices as the basically good hero, corrupted only through weakness and the designs of a villain, the faithful friend, the good, suffering woman, help arriving just too late, and so on. Moore took from Lillo his prison setting and his pair of servants who betray the villain; in both plays the hero lies down on the ground and indulges in excesses of grief. In *The Gamester*, the trusty old retainer, Jarvis, exists solely to evoke emotional responses, as do the lengthy descriptions of Beverley's arrest and suffering in prison. The feelings that Moore wanted to arouse in audiences can be summed up in Mrs. Beverley's words to her maid: 'Thy sympathizing Heart bleeds for the Ills of others.' Nevertheless, *The Gamester* is a better play than *The London Merchant*. The morality is less overt, the tragic effect more powerful, the tension tighter, the language less stilted, and the sentimentality more under control. The dramatic climax of *The London Merchant* (though not its emotional one) comes in Act IV with the arrest of Barnwell and Millwood; the remainder of the play is static. In *The Gamester* the climax is delayed until the death of Beverley at the end of Act V. Suspense is an important element of dramatic effect, whereas in *The London Merchant* it is almost non-existent. Of course, Beverley is not a tragic figure, but then neither is Barnwell. The hero of true tragic stature appears rarely in eighteenth-century drama.

The new direction in tragedy taken by these plays was not followed up. This is unfortunate, because they represented an original kind of tragedy for the time, capable of powerful effects. For the next appearance of tragedies of social realism England had to wait for well over a hundred years.

If *The London Merchant* and *The Gamester* came from a new vein of tragedy, Samuel Johnson extracted *Irene* (1749) from one that had been pretty thoroughly worked out. The classical tragedy as English writers of the eighteenth century practised it was never generally popular in the theatre. The best play of the type, Addison's *Cato* (already printed in the World's Classics' volume of Restoration tragedies), owed its immediate success to political factors and the reputation of its author; its retention in the repertory for more than a century, however, indicates durable dramatic qualities. The fact that Kemble, at the end of the century, was a great Cato doubtless had something to do with it. Only two or three plays of this kind were regularly revived, and *Irene* never appeared again after an initial run prolonged to nine nights by the determined efforts of Garrick. The reasons are not hard to find. *Irene*'s faults are partly those of the classical genre: the unities preserved at the expense of a complete lack of action, the verse mechanical and declamatory. (Judging by the quality of the prologue, it is a pity that Johnson did not write the play in his beloved couplets.) Yet *Irene* is crippled in a characteristically Johnsonian way. Johnson is not interested in the love element, the conspiracy, or the possibility of a fight. What really concerns him is the moral and religious issue, and Irene herself becomes an inert figure, a battleground between the forces of moral right and human corruption. A totally passive heroine does not make a good tragedy; neither does the inhumanity of Johnson's moral mouthpiece, the stern Aspasia, who might have stepped straight into one of the weightier numbers of the *Rambler*. Those who stand up for virtue escape unharmed to a better life, while Irene, who succumbs to heathen luxury, pays with her neck. Johnson thus strictly enforces his belief in poetic justice in tragedy. The failure of *Irene*, then, is essentially not one of type, for Addison had shown that one could succeed with this sort of play. It is because of the attempt to dramatize Johnsonian morality in a way that rejects any exploitation of the potentially theatrical elements in the play. This

attempt is not surprising from one who criticized Shakespeare for writing without any moral purpose. *Irene* reflects
the eighteenth-century concern with morality in art to a
far more uncompromising extent than *The London Merchant*
and *The Gamester*. It is little wonder that it did not become
a stock play.

John Home's *Douglas* (1756) is a very different play.
Although it preserves the classical unities as strictly as
Irene, *Douglas* possesses theatrical excitement as well as
a real dignity and elevation. The grand passion of Lady
Randolph and the impetuous valour of Young Norval mark
two of the best characterizations in eighteenth-century
tragedy, though the play is weakened by a hackneyed
Machiavellian villain and action determined by chance
rather than character. One of the reasons for the popularity
of *Douglas* was the vague medievalism and romanticism of
its setting, qualities that were becoming fashionable in the
literary world. The note of romantic melancholy is sounded
at once:

> Ye woods and wilds, whose melancholy gloom
> Accords with my soul's sadness, and draws forth
> The voice of sorrow from my bursting heart,
> Farewel a while.

Although the verse of eighteenth-century tragedies is
usually execrable, this is not true of Home's dramatic
poetry, which in *Douglas* has a genuine strength combined
with a sense of economy sadly unpractised by the dramatic
poets of the age. It is true that there is too much talk
and too little action; this was a common failing in contemporary tragedy, whose authors experienced great difficulty
in making character reveal itself through relevant action
rather than through dialogue.

The last play in this selection, George Colman the
Younger's *The Iron Chest* (1796), has affinities with the
others, while at the same time containing something new.
Like Lillo and Moore, Colman used for his main character
a basically good man struck down by one dreadful fault, and

employed the common feature of the virtuous woman who unreservedly loves the faltering hero. Like Home, he used romantic elements in his setting. The gloomy hero with a mysterious past and tremendous passions is a truly romantic conception; indeed, Kean, the best of romantic actors, found Mortimer one of his best parts. Such a character belongs to nineteenth-century melodrama rather than eighteenth-century tragedy, and other aspects of *The Iron Chest* point forward to this melodrama: the mystery and suspense centred on the iron chest, the robber band, the extensive comic relief. One cannot really class *The Iron Chest* as a tragedy at all (it even has a happy ending); its tragic effects are dissipated among non-tragic material. This mixture sharply separates the play from the others in the edition. They are unmistakably single-effect tragedies. *The Iron Chest* is representative of the confusion of categories that marked dramatic writing around 1800, and in this respect is a fitting conclusion to a selection of eighteenth-century tragedies.

MICHAEL R. BOOTH

Royal Military College of Canada
June 1964

A NOTE ON THE TEXT

ALL the plays are printed from first editions, with the exception of *The Iron Chest*, where the third edition (the first to omit Colman's lengthy preface attacking Kemble) has been employed. I have used the Edinburgh edition of *Douglas*, which actually appeared a few days after the London edition, in order that I might be able to incorporate the details of the Covent Garden production which it contains; it is, moreover, the fuller text, the London one being a slightly abbreviated acting edition. The original texts are unaltered except for the correction of misprints and changes in punctuation for the sake of clarity.

M. R. B.

THE
LONDON
MERCHANT:

WITH THE
TRAGICAL HISTORY
OF
GEORGE BARNWELL.

Written by Mr. LILLO.

LONDON,
Printed in the year
MDCCXXXI.

Sir JOHN EYLES, Bart.

Member of Parliament for, & Alderman
of the City of *London*, and Sub-Governor
of the *South-Sea* Company

SIR,

IF Tragick Poetry be, as Mr. *Dryden* has some where said, the most excellent and most useful kind of writing, the more extensively useful the Moral of any Tragedy is, the more excellent that piece must be of its kind.

I hope I shall not be thought to insinuate that this, to which I have presumed to prefix your Name, is such; that depends on its fitness to answer the end of Tragedy, the exciting of the Passions, in order to the correcting such of them as are criminal, either in their nature, or through their excess. Whether the following Scenes do this in any tolerable degree, is, with the deference that becomes one who wou'd not be thought vain, submitted to your candid and impartial judgment.

What I wou'd infer is this, I think, evident truth; that Tragedy is so far from losing its dignity, by being accommodated to the circumstances of the generality of Mankind, that it is more truly august in proportion to the extent of its influence, & the numbers that are properly affected by it. As it is more truly great to be the instrument of good to many, who stand in need of our assistance, than to a very small part of that number.

If Princes, &c. were alone liable to misfortunes, arising from vice, or weakness in themselves, or others, there wou'd be good reason for confining the characters in Tragedy to those of superior rank; but, since the contrary is evident, nothing can be more reasonable than to proportion the remedy to the disease.

I am far from denying that Tragedies, founded on any instructive & extraordinary events in History, or a well-invented Fable, where the Persons introduced are of the highest rank, are without their use, even to the bulk of the audience. The strong contrast between a *Tamerlane* & a *Bajazet*, may have its weight with an unsteady People, and contribute to the fixing of them in the interest of a Prince of the character of the former, when, thro' their own levity, or the arts of designing Men, they are render'd factious and uneasy, tho' they have the highest reason to be satisfied. The sentiments and example of a *Cato*, may inspire his spectators with a just sense of the value of Liberty, when they see that honest Patriot prefer Death to an obligation from a Tyrant, who wou'd sacrifice the Constitution of his Country, and the Liberties of Mankind, to his Ambition or Revenge. I have attempted, indeed, to enlarge the province of the graver kind of Poetry, and should be glad to see it carried on by some abler hand. Plays, founded on moral Tales in private life, may be of admirable use, by carrying conviction to the mind, with such irresistible force, as to engage all the faculties & powers of the soul in the cause of Virtue, by stifling Vice in its first principles. They who imagine this to be too much to be attributed to Tragedy, must be strangers to the energy of that noble species of Poetry. *Shakespear*, who has given such amazing proofs of his genius, in that as well as in Comedy, in his *Hamlet*, has the following lines:

> *Had he the motive and the cause for Passion*
> *That I have ; he wou'd drown the Stage with tears ;*
> *And cleave the general Ear with horrid speech ;*
> *Make mad the Guilty, and appale the Free,*
> *Confound the Ignorant, and amaze indeed*
> *The very faculty of eyes and ears.*

And farther, in the same Speech,

> *I've heard that guilty Creatures at a Play,*
> *Have, by the very cunning of the Scene,*
> *Been so struck to the Soul, that presently*
> *They have proclaim'd their malefactions.*

Prodigious! yet strictly just. But I shan't take up your valuable time with my remarks; only give me leave just to observe, that he seems so firmly perswaded of the power of a well wrote Piece to produce the effect here ascribed to it, as to make *Hamlet* venture his Soul on the event, and rather trust that, than a Messenger from the other World, tho' it assumed, as he expresses it, his noble Father's form, and assured him, that it was his Spirit. I'll have, says *Hamlet*, grounds more relative.

> . . . *The Play's the thing,*
> *Wherein I'll catch the Conscience of the King.*

Such Plays are the best answers to them who deny the lawfulness of the Stage.

Considering the novelty of this attempt, I thought it would be expected from me to say something in its excuse; and I was unwilling to lose the opportunity of saying something of the usefulness of Tragedy in general, and what may be reasonably expected from the farther improvement of this excellent kind of Poetry.

SIR, I hope you will not think I have said too much of an Art, a mean specimen of which I am ambitious enough to recommend to your favour & protection. A Mind, conscious of superior worth, as much despises flattery, as it is above it. Had I found in my self an inclination to so contemptible a vice, I should not have chose Sir JOHN EYLES for my Patron. And indeed the best writ Panegyrick, tho' strictly true, must place you in a light, much inferior to that in which you have long been fix'd, by the love and esteem of your Fellow Citizens; whose choice of you for one of their Representatives in Parliament, has sufficiently declared their sense of your merit. Nor hath the knowledge of your worth been confined to the City. The Proprietors in the *South-Sea* Company, in which are included numbers of Persons, as considerable for their rank, fortune, and understanding, as any in the Kingdom, gave the greatest proof of their confidence, in your capacity and probity, when they chose you Sub-Governor of their Company, at a time when their affairs were in the utmost confusion, & their Properties in the greatest danger. Nor is the Court insensible of your importance. I shall not therefore attempt your Character, nor pretend to add any thing to a Reputation so well established.

Whatever others may think of a Dedication, wherein there is so much said of other things, & so little of the Person to whom it is address'd, I have reason to believe that you will the more easily pardon it on that very account.

I am, SIR,

Your most obedient humble Servant

GEORGE LILLO.

PROLOGUE

Spoke by Mr. CIBBER, Jun.

The Tragick Muse, sublime, delights to show
Princes distrest, and Scenes of Royal Woe;
In awful Pomp, Majestick, to relate
The Fall of Nations, or some Heroe's Fate:
That Scepter'd Chiefs may by example know
The strange Vicissitude of things below:
What dangers on security attend;
How Pride and Cruelty in Ruin end:
Hence Providence Supream to know; and own
Humanity adds Glory to a Throne.
  In ev'ry former Age, and Foreign Tongue,
With native grandure thus the Goddess sung.
Upon our Stage indeed, with wish'd success,
You've sometimes seen her in a humbler dress;
Great only in distress. When she complains
In Southern's, Rowe's, or Otway's moving strains,
The brillant drops, that fall from each bright eye,
The absent pomp, with brighter gems, supply.
Forgive us then, if we attempt to show,
In artless strains, a Tale of private woe.
A London Prentice ruin'd is our theme,
Drawn from the fam'd old Song, that bears his name.
We hope your taste is not so high to scorn
A moral Tale, esteem'd e'er you were born;
Which for a Century of rolling years,
Has fill'd a thousand-thousand eyes with tears.
If thoughtless Youth to warn, and shame the Age
From Vice destructive, well becomes the Stage;
If this Example Innocence secure,
Prevent our guilt, or by reflection cure;
If Millwood's dreadful guilt, and sad despair,
Commend the Virtue of the Good and Fair,
Tho' Art be wanting, and our Numbers fail,
Indulge th' attempt in justice to the Tale.

DRAMATIS PERSONÆ

MEN

THOROWGOOD	Mr. *Bridgwater*
BARNWELL	*Uncle to* GEORGE, Mr. *Roberts*
GEORGE BARNWELL	Mr. *Cibber*, Jun.
TRUEMAN	Mr. *W. Mills*
BLUNT	Mr. *R. Wetherilt*

WOMEN

MARIA	Mrs. *Cibber*
MILLWOOD	Mrs. *Butler*
LUCY	Mrs. *Charke*

Officers with their Attendants, Keeper, & Footmen

SCENE London, *and an adjacent Village*

THE

LONDON MERCHANT

OR, THE

HISTORY

OF

GEORGE BARNWELL

ACT I. SCENE I

A Room in Thorowgood's *House*

THOROWGOOD *and* TRUEMAN

Tr. Sir, the Packet from *Genoa* is arriv'd.   (*Gives Letters.*

Thor. Heav'n be praised, the Storm that threaten'd our Royal Mistress, pure Religion, Liberty, & Laws, is for a time diverted; the haughty and revengeful *Spaniard*, disappointed of the Loan on which he depended from *Genoa*, must now attend the slow return of wealth from his new World, to supply his empty coffers, e'er he can execute his purpos'd Invasion of our happy Island; by which means time is gain'd to make such preparations on our part, as may, Heav'n concurring, prevent his malice, or turn the meditated mischief on himself.

Tr. He must be insensible indeed, who is not affected when the safety of his Country is concern'd.—Sir, may I know by what means—if I am too bold—

Thor. Your curiosity is laudable; and I gratify it with the greater pleasure, because from thence you may learn, how honest Merchants, as such, may sometimes contribute to the safety of their Country, as they do at all times to its happiness; that if hereafter you should be tempted to any action that has the appearance of vice or meanness in it, upon reflecting on the Dignity of our Profession, you may with honest scorn reject whatever is unworthy of it.

Tr. Shou'd *Barnwell*, or I, who have the benefit of your Example, by our ill conduct bring any imputation on that honourable Name, we must be left without excuse.

Thor. You complement, young Man.—

(Trueman *bows respectfully.*
Nay, I'm not offended. As the Name of Merchant never degrades the Gentleman, so by no means does it exclude him; only take heed not to purchase the character of complaisant at the expence of your sincerity.—But to answer your question,—The Bank of *Genoa* had agreed, at excessive Interest & on good Security, to advance the King of *Spain* a Sum of money sufficient to equip his vast Armado,—of which our peerless *Elizabeth* (more than in name the Mother of her People) being well informed, sent *Walsingham*, her wise and faithful Secretary, to consult the Merchants of this loyal City, who all agreed to direct their several Agents to influence, if possible, the *Genoese* to break their Contract with the *Spanish* Court. 'Tis done, the State and Bank of *Genoa*, having maturely weigh'd and rightly judged of their true interest, prefer the friendship of the Merchants of *London*, to that of a Monarch, who proudly stiles himself King of both *Indies*.

Tr. Happy success of prudent Councils. What an expence of Blood and Treasure is here saved!—Excellent Queen! O how unlike to former Princes, who made the danger of foreign Enemies a pretence to oppress their Subjects, by Taxes great & grievous to be born.

Thor. Not so our gracious Queen, whose richest Exchequer is her Peoples love, as their happiness her greatest Glory.

Tr. On these terms to defend us, is to make our protection a benefit worthy her who confers it, and well worth our acceptance.—Sir, have you any commands for me at this time?

Thor. Only to look carefully over the files to see whether there are any Trades-mens Bills unpaid; & if there are, to send & discharge 'em. We must not let Artificers lose their time, so useful to the Publick and their Families, in unnecessary attendance.

SCENE II

THOROWGOOD *and* MARIA

Thor. Well, *Maria*, have you given orders for the Entertainment? I would have it in some measure worthy the Guests. Let there be plenty, and of the best; that the Courtiers, tho' they should deny us Citizens politeness, may at least commend our Hospitality.

Ma. Sir, I have endeavoured not to wrong your well-known Generosity by an ill-tim'd Parsimony.

Thor. Nay, 'twas a needless caution, I have no cause to doubt your prudence.

Ma. Sir, I find my self unfit for conversation at present, I should but increase the number of the company, without adding to their satisfaction.

Thor. Nay, My Child, this melancholy must not be indulged.

Ma. Company will but increase it. I wish you would dispense with my absence; Solitude best suits my present temper.

Thor. You are not insensible that it is chiefly on your account these noble Lords do me the Honour so frequently to grace my Board; shou'd you be absent, the disappointment may make them repent their condescension, and think their labour lost.

Ma. He that shall think his time or Honour lost in visiting you, can set no real value on your Daughter's company, whose only merit is that she is yours. The Man of Quality, who chuses to converse with a Gentleman & Merchant of your worth & character, may confer Honour by so doing, but he loses none.

Thor. Come, come, *Maria*, I need not tell you that a young Gentleman may prefer your conversation to mine, yet intend me no disrespect at all; for tho' he may lose no Honour in my company, 'tis very natural for him to expect more pleasure in yours. I remember the time, when the company of the greatest and wisest Man in the Kingdom would have been insipid and tiresome to me, if it had deprived me of an opportunity of enjoying your Mother's.

Ma. Your's no doubt was as agreeable to her; for generous Minds know no pleasure in society but where 'tis mutual.

Thor. Thou know'st I have no Heir, no Child but thee; the fruits of many years successful industry must all be thine; now it would give me pleasure great as my love, to see on whom you would bestow it. I am daily solicited by Men of the greatest rank and merit for leave to address you, but I have hitherto declin'd it, in hopes that by observation I shou'd learn which way your inclination tends; for as I know love to be essential to happiness in the marriage state, I had rather my approbation should confirm your choice, than direct it.

Ma. What can I say? How shall I answer, as I ought, this tenderness, so uncommon, even in the best of Parents? But you are without example: yet had you been less indulgent, I had been most wretched. That I look on the Croud of Courtiers, that visit here, with equal esteem, but equal indifference, you have observed, and I must needs confess; yet had you asserted your authority, & insisted on a Parent's right to be obey'd, I had submitted, & to my Duty sacrificed my Peace.

Thor. From your perfect obedience in every other instance, I fear'd as much; & therefore wou'd leave you without a byass in an affair wherein your happiness is so immediately concern'd.

Ma. Whether from a want of that just ambition that wou'd become your Daughter, or from some other cause I know not; but, I find high birth and Titles don't recommend the Man, who owns them, to my affections.

Thor. I wou'd not that they shou'd, unless his merit recommends him more. A noble birth and fortune, tho' they make not a bad Man good, yet they are a real advantage to a worthy one, & place his Virtues in the fairest light.

Ma. I cannot answer for my inclinations, but they shall ever be submitted to your wisdom & authority; and as you will not compel me to marry where I cannot love, so Love shall never make me act contrary to my Duty. Sir, have I your permission to retire?

Thor. I'll see you to your chamber.

SCENE III. *A Room in* Millwood's *House*

MILLWOOD. LUCY *Waiting*

Mill. How do I look to-day, *Lucy*?

Lucy. O, killingly, Madam!—A little more red, and you'll be irresistible!—But why this more than ordinary care of your Dress and Complexion? What new Conquest are you aiming at?

Mill. A Conquest wou'd be new indeed!

Lucy. Not to you, who make 'em every day,—but to me.—Well! 'tis what I'm never to expect,—unfortunate as I am:—But your Wit and Beauty—

Mill. First made me a Wretch, and still continue me so.—Men, however generous or sincere to one another, are all selfish Hypocrites in their affairs with us. We are no otherwise esteemed or regarded by them, but as we contribute to their satisfaction.

Lucy. You are certainly, Madam, on the wrong side in this argument: Is not the expence all theirs? And I am sure it is our own fault if we hav'n't our share of the pleasure.

Mill. We are but Slaves to Men.

Lucy. Nay, 'tis they that are Slaves most certainly; for we lay them under contribution.

Mill. Slaves have no property: no, not even in themselves.—All is the Victors.

Lucy. You are strangely arbitrary in your Principles, Madam.

Mill. I would have my Conquests compleat, like those of the *Spaniards* in the New-World; who first plunder'd the Natives of all the wealth they had, and then condemn'd the Wretches to the Mines for life, to work for more.

Lucy. Well, I shall never approve of your scheme of Government: I should think it much more politick, as well as just, to find my Subjects an easier imployment.

Mill. It's a general maxim among the knowing part of Mankind, that a Woman without Virtue, like a Man without Honour or Honesty, is capable of any action, tho' never so vile: And yet what pains will they not take, what arts not use, to seduce us from our innocence, & make us contemptible & wicked, even in their own opinions? Then is it not just, the Villains, to their cost, should find us so.—But guilt makes them suspicious, & keeps them on their guard; therefore we can take advantage only of the young & innocent part of the Sex, who having never injured Women, apprehend no injury from them.

Lucy. Ay, they must be young indeed.

Mill. Such a one, I think, I have found.—As I've passed thro' the City, I have often observ'd him receiving and paying considerable sums of Money; from thence I conclude he is employ'd in affairs of consequence.

Lucy. Is he handsome?

Mill. Ay, ay, the Stripling is well made.

Lucy. About—

Mill. Eighteen—

Lucy. Innocent, handsome, & about eighteen.—You'll be vastly happy.—Why, if you manage well, you may keep him to your self these two or three years.

Mill. If I manage well, I shall have done with him much sooner, having long had a design on him; & meeting him yesterday, I made a full stop, & gazing wishfully on his face, ask'd him his name: He blush'd, & bowing very low, answer'd, *George Barnwell.* I beg'd his pardon for the freedom I had taken, & told him, that he was the person I had

long wish'd to see, and to whom I had an affair of importance to communicate, at a proper time & place. He named
a Tavern; I talk'd of Honour and Reputation, and invited
him to my house: He swallow'd the bait, promis'd to come,
and this is the time I expect him. (*knocking at the door*.)
Some-body knocks,—d'ye hear; I am at home to no-body
to-day, but him.—

SCENE IV

Millwood

Mill. Less affairs must give way to those of more consequence; and I am strangely mistaken if this does not prove
of great importance to me & him too, before I have done
with him.—Now after what manner shall I receive him?
Let me consider—what manner of person am I to receive?—He is young, innocent, & bashful; therefore I
must take care not to shock him at first.—But then, if I
have any skill in phisiognomy, he is amorous, &, with a
little assistance, will soon get the better of his modesty.—
I'll trust to Nature, who does wonders in these matters.—
If to seem what one is not, in order to be the better liked
for what one really is; if to speak one thing, & mean the
direct contrary, be Art in a Woman, I know nothing of
Nature.

SCENE V

To her BARNWELL *bowing very low*, LUCY *at a distance*

Mill. Sir! the surprize and joy!—
Barn. Madam.—
Mill. This is such a favour,—   (*advancing.*
Barn. Pardon me, Madam,—
Mill. So unhop'd for,—   (*still advances.*
      (Barnwell *salutes her, and retires in confusion.*

Mill. To see you here.—Excuse the confusion.—

Barn. I fear I am too bold.—

Mill. Alas, Sir! All my apprehensions proceed from my fears of your thinking me so.—Please, Sir, to sit.— I am as much at a loss how to receive this honour as I ought, as I am surpriz'd at your goodness in confering it.

Barn. I thought you had expected me—I promis'd to come.

Mill. That is the more surprizing; few Men are such religious observers of their word.

Barn. All, who are honest, are.

Mill. To one another:—But we silly Women are seldom thought of consequence enough to gain a place in your remembrance.   *(Laying her hand on his, as by accident.*

Barn. Her disorder is so great, she don't perceive she has laid her hand on mine.—Heaven! how she trembles!— What can this mean!   *(Aside.*

Mill. The interest I have in all that relates to you, (the reason of which you shall know hereafter) excites my curiosity; and, were I sure you would pardon my presumption, I should desire to know your real sentiments on a very particular affair.

Barn. Madam, you may command my poor thoughts on any subject;—I have none that I would conceal.

Mill. You'll think me bold.

Barn. No, indeed.

Mill. What then are your thoughts of Love?

Barn. If you mean the Love of Women, I have not thought of it at all.—My youth and circumstances make such thoughts improper in me yet: But if you mean the general Love we owe to Mankind, I think no one has more of it in his temper than my self.—I don't know that Person in the world whose happiness I don't wish, and wou'dn't promote, were it in my power.—In an especial manner I love my Uncle, and my Master, but above all, my Friend.

Mill. You have a Friend then, whom you love?

Barn. As he does me, sincerely.

Mill. He is, no doubt, often bless'd with your company and conversation.—

Barn. We live in one house together, & both serve the same worthy Merchant.

Mill. Happy, happy Youth!—who e'er thou art, I envy thee, and so must all who see and know this Youth.— What have I lost, by being form'd a Woman!—I hate my Sex, my self.—Had I been a Man, I might, perhaps, have been as happy in your Friendship, as he who now enjoys it:—But as it is,—Oh!—

Barn. I never observ'd Women before, or this is sure the most beautiful of her Sex. (*Aside.*) You seem disorder'd, Madam! May I know the cause?

Mill. Do not ask me,—I can never speak it, whatever is the cause;—I wish for things impossible:—I wou'd be a Servant, bound to the same Master as you are, to live in one house with you.

Barn. How strange, and yet how kind, her words and actions are? And the effect they have on me is as strange.— I feel desires I never knew before;—I must be gone, while I have power to go. (*Aside.*) Madam, I humbly take my leave.—

Mill. You will not sure leave me so soon!

Barn. Indeed I must.

Mill. You cannot be so cruel!—I have prepar'd a poor supper, at which I promis'd my self your company.

Barn. I am sorry I must refuse the honour that you de- sign'd me,—but my duty to my Master calls me hence.—I never yet neglected his service: He is so gentle, and so good a Master, that should I wrong him, tho' he might forgive me, I never should forgive my self.

Mill. Am I refus'd, by the first Man, the second favour I ever stoop'd to ask?—Go then thou proud hard-hearted Youth.—But know, you are the only Man that cou'd be found, who would let me sue twice for greater favours.

Barn. What shall I do!—How shall I go or stay!

Mill. Yet do not, do not leave me.—I wish my Sex's pride wou'd meet your scorn:—But when I look upon you, when I behold those eyes,—Oh! spare my tongue, and let my blushes speak.—This flood of tears to that will force their way, and declare—what Woman's modesty should hide.

Barn. Oh, Heavens! she loves me, worthless as I am; her looks, her words, her flowing tears confess it: And can I leave her then?—Oh, never,—never.—Madam, dry up those tears.—You shall command me always;—I will stay here for ever, if you'd have me.

Lucy. So! she has wheedled him out of his virtue of obedience already, & will strip him of all the rest, one after another, 'till she has left him as few as her Ladyship, or my self.   (*Aside.*

Mill. Now you are kind, indeed; but I mean not to detain you always: I would have you shake off all slavish obedience to your Master;—but you may serve him still.

Lucy. Serve him still!—Aye, or he'll have no opportunity of fingering his Cash, & then he'll not serve your end, I'll be sworn.   (*Aside.*

SCENE VI

(*To them.*) BLUNT

Blunt. Madam, Supper's on the table.

Mill. Come, Sir, You'll excuse all defects.—My thoughts were too much employ'd on my Guest to observe the Entertainment.

SCENE VII

LUCY *and* BLUNT

Blunt. What, is all this preparation, this elegant Supper, variety of Wines, and Musick, for the entertainment of that young Fellow?

Lucy. So it seems.

Blunt. What, is our Mistress turn'd Fool at last? She's in love with him, I suppose.

Lucy. I suppose not,—but she designs to make him in love with her, if she can.

Blunt. What will she get by that? He seems under age, and can't be suppos'd to have much Money.

Lucy. But his Master has; & that's the same thing, as she'll manage it.

Blunt. I don't like this fooling with a handsome young Fellow; while she's endeavouring to ensnare him, she may be caught her self.

Lucy. Nay, were she like me, that would certainly be the consequence;—for, I confess, there is something in youth & innocence that moves me mightily.

Blunt. Yes, so does the smoothness and plumpness of a Partridge move a mighty desire in the Hawk to be the destruction of it.

Lucy. Why, Birds are their prey, as Men are ours; though, as you observ'd, we are sometimes caught our selves:— But that I dare say will never be the case with our Mistress.

Blunt. I wish it may prove so; for you know we all depend upon her: Should she trifle away her time with a young Fellow, that there's nothing to be got by, we must all starve.

Lucy. There's no danger of that, for I am sure she has no view in this affair, but interest.

Blunt. Well, and what hopes are there of success in that?

Lucy. The most promising that can be.—'Tis true, the Youth has his scruples; but she'll soon teach him to answer them, by stifling his Conscience.—O, the Lad is in a hopeful way, depend upon't.

SCENE VIII

BARNWELL *and* MILLWOOD *at an Entertainment*

Barn. What can I answer!—All that I know is, that you are fair, and I am miserable.

Mill. We are both so, and yet the fault is in our selves.

Barn. To ease our present anguish, by plunging into guilt, is to buy a moment's pleasure with an age of pain.

Mill. I should have thought the joys of love as lasting as they are great: If ours prove otherwise, 'tis your inconstancy must make them so.

Barn. The Law of Heaven will not be revers'd; and that requires us to govern our Passions.

Mill. To give us sense of beauty and desires, and yet forbid us to taste and be happy, is cruelty to Nature.—Have we Passions only to torment us!

Barn. To hear you talk,—tho' in the cause of Vice,— to gaze upon your Beauty,—press your hand,—and see your snow-white bosom heave and fall,—enflames my wishes;—my pulse beats high,—my senses all are in a hurry, & I am on the rack of wild desire;—yet for a moment's guilty pleasure, shall I lose my innocence, my peace of mind, and hopes of solid happiness?

Mill. Chimeras all,—

  —Come on with me and prove,
  No joy's like Woman kind, nor Heav'n like Love.

Barn. I wou'd not,—yet I must on.—

Reluctant thus, the Merchant quits his ease,
And trusts to rocks, and sands, and stormy Seas;
In hopes some unknown golden coast to find,
Commits himself, tho' doubtful, to the wind,
Longs much for joys to come, yet mourns those left behind.

ACT II. SCENE I

A Room in Thorowgood's *House*

BARNWELL

Barn. How strange are all things round me? Like some Thief, who treads forbidden ground, fearful I enter each apartment of this well known house. To guilty love, as if that was too little, already have I added breach of trust.—A Thief!—Can I know my self that wretched thing, and look my honest Friend and injured Master in the face?—Tho' Hypocrisy may a while conceal my guilt, at length it will be known, and publick shame & ruin must ensue. In the mean time, what must be my life? ever to speak a language foreign to my heart; hourly to add to the number of my crimes in order to conceal 'em.—Sure such was the condition of the grand Apostate, when first he lost his purity; like me disconsolate he wander'd, and while yet in Heaven, bore all his future Hell about him.

SCENE II

BARNWELL *and* TRUEMAN

Tr. Barnwell! O how I rejoice to see you safe! so will our Master & his gentle Daughter, who during your absence often inquir'd after you.

Barn. Wou'd he were gone, his officious love will pry into the secrets of my soul. *(Aside.*

Tr. Unless you knew the pain the whole Family has felt on your account, you can't conceive how much you are belov'd; but why thus cold & silent? when my heart is full of joy for your return, why do you turn away? why thus avoid me? what have I done? how am I alter'd since you saw me last? Or rather what have you done? and why are you thus changed? for I am still the same.

Barn. What have I done indeed?   (*Aside.*

Tr. Not speak, nor look upon me!

Barn. By my face he will discover all I wou'd conceal; methinks already I begin to hate him.   (*Aside.*

Tr. I cannot bear this usage from a Friend, one whom till now I ever found so loving, whom yet I love, tho' this unkindness strikes at the root of Friendship, and might destroy it in any breast but mine.

Barn. I am not well. (*Turning to him.*) Sleep has been a stranger to these eyes since you beheld them last.

Tr. Heavy they look indeed, & swoln with tears;—now they o'erflow;—rightly did my sympathizing heart forebode last night when thou wast absent, something fatal to our peace.

Barn. Your Friendship ingages you too far. My troubles, whate'er they are, are mine alone; you have no interest in them, nor ought your concern for me to give you a moment's pain.

Tr. You speak as if you knew of Friendship nothing but the name. Before I saw your grief I felt it. Since we parted last I have slept no more than you, but pensive in my chamber sat alone, and spent the tedious night in wishes for your safety and return; e'en new, tho' ignorant of the cause, your sorrow wounds me to the heart.

Barn. 'Twill not be always thus. Friendship and all engagements cease, as circumstances and occasions vary; and since you once may hate me, perhaps it might be better for us both that now you lov'd me less.

Tr. Sure I but dream; without a cause would *Barnwell* use me thus? Ungenerous and ungrateful Youth, farewell;—I shall endeavour to follow your advice.—(*Going.*) Yet stay, perhaps I am too rash, and angry when the cause demands compassion. Some unforeseen calamity may have befaln him too great to bear.

Barn. What part am I reduc'd to act;—'tis vile & base to move his temper thus, the best of Friends & Men.

Tr. I am to blame, prithee forgive me *Barnwell*—Try to compose your rufled mind, & let me know the cause that thus transports you from your self; my friendly counsel may restore your peace.

Barn. All that is possible for Man to do for Man, your generous Friendship may effect; but here even that's in vain.

Tr. Something dreadful is labouring in your breast. O give it vent & let me share your grief; 'twill ease your pain shou'd it admit no cure; & make it lighter by the part I bear.

Barn. Vain supposition! my woes increase by being observ'd; shou'd the cause be known they wou'd exceed all bounds.

Tr. So well I know thy honest heart, guilt cannot harbour there.

Barn. O torture insupportable!   (*Aside.*

Tr. Then why am I excluded? have I a thought I would conceal from you?

Barn. If still you urge me on this hated subject, I'll never enter more beneath this roof, nor see your face again.

Tr. 'Tis strange,—but I have done, say but you hate me not.

Barn. Hate you!—I am not that Monster yet.

Tr. Shall our Friendship still continue.

Barn. It's a blessing I never was worthy of, yet now must stand on terms; and but upon conditions can confirm it.

Tr. What are they?

Barn. Never hereafter, tho' you shou'd wonder at my conduct, desire to know more than I am willing to reveal.

Tr. 'Tis hard, but upon any conditions I must be your Friend.

Barn. Then, as much as one lost to himself can be another's, I am yours.   (*Embracing.*

Tr. Be ever so, & may Heav'n restore your peace.

Barn. Will yesterday return?—We have heard the glorious Sun, that till then incessant roll'd, once stopp'd his rapid course, and once went back: The dead have risen; and parched rocks pour'd forth a liquid stream to quench a Peoples thirst: The Sea divided, and form'd walls of water, while a whole Nation pass'd in safety thro' its sandy bosom: Hungry Lions have refus'd their prey: And Men unhurt have walk'd amidst consuming flames; but never yet did Time once past, return.

Tr. Tho' the continued chain of Time has never once been broke, nor ever will, but uninterrupted must keep on its course, till lost in Eternity it ends there where it first begun; yet as Heav'n can repair whatever evils Time can bring upon us, he who trusts Heaven ought never to despair. But busines requires our attendance, Business the Youth's best preservative from ill, as idleness his worst of snares. Will you go with me?

Barn. I'll take a little time to reflect on what has past, and follow you.

SCENE III

BARNWELL

I might have trusted *Trueman* to have applied to my Uncle to have repaired the wrong I have done my Master; but what of *Millwood*? must I expose her too? ungenerous and base! then Heav'n requires it not.—But Heaven requires that I forsake her. What! never see her more! Does Heaven require that,—I hope I may see her, and Heav'n not be offended. Presumptuous hope,—dearly already have I prov'd my frailty; should I once more tempt Heav'n, I may be left to fall, never to rise again. Yet shall I leave her, for ever leave her, and not let her know the cause? She who loves me with such a boundless passion; can cruelty be duty? I judge of what she then must feel, by what I now indure. The love of life & fear of shame, oppos'd by inclination strong as death or shame, like wind and tide in raging conflict met, when neither can prevail, keep me in doubt.—How then can I determine?

SCENE IV

THOROWGOOD *and* BARNWELL

Thor. Without a cause assign'd, or notice given, to absent your self last night was a fault, young Man, and I came to chide you for it, but hope I am prevented; that modest blush, the confusion so visible in your face, speak grief and shame: When we have offended Heaven, it requires no more; & shall Man, who needs himself to be forgiven, be harder to appease? If my pardon or love be of moment to your peace, look up secure of both.

Barn. This goodness has o'ercome me. (*Aside.*) O Sir! you know not the nature and extent of my offence; and I shou'd abuse your mistaken bounty to receive 'em. Tho' I had rather die than speak my shame; tho' Racks could not have forced the guilty secret from my breast, your kindness has.

Thor. Enough, enough, whate'er it be, this concern shews you're convinc'd, & I am satisfied. How painful is the sense of Guilt to an ingenuous Mind;—some youthful folly, which it were prudent not to enquire into.—When we consider the frail condition of Humanity, it may raise our pity, not our wonder, that Youth should go astray; when Reason, weak at the best when oppos'd to Inclination, scarce form'd, & wholly unassisted by Experience, faintly contends, or willingly becomes the slave of Sense. The state of Youth is much to be deplored; and the more so because they see it not; they being then to danger most expos'd, when they are least prepar'd for their defence.

Barn. It will be known, & you recall your pardon and abhor me.

Thor. I never will; so Heav'n confirm to me the pardon of my offences. Yet be upon your guard in this gay thoughtless season of your life; now, when the sense of pleasure's quick, and passion high, the voluptuous appetites raging and fierce demand the strongest curb; take heed of a relapse: When Vice becomes habitual, the very power of leaving it is lost.

Barn. Hear me then on my knees confess.

Thor. I will not hear a syllable more upon this subject; it were not mercy, but cruelty, to hear what must give you such torment to reveal.

Barn. This Generosity amazes and distracts me.

Thor. This remorse makes thee dearer to me than if thou hadst never offended; whatever is your fault, of this I'm certain, 'twas harder for you to offend than me to pardon.

SCENE V

BARNWELL

Barn. Villain, Villain, Villain! basely to wrong so excellent a Man. Shou'd I again return to folly—detested thought; but what of *Millwood* then?—Why, I renounce her;—I give her up;—the struggle's over, & Virtue has prevail'd. Reason may convince, but Gratitude compels. This unlook'd for generosity has sav'd me from destruction.   *Going.*

SCENE VI

To him a FOOTMAN

Foot. Sir, two Ladies, from your Uncle in the Country, desire to see you.

Barn. Who shou'd they be? (*Aside.*) Tell them I'll wait upon 'em.

SCENE VII

BARNWELL

Barn. Methinks I dread to see 'em.—Guilt, what a Coward hast thou made me?—Now every thing alarms me.

SCENE VIII

Another Room in Thorowgood's *House*

MILLWOOD *and* LUCY, *and to them a* FOOTMAN

Foot. Ladies, he'll wait upon you immediately.
Mill. 'Tis very well.—I thank you.

SCENE IX

BARNWELL, MILLWOOD, *and* LUCY

Barn. Confusion! *Millwood!*

Mill. That angry look tells me that here I'm an unwelcome Guest; I fear'd as much,—the unhappy are so every where.

Barn. Will nothing but my utter ruin content you?

Mill. Unkind & cruel! lost my self, your happiness is now my only care.

Barn. How did you gain admission?

Mill. Saying we were desir'd by your Uncle to visit and deliver a Message to you, we were receiv'd by the Family without suspicion, and with much respect directed here.

Barn. Why did you come at all?

Mill. I never shall trouble you more, I'm come to take my leave for ever. Such is the malice of my Fate. I go hopeless, despairing ever to return. This hour is all I have left me. One short hour is all I have to bestow on Love & you, for whom I thought the longest life too short.

Barn. Then we are met to part for ever?

Mill. It must be so;—yet think not that time or absence ever shall put a period to my grief, or make me love you less; tho' I must leave you, yet condemn me not.

Barn. Condemn you? No, I approve your resolution, & rejoice to hear it; 'tis just,—'tis necessary,—I have well weigh'd, and found it so.

Lucy. I'm afraid the young Man has more sense than she thought he had.   (*Aside.*

Barn. Before you came I had determin'd never to see you more.

Mill. Confusion!   (*Aside.*

Lucy. Ay! we are all out; this is a turn so unexpected, that I shall make nothing of my part, they must e'en play the Scene betwixt themselves.   (*Aside.*

Mill. 'Twas some relief to think, tho' absent, you would love me still; but to find, tho' Fortune had been kind, that you, more cruel & inconstant, had resolv'd to cast me off.— This, as I never cou'd expect, I have not learnt to bear.

Barn. I am sorry to hear you blame in me, a resolution that so well becomes us both.

Mill. I have reason for what I do, but you have none.

Barn. Can we want a reason for parting, who have so many to wish we never had met.

Mill. Look on me *Barnwell*, am I deform'd or old, that satiety so soon succeeds enjoyment? nay, look again, am I not she whom yesternight you thought the fairest and the kindest of her Sex? whose hand, trembling with extacy, you prest and moulded thus, while on my eyes you gazed with such delight, as if desire increas'd by being fed?

Barn. No more; let me repent my former follies, if possible, without remembring what they were.

Mill. Why?

Barn. Such is my frailty that 'tis dangerous.

Mill. Where is the danger, since we are to part?

Barn. The thought of that already is too painful.

Mill. If it be painful to part, then I may hope at least you do not hate me?

Barn. No,—no,—I never said I did,—O my Heart!—

Mill. Perhaps you pity me?

Barn. I do,—I do,—indeed, I do.

Mill. You'll think upon me?

Barn. Doubt it not while I can think at all.

Mill. You may judge an embrace at parting too great a favour, though it would be the last? (*He draws back.*) A look shall then suffice,—farewell for ever.

SCENE X

BARNWELL

Barn. If to resolve to suffer be to conquer, I have con-quer'd. Painful Victory!

SCENE XI

BARNWELL, MILLWOOD, *and* LUCY

Mill. One thing I had forgot,—I never must return to my own house again. This I thought proper to let you know, lest your mind should change, & you shoud seek in vain to find me there. Forgive me this second intrusion; I only came to give you this caution, and that perhaps was needless.

Barn. I hope it was, yet it is kind, and I must thank you for it.

Mill. My Friend, your arm. (*To* Lucy.) Now I am gone for ever. (*Going.*

Barn. One thing more;—sure there's no danger in my knowing where you go? If you think otherwise—

Mill. Alas! (*Weeping.*

Lucy. We are right I find, that's my cue. (*Aside.*) Ah; dear Sir, she's going she knows not whither; but go she must.

Barn. Humanity obliges me to wish you well; why will you thus expose your self to needless troubles?

Lucy. Nay, there's no help for it: She must quit the Town immediately, and the Kingdom as soon as possible: it was no small matter, you may be sure, that could make her resolve to leave you.

Mill. No more, my Friend; since he for whose dear sake alone I suffer, and am content to suffer, is kind and pities me. Where'er I wander through wilds & desarts, benighted & forlorn, that thought shall give me comfort.

Barn. For my sake! O tell me how; which way am I so curs'd as to bring such ruin on thee?

Mill. No matter, I am contented with my lot.

Barn. Leave me not in this incertainty.

Mill. I have said too much.

Barn. How, how am I the cause of your undoing?

Mill. 'Twill but increase your troubles.

Barn. My troubles can't be greater than they are.

Lucy. Well, well, Sir, if she won't satisfy you, I will.

Barn. I am bound to you beyond expression.

Mill. Remember, Sir, that I desir'd you not to hear it.

Barn. Begin, and ease my racking expectation.

Lucy. Why you must know, my Lady here was an only Child; but her Parents dying while she was young, left her and her Fortune, (no inconsiderable one, I assure you) to the care of a Gentleman, who has a good Estate of his own.

Mill. Ay, ay, the barbarous Man is rich enough;—but what are Riches when compared to Love?

Lucy. For a while he perform'd the office of a faithful Guardian, settled her in a house, hir'd her Servants:—but you have seen in what manner she liv'd, so I need say no more of that.

Mill. How I shall live hereafter, Heaven knows.

Lucy. All things went on as one cou'd wish, till, some time ago, his Wife dying, he fell violently in love with his charge, and wou'd fain have marry'd her: Now the Man is neither old nor ugly, but a good personable sort of a Man; but I don't know how it was, she cou'd never endure him; in short, her ill usage so provok'd him, that he brought in an account of his Executorship, wherein he makes her debtor to him.—

Mill. A trifle in it self, but more than enough to ruin me, whom, by this unjust account, he had stripp'd of all before.

Lucy. Now she having neither money, nor Friend, except me, who am as unfortunate as her self, he compell'd her to pass his account, and give Bond for the sum he demanded; but still provided handsomely for her, and continued his courtship; till being inform'd by his Spies (truly I suspect some in her own Family) that you were entertain'd at her house, and stay'd with her all night, he came this morning raving & storming like a Madman, talks no more of

Marriage; so there's no hopes of making up matters that way, but vows her ruin, unless she'll allow him the same favour that he supposes she granted you.

Barn. Must she be ruin'd, or find her refuge in another's arms?

Mill. He gave me but an hour to resolve in, that's happily spent with you;—and now I go.—

Barn. To be expos'd to all the rigours of the various seasons; the Summer's parching heat, and Winter's cold, unhous'd to wander friendless thro' the unhospitable world, in misery & want; attended with fear and danger, and pursu'd by malice and revenge; woud'st thou endure all this for me, and can I do nothing to prevent it?

Lucy. 'Tis really a pity, there can be no way found out.

Barn. O where are all my resolutions now; like early vapours, or the morning dew, chas'd by the Sun's warm beams they're vanish'd and lost, as tho' they had never been.

Lucy. Now I advis'd her, Sir, to comply with the Gentleman; that wou'd not only put an end to her troubles, but make her Fortune at once.

Barn. Tormenting Fiend, away.—I had rather perish, nay, see her perish, than have her sav'd by him. I will my self prevent her ruin, tho' with my own. A moment's patience, I'll return immediately.—

SCENE XII

Millwood *and* Lucy

Lucy. 'Twas well you came, or, by what I can perceive, you had lost him.

Mill. That, I must confess, was a danger I did not foresee; I was only afraid he should have come without money. You know a house of entertainment, like mine, is not kept with nothing.

Lucy. That's very true, but then you shou'd be reasonable in your demands, 'tis pity to discourage a young Man.

SCENE XIII

BARNWELL, MILLWOOD, *and* LUCY

Barn. What am I about to do?—Now you, who boast your Reason all-sufficient, suppose your selves in my condition, and determine for me; whether it's right to let her suffer for my faults, or, by this small addition to my guilt, prevent the ill effects of what is past.

Lucy. These young Sinners think every thing in the ways of wickedness so strange,—but I cou'd tell him that this is nothing but what's very common; for one Vice as naturally begets another, as a Father a Son:—But he'll find out that himself, if he lives long enough.

Barn. Here take this, and with it purchase your deliverance; return to your house, and live in peace and safety.

Mill. So I may hope to see you there again.

Barn. Answer me not,—but fly, lest, in the agonies of my remorse, I take again what is not mine to give, & abandon thee to want & misery.

Mill. Say but you'll come.—

Barn. You are my Fate, my Heaven, or my Hell; only leave me now, dispose of me hereafter as you please.

SCENE XIV

BARNWELL

What have I done?—Were my resolutions founded on Reason, & sincerely made,—why then has Heaven suffer'd me to fall? I sought not the occasion; and, if my heart deceives me not, compassion and generosity were my motives.—Is Virtue inconsistent with it self, or are Vice and Virtue only empty names? Or do they depend on accidents, beyond our power to produce, or to prevent,— wherein we have no part, & yet must be determin'd by the event? But why should I attempt to reason? All is confusion, horror, and remorse;—I find I am lost, cast down from all

my late erected hopes, and plung'd again in guilt, yet scarce
know how or why—

> *Such undistinguish'd horrors make my brain,*
> *Like Hell, the seat of darkness, and of pain.*

ACT III. SCENE I

THOROWGOOD *and* TRUEMAN

Thor. Methinks I wou'd not have you only learn the method
of Merchandize, & practise it hereafter, merely as a means
of getting wealth.—'Twill be well worth your pains to
study it as a Science.—See how it is founded in Reason,
& the Nature of things.—How it has promoted Humanity,
as it has opened and yet keeps up an intercourse between
Nations, far remote from one another in situation, customs
and Religion; promoting Arts, Industry, Peace and Plenty;
by mutual benefits diffusing mutual Love from Pole to
Pole.

Tr. Something of this I have consider'd, & hope, by your
assistance, to extend my thoughts much farther. I have
observ'd those Countries, where Trade is promoted and
encouraged, do not make discoveries to destroy, but to
improve Mankind,—by Love and Friendship, to tame the
fierce, and polish the most savage, to teach them the ad-
vantages of honest Traffick, by taking from them, with
their own consent, their useless superfluities, & giving
them, in return, what, from their ignorance in manual
arts, their situation, or some other accident they stand in
need of.

Thor. 'Tis justly observ'd:—The populous East, luxuriant,
abounds with glittering Gems, bright Pearls, aromatick
Spices, and health-restoring Drugs: The late found Western
World glows with unnumber'd Veins of Gold and Silver
Ore.—On every Climate, and on every Country, Heaven

has bestowed some good peculiar to it self.—It is the industrious Merchant's business to collect the various blessings of each soil & climate, and, with the product of the whole, to enrich his native Country.—Well! I have examin'd your Accounts: They are not only just, as I have always found them, but regularly kept, and fairly enter'd.—I commend your diligence. Method in business is the surest guide. He, who neglects it, frequently stumbles, and always wanders perplex'd, uncertain, and in danger. Are *Barnwell's* Accounts ready for my inspection? He does not use to be the last on these occasions.

Tr. Upon receiving your orders he retir'd, I thought in some confusion.—If you please, I'll go & hasten him.— I hope he hasn't been guilty of any neglect.

Thor. I'm now going to the *Exchange*; let him know, at my return, I expect to find him ready.

SCENE II

MARIA *with a Book sits and reads*

Ma. How forcible is Truth! The weakest mind, inspir'd with love of that,—fix'd and collected in it self, with indifference beholds the united force of Earth and Hell opposing: Such Souls are rais'd above the sense of pain, or so supported, that they regard it not. The Martyr cheaply purchases his Heaven.—Small are his sufferings, great is his reward;—not so the Wretch, who combats Love with Duty; when the mind, weaken'd and dissolved by the soft passion, feeble & hopeless opposes its own desires.— What is an hour, a day, a year of pain, to a whole life of tortures, such as these?

SCENE III

TRUEMAN *and* MARIA

Tr. O, *Barnwell*!—O, my Friend, how art thou fallen?

Ma. Ha! *Barnwell*! What of him? Speak, say what of *Barnwell*.

Tr. 'Tis not to be conceal'd.—I've news to tell of him that will afflict your generous Father, your self, and all who knew him.

Ma. Defend us Heaven!

Tr. I cannot speak it.—See there.

(*Gives a Letter*, Maria *reads*.

Trueman,

I know my absence will surprize my honour'd Master, & your self, and the more, when you shall understand that the reason of my withdrawing, is my having embezzled part of the Cash with which I was entrusted. After this, 'tis needless to inform you that I intend never to return again: though this might have been known, by examining my Accounts; yet, to prevent that unnecessary trouble, & to cut off all fruitless expectations of my return, I have left this from the lost

George Barnwell.

Tr. Lost indeed! Yet how he shou'd be guilty of what he there charges himself withal, raises my wonder equal to my grief.—Never had Youth a higher sense of Virtue— justly he thought, & as he thought he practised; never was life more regular than his, an understanding uncommon at his years; an open, generous manliness of temper; his manners easy, unaffected and engaging.

Ma. This & much more you might have said with truth.— He was the delight of every eye, & joy of every heart that knew him.

Tr. Since such he was, and was my Friend, can I support his loss?—See the fairest and happiest Maid this wealthy City boasts, kindly condescends to weep for thy unhappy fate, poor ruin'd *Barnwell*!

Ma. Trueman, Do you think a Soul so delicate as his, so sensible of shame, can e'er submit to live a Slave to Vice?

Tr. Never, never. So well I know him, I'm sure this act of his, so contrary to his nature, must have been caused by some unavoidable necessity.

Ma. Is there no means yet to preserve him?

Tr. O! that there were.—But few Men recover Reputation lost.—A Merchant never.—Nor wou'd he, I fear, though I shou'd find him, ever be brought to look his injur'd Master in the face.

Ma. I fear as much,—& therefore wou'd never have my Father know it.

Tr. That's impossible.

Ma. What's the Sum?

Tr. 'Tis considerable.—I've mark'd it here, to show it, with the Letter, to your Father, at his return.

Ma. If I shou'd supply the money, cou'd you so dispose of that, and the account, as to conceal this unhappy mismanagement from my Father?

Tr. Nothing more easy:—But can you intend it? Will you save a helpless Wretch from ruin? Oh! 'twere an act worthy such exalted Virtue, as *Maria*'s. Sure Heaven, in mercy to my Friend, inspired the generous thought.

Ma. Doubt not but I wou'd purchase so great a happiness at a much dearer price.—But how shall he be found?

Tr. Trust to my diligence for that.—In the mean time, I'll conceal his absence from your Father, or find such excuses for it, that the real cause shall never be suspected.

Ma. In attempting to save from shame, one whom we hope may yet return to virtue, to Heaven, & you, the Judges of this action, I appeal, whether I have done any thing misbecoming my Sex & character.

Tr. Earth must approve the deed, and Heaven, I doubt not, will reward it.

Ma. If Heaven succeed it, I am well rewarded. A Virgin's Fame is sullied by suspicion's slightest breath; & therefore as this must be a secret from my Father, and the world, for *Barnwell*'s sake, for mine, let it be so to him.

SCENE IV. Millwood's *House*

LUCY *and* BLUNT

Lucy. Well! what do you think of *Millwood's* conduct now?

Blunt. I own it is surprizing: I don't know which to admire most, her feign'd, or his real passion, tho' I have sometimes been afraid that her avarice wou'd discover her:—But his youth & want of experience make it the easier to impose on him.

Lucy. No, it is his Love. To do him justice, notwithstanding his youth, he don't want understanding; but you Men are much easier imposed on, in these affairs, than your vanity will allow you to believe.—Let me see the wisest of you all, as much in love with me, as *Barnwell* is with *Millwood*, & I'll engage to make as great a fool of him.

Blunt. And all circumstances considerd, to make as much money of him too.

Lucy. I can't answer for that. Her artifice in making him rob his Master at first, & the various stratagems, by which she has obliged him to continue in that course, astonish even me, who know her so well.—

Blunt. But then you are to consider that the money was his Master's.

Lucy. There was the difficulty of it.—Had it been his own, it had been nothing.—Were the World his, she might have it for a smile.—But those golden days are done;—he's ruin'd, and *Millwood's* hopes of farther profits there, are at an end.

Blunt. That's no more than we all expected.

Lucy. Being call'd, by his Master, to make up his Accounts, he was forc'd to quit his house & service, and wisely flies to *Millwood* for relief and entertainment.

Blunt. I have not heard of this before! How did she receive him?

Lucy. As you wou'd expect.—She wonder'd what he

meant, was astonish'd at his impudence,—and, with an air of modesty peculiar to her self, swore so heartily, that she never saw him before,—that she put me out of countenance.

Blunt. That's much indeed! But how did *Barnwell* behave?

Lucy. He griev'd, and, at length, enrag'd at this barbarous treatment, was preparing to be gone; and, making toward the door, show'd a bag of Money, which he had stol'n from his Master,—the last he's ever like to have from thence.

Blunt. But then *Millwood*?

Lucy. Aye, she, with her usual address, return'd to her old arts of lying, swearing, & dissembling.—Hung on his neck, and wept, & swore 'twas meant in jest, till the easy Fool, melted into tears, threw the Money into her lap, & swore he had rather die, than think her false.

Blunt. Strange infatuation!

Lucy. But what follow'd was stranger still. As doubts and fears, follow'd by reconcilement, ever increase love, where the passion is sincere, so in him it caus'd so wild a transport of excessive fondness, such joy, such grief, such pleasure, and such anguish, that Nature in him seem'd sinking with the weight, and the charm'd Soul dispos'd to quit his breast for hers.—Just then, when every passion with lawless anarchy prevail'd, and Reason was in the raging tempest lost,—the cruel artful *Millwood* prevail'd upon the wretched Youth to promise what I tremble but to think on.

Blunt. I am amaz'd! what can it be?

Lucy. You will be more so, to hear it is to attempt the life of his nearest Relation, & best Benefactor.—

Blunt. His Uncle, whom we have often heard him speak of, as a Gentleman of a large Estate, and fair Character in the Country, where he lives.

Lucy. The same.—She was no sooner possess'd of the last dear purchase of his ruin, but her avarice, insatiate as the grave, demands this horrid sacrifice.—*Barnwell*'s near relation, and unsuspected Virtue must give too easy means to seize the good Man's Treasure; whose blood must seal the dreadful secret, and prevent the terrors of her guilty fears.

Blunt. Is it possible she cou'd perswade him to do an act like that! He is, by nature, honest, grateful, compassionate, and generous: And though his love, & her artful perswasions, have wrought him to practise what he most abhors; yet we all can witness for him, with what reluctance he has still comply'd! So many tears he shed o'er each offence, as might, if possible, sanctify theft, and make a merit of a crime.

Lucy. 'Tis true, at the naming the murder of his Uncle, he started into rage; and, breaking from her arms, where she till then had held him, with well dissembled love and false endearments, call'd her, cruel Monster, Devil, & told her she was born for his destruction.—She thought it not for her purpose to meet his rage with rage, but affected a most passionate fit of grief;—rail'd at her Fate, and curs'd her wayward Stars,—that still her wants shou'd force her to press him to act such deeds, as she must needs abhor, as well as he; but told him Necessity had no law, and Love no bounds; that therefore he never truly lov'd, but meant, in her necessity, to forsake her;—then kneel'd and swore, that since, by his refusal, he had given her cause to doubt his love, she never wou'd see him more; unless, to prove it true, he robb'd his Uncle to supply her wants, & murder'd him, to keep it from discovery.

Blunt. I am astonish'd! What said he?

Lucy. Speechless he stood, but in his face you might have read, that various passions tore his very Soul. Oft he, in anguish, threw his eyes towards Heaven, & then as often bent their beams on her; then wept & groan'd, & beat his breast; at length, with horror, not to be express'd, he cry'd, Thou cursed Fair! have I not given dreadful proofs of love! What drew me from my youthful innocence, to stain my then unspotted Soul, but Love? What caus'd me to rob my gentle Master, but cursed Love? What makes me now a fugitive from his service, loath'd by my self, and scorn'd by all the world, but Love? What fills my eyes with tears, my Soul with torture, never felt on this side death before? Why Love, Love, Love. And why, above all, do I resolve, (for, tearing his hair, he cry'd I do resolve) to kill my Uncle?

Blunt. Was she not mov'd? It makes me weep to hear the sad relation.

Lucy. Yes, with joy, that she had gain'd her point.—She gave him no time to cool, but urg'd him to attempt it instantly. He's now gone: if he performs it, and escapes, there's more money for her; if not, he'll ne'er return, and then she's fairly rid of him.

Blunt. 'Tis time the World was rid of such a Monster.—

Lucy. If we don't do our endeavours to prevent this murder, we are as bad as she.

Blunt. I'm afraid it is too late.

Lucy. Perhaps not.—Her barbarity to *Barnwell* makes me hate her.—We've run too great a length with her already. —I did not think her or my self so wicked, as I find, upon reflection, we are.

Blunt. 'Tis true; we have all been too much so.—But there is something so horrid in murder,—that all other crimes seem nothing when compared to that.—I wou'd not be involv'd in the guilt of that for all the world.

Lucy. Nor I, Heaven knows,—therefore let us clear our selves, by doing all that is in our power to prevent it. I have just thought of a way, that, to me, seems probable.—Will you join with me to detect this curs'd design?

Blunt. With all my heart.—How else shall I clear my self? He who knows of a murder intended to be committed, and does not discover it, in the eye of the Law, and Reason, is a Murderer.

Lucy. Let us lose no time,—I'll acquaint you with the particulars as we go.

SCENE V

A Walk at some distance from a Country Seat

BARNWELL

A dismal gloom obscures the face of Day; either the Sun has slip'd behind a cloud, or journeys down the west of Heaven, with more than common speed, to avoid the sight of what I'm doom'd to act. Since I set forth on this accursed design, where'er I tread, methinks, the solid Earth trembles beneath my feet.—Yonder limpid stream, whose hoary fall has made a natural cascade, as I pass'd by, in doleful accents seem'd to murmur, murder. The Earth, the Air, and Water, seem concern'd; but that's not strange, the World is punish'd, and Nature feels the shock, when Providence permits a good Man's fall!—Just Heaven! Then what shou'd I be for him that was my Father's only Brother, & since his death has been to me a Father, who took me up an Infant, & an Orphan, rear'd me with tenderest care, & still indulged me with most paternal fondness?—Yet here I stand avow'd his destin'd Murderer:—I stiffen with horror at my own impiety.—'Tis yet unperform'd.—What if I quit my bloody purpose, & fly the place? (*Going, then stops.*)—But whither, O whither, shall I fly!—My Master's once friendly doors are ever shut against me, & without money *Millwood* will never see me more, & life is not to be endured without her:—She's got such firm possession of my Heart, and governs there with such despotick sway.—Aye, there's the cause of all my sin and sorrow:—'Tis more than Love, 'tis the fever of the Soul, and madness of desire.—In vain does Nature, Reason, Conscience, all oppose it, the impetuous Passion bears down all before it, and drives me on to lust, to theft, and murder.—Oh Conscience! feeble guide to Virtue, who only shows us when we go astray, but wants the power to stop us in our course.—Ha! in yonder shady Walk I see my Uncle.—He's alone.—Now for my disguise. —(*Plucks out a vizor.*) This is his hour of private meditation. Thus daily he prepares his Soul for Heaven,—whilst I—

But what have I to do with Heaven!—Ha! No struggles, Conscience.—

> *Hence! Hence remorse, & ev'ry thought that's good;*
> *The storm that lust began, must end in blood.*

(*Puts on the vizor, & draws a pistol.*

SCENE VI

A close Walk in a Wood

UNCLE

If I was superstitious, I shou'd fear some danger lurk'd unseen, or Death were nigh:—A heavy melancholy clouds my spirits, my imagination is fill'd with gashly forms of dreary graves, & bodies chang'd by Death,—when the pale lengthen'd visage attracts each weeping eye,—and fills the musing Soul, at once, with grief and horror, pity and aversion.—I will indulge the thought. The wise Man prepares himself for Death, by making it familiar to his mind.—When strong reflexions hold the mirror near,—& the Living in the Dead behold their future selves, how does each inordinate passion and desire cease or sicken at the view?—The mind scarce moves.—The blood, curdling, & chill'd, creeps slowly thro' the veins, fix'd, still, & motionless, like the solemn object of our thoughts.—We are almost at present—what we must be hereafter, 'till curiosity awakes the Soul, and sets it on inquiry.—

SCENE VII

UNCLE, GEORGE BARNWELL *at a distance*

Uncle. O Death, thou strange mysterious Power,—seen every day, yet never understood—but by the incommunicative dead. What are thou?—The extensive mind of Man, that with a thought circles the Earth's vast globe,—sinks to the centre, or ascends above the Stars, that Worlds exotick finds, or thinks it finds, thy thick clouds attempts to pass in vain, lost and bewilder'd in the horrid gloom,—defeated she returns more doubtful than before, of nothing certain, but of labour lost.

(*During this Speech*, Barnwell *sometimes presents the pistol, & draws it back again, at last he drops it,—at which his Uncle starts, & draws his sword.*

Barn. Oh, 'tis impossible!

Uncle. A Man so near me, arm'd and masqu'd!

Barn. Nay, then there's no retreat.

(*Plucks a Poniard from his bosom, & stabs him.*

Uncle. Oh! I am slain! All gracious Heaven regard the prayer of thy dying Servant. Bless, with thy choicest blessings, my dearest Nephew; forgive my murderer, and take my fleeting Soul to endless mercy.

(Barnwell *throws off his mask, runs to him, and, kneeling by him, raises and chafes him.*

Barn. Expiring Saint! Oh, murder'd, martyr'd Uncle! Lift up your dying eyes, & view your Nephew in your Murderer.—O do not look so tenderly upon me.—Let indignation lighten from your eyes, and blast me e're you die.—By Heaven, he weeps in pity of my woes.—Tears,—Tears, for blood.—The Murder'd, in the agonies of Death, weeps for his Murderer.—O, speak your pious purpose,—pronounce my pardon then,—and take me with you.—He wou'd, but cannot.—O why, with such fond affection do you press my murdering hand!—What! will you kiss me?

(*Kisses him. Uncle groans and dies.*

Barn. He's gone for ever,—and oh! I follow.—(*Swoons away upon his Uncle's dead body.*) Do I still live to press the suffering bosom of the Earth?—Do I still breath, and taint with my infectious breath the wholesome air? Let Heaven, from its high Throne, in Justice or in Mercy, now look down on that dear murder'd Saint, & me the Murderer.—And, if his Vengeance spares,—let Pity strike and end my wretched being.—Murder the worst of crimes, and

Parricide the worst of Murders, and this the worst of Parricides. *Cain*, who stands on record from the birth of Time, & must to its last final period, as accurs'd, slew a Brother, favour'd above him.—Detested *Nero*, by another's hand, dispatch'd a Mother, that he fear'd and hated.—But I, with my own hand, have murder'd a Brother, Mother, Father, and a Friend, most loving & belov'd.—This execrable act of mine's without a parallel.—O may it ever stand alone,— the last of Murders, as it is the worst.—

> *The rich Man thus, in torment and despair,*
> *Prefer'd his vain, but charitable prayer.*
> *The Fool, his own Soul lost, wou'd fain be wise*
> *For others good ; but Heaven his suit denies.*
> *By Laws and means well known we stand or fall,*
> *And one eternal rule remains for all.*

ACT IV. SCENE I

MARIA

How falsly do they judge who censure or applaud, as we're afflicted or rewarded here. I know I am unhappy, yet cannot charge my self with any crime, more than the common frailties of our kind, that shou'd provoke just Heaven to mark me out for sufferings so uncommon & severe. Falsly to accuse our selves, Heaven must abhor; then it is just & right that Innocence should suffer; for Heaven must be just in all its ways.—Perhaps by that they are kept from moral evils, much worse than penal, or more improv'd in Virtue. Or may not the lesser ills that they sustain, be the means of greater good to others? Might all the joyless days & sleepless nights that I have past, but purchase peace for thee—

Thou dear, dear cause of all my grief and pain,
Small were the loss, and infinite the gain:
Tho' to the grave in secret love I pine,
So life, and Fame, and happiness were thine.

SCENE II

TRUEMAN *and* MARIA

Ma. What news of *Barnwell*?

Tr. None.—I have sought him with the greatest diligence, but all in vain.

Ma. Doth my Father yet suspect the cause of his absenting himself?

Tr. All appear'd so just and fair to him, it is not possible he ever shou'd; but his absence will no longer be conceal'd. Your Father's wise, and though he seems to hearken to the friendly excuses, I wou'd make for *Barnwell*; yet, I am afraid, he regards 'em only as such, without suffering them to influence his judgment.

Ma. How does the unhappy Youth defeat all our designs to serve him; yet I can never repent what we have done. Shou'd he return, 'twill make his reconciliation with my Father easier, and preserve him from future reproach from a malicious unforgiving world.

SCENE III

(*To them.*) THOROWGOOD *and* LUCY

Thor. This Woman here has given me a sad, (and bating some circumstances) too probable account of *Barnwell*'s defection.

Lucy. I am sorry, Sir, that my frank confession of my former unhappy course of life shou'd cause you to suspect my truth on this occasion.

Thor. It is not that; your confession has in it all the appearance of truth. (*To them.*) Among many other particulars, she informs me that *Barnwell* has been influenc'd to break his trust, and wrong me, at several times, of considerable sums of Money; now, as I know this to be false, I wou'd fain doubt the whole of her relation,—too dreadful to be willingly believ'd.

Ma. Sir, your pardon, I find my self on a sudden so indispos'd, that I must retire.—Providence opposes all attempts to save him.—Poor ruin'd *Barnwell*!—Wretched lost *Maria*!—   (*Aside.*

SCENE IV

THOROWGOOD, TRUEMAN, *and* LUCY

Thor. How am I distress'd on every side! Pity for that unhappy Youth, fear for the life of a much valued Friend— and then my Child—the only joy & hope of my declining life. Her melancholy increases hourly, and gives me painful apprehensions of her loss.—O *Trueman*! this person informs me, that your Friend, at the instigation of an impious Woman, is gone to rob and murder his venerable Uncle.

Tr. O execrable deed, I am blasted with the horror of the thought.

Lucy. This delay may ruin all.

Thor. What to do or think I know not; that he ever wrong'd me, I know is false,—the rest may be so too, there's all my hope.

Tr. Trust not to that, rather suppose all true than lose a moment's time; even now the horrid deed may be a doing, —dreadful imagination,—or it may be done, and we are vainly debating on the means to prevent what is already past.

Thor. This earnestness convinces me that he knows more than he has yet discover'd. What ho! without there! who waits?

(To them.) A Servant

Thor. Order the Groom to saddle the swiftest horse, and prepare himself to set out with speed.—An affair of life and death demands his diligence. For you, whose behaviour on this occasion I have no time to commend as it deserves, I must ingage your farther assistance.—Return & observe this *Millwood* till I come. I have your directions, & will follow you as soon as possible.   (*Exit* Lucy.

Thor. Trueman, you I am sure wou'd not be idle on this occasion.

Tr. He only who is a Friend can judge of my distress.

SCENE V. Millwood's *House*

Millwood

I wish I knew the event of his design;—the attempt without success would ruin him.—Well! what have I to apprehend from that? I fear too much. The mischief being only intended, his Friends, in pity of his youth, turn all their rage on me. I should have thought of that before.— Suppose the deed done, then, and then only I shall be secure; or what if he returns without attempting it at all?

Enter Barnwell *bloody*

Mill. But he is here, & I have done him wrong: his bloody hands show he has done the deed, but show he wants the prudence to conceal it.

Barn. Where shall I hide me? whither shall I fly to avoid the swift unerring hand of Justice?

Mill. Dismiss those fears; tho' Thousands had pursu'd you to the door, yet being enter'd here you are safe as Innocence: I have such a cavern, by art so cunningly contriv'd, that the piercing eyes of Jealousy & Revenge may search in vain, nor find the entrance to the safe retreat; there will I hide you if any danger's near.

Barn. O hide me from my self if it be possible, for while I bear my Conscience in my bosom, tho' I were hid where Man's eye never saw, nor light e'er dawn'd, 'twere all in vain. For that inmate,—that impartial Judge, will try, convict, & sentence me for Murder; and execute me with never ending torments. Behold these hands all crimson'd o'er with my dear Uncle's blood! Here's a sight to make a Statue start with horror, or turn a living Man into a Statue.

Mill. Ridiculous! Then it seems you are afraid of your own shadow, or what's less than a shadow, your Conscience.

Barn. Tho' to Man unknown I did the accursed act, what can we hide from Heav'ns omniscient eye?

Mill. No more of this stuff,—what advantage have you made of his death? or what advantage may yet be made of it?—did you secure the keys of his Treasure,—those no doubt were about him?—what Gold, what Jewels, or what else of value have you brought me?

Barn. Think you I added Sacrilege to Murder? Oh! had you seen him as his life flowed from him in a crimson flood, & heard him praying for me by the double name of Nephew and of Murderer; alas, alas! he knew not then that his Nephew was his Murderer; how wou'd you have wish'd as I did, tho' you had a thousand years of life to come, to have given them all to have lengthen'd his one hour. But being dead, I fled the sight of what my hands had done, nor cou'd I to have gain'd the Empire of the World, have violated by theft his sacred corps.

Mill. Whining preposterous canting Villain, to murder your Uncle, rob him of Life, Natures first, last, dear Prerogative, after which there's no injury, then fear to take what he no longer wanted; & bring to me your penury & guilt. Do you think I'll hazard my Reputation; nay my Life to entertain you?

Barn. Oh!—*Millwood!*—this from thee;—but I have done, if you hate me, if you wish me dead; then are you happy,—for Oh! 'tis sure my grief will quickly end me.

Mill. In his madness he will discover all, and involve me

in his ruin;—we are on a precipice from whence there's no retreat for both,—then to preserve my self—(*Pauses.*) there is no other way,—'tis dreadful,—but reflection comes too late when danger's pressing, and there's no room for choice. —It must be done.   (*Stamps.*

(*To them.*) A SERVANT

Mill. Fetch me an Officer and seize this Villain; he has confess'd himself a Murderer. Shou'd I let him escape, I justly might be thought as bad as he.

Barn. O *Millwood*! sure thou dost not, cannot mean it. Stop the Messenger, upon my knees I beg you, call him back. 'Tis fit I die indeed, but not by you. I will this instant deliver my self into the hands of Justice, indeed I will, for Death is all I wish. But thy ingratitude so tears my wounded Soul, 'tis worse ten thousand times than Death with Torture.

Mill. Call it what you will, I am willing to live, and live secure; which nothing but your death can warrant.

Barn. If there be a pitch of wickedness that seats the Author beyond the reach of Vengeance, you must be secure. But what remains for me, but a dismal dungeon, hard-galling fetters, an awful Tryal, and ignominious Death, justly to fall unpitied & abhorr'd?—After death to be sus-pended between Heaven and Earth, a dreadful Spectacle, the warning and horror of a gaping Croud. This I cou'd bear, nay wish not to avoid, had it but come from any hand but thine.—

SCENE VI

MILLWOOD, BARNWELL, BLUNT, *Officer & Attendants*

Mill. Heaven defend me! Conceal a Murderer! Here, Sir, take this Youth into your custody; I accuse him of Mur-der, and will appear to make good my charge. (*They seize him.*

Barn. To whom, of what, or how shall I complain? I'll not

accuse her, the hand of Heav'n is in it, and this the punishment of Lust and Parricide; yet Heav'n that justly cuts me off, still suffers her to live, perhaps to punish others: tremendous Mercy! so Fiends are curs'd with immortality, to be the Executioners of Heaven.—

> *Be warn'd ye Youths, who see my sad despair,*
> *Avoid lewd Women, false as they are fair.*
> *By Reason guided, honest joys pursue :*
> *The Fair to Honour, and to Virtue true,* ⎫
> *Just to her self, will ne'er be false to you.* ⎭
> *By my example learn to shun my Fate,*
> *(How wretched is the Man who's wise too late !)*
> *E'er Innocence, and Fame, and Life be lost,*
> *Here purchase Wisdom, cheaply, at my cost.*

(Exit with Officer, &c.

Mill. Where's *Lucy*, why is she absent at such a Time?
Blunt. Wou'd I had been so too, thou Devil!
Mill. Insolent! this to me?
Blunt. The worst that we know of the Devil is that he first seduces to sin, & then betrays to punishment.

(Exit Blunt.

Mill. They disapprove of my conduct,—& mean to take this opportunity to set up for themselves.—My ruin is resolv'd; I see my danger, but scorn both it and them.—I was not born to fall by such weak instruments.— *(Going.*

SCENE VII

THOROWGOOD *and* MILLWOOD

Thor. Where is this scandal of her own Sex, and curse of ours?
Mill. What means this insolence? Who do you seek?
Thor. Millwood.
Mill. Well, you have found her then.—I am *Millwood.*—

Thor. Then you are the most impious wretch that e'er the Sun beheld.

Mill. From your appearance I shou'd have expected wisdom & moderation, but your manners bely your aspect.— What is your business here? I know you not.

Thor. Hereafter you may know me better; I am *Barnwell*'s Master.

Mill. Then you are Master to a Villain; which, I think, is not much to your credit.

Thor. Had he been as much above thy arts, as my credit is superior to thy malice, I need not blush to own him.

Mill. My arts?—I don't understand you, Sir! If he has done amiss, what's that to me? Was he my Servant, or yours? —You shou'd have taught him better.

Thor. Why shou'd I wonder to find such uncommon impudence in one arriv'd to such a height of wickedness.— When Innocence is banish'd, Modesty soon follows. Know, Sorceress, I'm not ignorant of any of your arts, by which you first deceiv'd the unwary Youth: I know how, step by step, you've led him on, (reluctant & unwilling) from crime to crime, to this last horrid act, which you contriv'd, and, by your curs'd wiles, even forced him to commit, and then betray'd him.

Mill. Ha! *Lucy* has got the advantage of me, and accused me first; unless I can turn the accusation, & fix it upon her and *Blunt*, I am lost.   (*Aside.*

Thor. Had I known your cruel design sooner, it had been prevented. To see you punish'd as the Law directs, is all that now remains.—Poor satisfaction,—for he, innocent as he is, compared to you, must suffer too. But Heaven, who knows our frame, and graciously distinguishes between frailty and presumption, will make a difference, tho' Man cannot, who sees not the heart, but only judges by the outward action.—

Mill. I find, Sir, we are both unhappy in our Servants. I was surpriz'd at such ill treatment, from a Gentleman of your appearance, without cause, and therefore too hastily return'd it; for which I ask your pardon. I now perceive you have been so far impos'd on, as to think me engaged in a former correspondence with your Servant, and, some way or other, accessary to his undoing.

Thor. I charge you as the Cause, the sole Cause of all his Guilt, and all his Suffering, of all he now endures, and must endure, till a violent and shameful Death shall put a dreadful period to his life and miseries together.

Mill. 'Tis very strange; but who's secure from scandal and detraction?—So far from contributing to his ruin, I never spoke to him till since that fatal accident, which I lament as much as you: 'Tis true, I have a Servant, on whose account he has of late frequented my house; if she has abus'd my good opinion of her, am I to blame? Hasn't *Barnwell* done the same by you?

Thor. I hear you; pray go on.

Mill. I have been inform'd he had a violent passion for her, and she for him; but I always thought it innocent. I know her poor, and given to expensive pleasures. Now who can tell but she may have influenced the amorous Youth to commit this Murder, to supply her extravagancies; it must be so.—I now recollect a thousand circumstances that confirm it: I'll have her and a Man Servant, that I suspect as an accomplice, secured immediately. I hope, Sir, you will lay aside your ill-grounded suspicions of me, and join to punish the real contrivers of this bloody deed. (*Offers to go.*

Thor. Madam, you pass not this way: I see your design, but shall protect them from your malice.

Mill. I hope you will not use your influence, and the credit of your Name, to skreen such guilty Wretches. Consider, Sir, the wickedness of perswading a thoughtless Youth to such a Crime.

Thor. I do,—and of betraying him when it was done.

Mill. That which you call betraying him, may convince you of my innocence. She who loves him, tho' she contriv'd the Murder, would never have deliver'd him into the hands of Justice, as I (struck with the horror of his crimes) have done.—

Thor. How shou'd an unexperienc'd Youth escape her

snares? The powerful Magick of her Wit & Form, might betray the wisest to simple dotage, and fire the blood that Age had froze long since. Even I, that with just prejudice came prepared, had, by her artful story, been deceiv'd, but that my strong conviction of her guilt makes even a doubt impossible. Those whom subtilly you wou'd accuse, you know are your Accusers; and what proves unanswerably their innocence, and your guilt; they accus'd you before the deed was done, and did all that was in their power to have prevented it.

Mill. Sir, you are very hard to be convinc'd; but I have such a proof, which, when produced, will silence all objections.   (*Exit.*

SCENE VIII

THOROWGOOD, LUCY, TRUEMAN, BLUNT, OFFICERS, &c.

Lucy. Gentlemen, pray place your selves, some on one side of that door, and some on the other, watch her entrance, and act as your prudence shall direct you.—This way—(*to* Thorowgood) and note her behaviour; I have observ'd her, she's driven to the last extremity, and is forming some desperate resolution.—I guess at her design.—

To them, Millwood *with a Pistol.*—

Trueman *secures her.*

Tr. Here thy power of doing mischief ends, deceitful, cruel, bloody Woman!

Mill. Fool, Hypocrite, Villain.—Man! thou can'st not call me that.

Tr. To call thee Woman, were to wrong the Sex, thou Devil!

Mill. That imaginary Being is an Emblem of thy cursed Sex collected. A Mirrour, wherein each particular Man may see his own likeness, and that of all Mankind.

Tr. Think not by aggravating the fault of others to

extenuate thy own, of which the abuse of such uncommon perfections of mind and body is not the least.

Mill. If such I had, well may I curse your barbarous Sex, who robb'd me of 'em, e'er I knew their worth; then left me, too late, to count their value by their loss. Another and another Spoiler came, & all my gain was poverty and reproach. My Soul disdain'd, and yet disdains dependance & contempt. Riches, no matter by what means obtain'd, I saw secur'd the worst of Men from both; I found it therefore necessary to be rich; and, to that end, I summon'd all my Arts. You call 'em wicked, be it so, they were such as my conversation with your sex had furnish'd me withal.

Thor. Sure none but the worst of Men convers'd with thee.

Mill. Men of all Degrees & all Professions I have known; yet found no difference, but in their several capacities; all were alike wicked to the utmost of their power. In pride, contention, avarice, cruelty, and revenge, the Reverend Priesthood were my unerring Guides. From Suburb-Magistrates, who live by ruin'd Reputations, as the unhospitable Natives of *Cornwall* do by Ship-wrecks, I learn'd, that to charge my innocent Neighbours with my crimes, was to merit their protection; for to skreen the guilty, is the less scandalous, when many are suspected, and Detraction, like Darkness and Death, blackens all objects, and levels all distinction. Such are your venal Magistrates, who favour none but such as, by their office, they are sworn to punish: With them not to be guilty, is the worst of crimes, and large fees privately paid, is every needful Virtue.

Thor. Your practice has sufficiently discover'd your contempt of Laws, both human & divine; no wonder then that you shou'd hate the Officers of both.

Mill. I hate you all, I know you, and expect no mercy; nay, I ask for none; I have done nothing that I am sorry for; I follow'd my inclinations, and that the best of you does every day. All actions are alike natural and indifferent to Man and Beast, who devour, or are devour'd, as they meet with others weaker or stronger than themselves.

Thor. What pity it is, a Mind so comprehensive, daring and inquisitive, shou'd be a stranger to Religion's sweet, but powerful charms.

Mill. I am not Fool enough to be an Atheist, tho' I have known enough of Men's Hypocrisy to make a thousand simple Women so. Whatever Religion is in it self, as practis'd by Mankind, it has caus'd the evils, you say, it was design'd to cure. War, Plague, & Famine has not destroy'd so many of the human Race, as this pretended Piety has done; & with such barbarous cruelty, as if the only way to honour Heaven, were to turn the present World into Hell.

Thor. Truth is Truth, tho' from an Enemy, and spoke in malice. You bloody, blind, & superstitious Bigots, how will you answer this?

Mill. What are your Laws, of which you make your boast, but the Fool's Wisdom, & the Coward's Valour; the instrument and skreen of all your Villanies, by which you punish in others what you act your selves, or wou'd have acted, had you been in their circumstances. The Judge who condemns the poor Man for being a Thief, had been a Thief himself had he been poor. Thus you go on deceiving, & being deceiv'd, harrassing, plaguing, & destroying one another, but Women are your universal prey.

> *Women, by whom you are, the source of joy,*
> *With cruel arts you labour to destroy;*
> *A thousand ways our ruin you pursue,*
> *Yet blame in us those Arts, first taught by you.*
> *O may, from hence, each violated Maid,*
> *By flatt'ring, faithless, barb'rous Man betray'd,*
> *When robb'd of Innocence, and Virgin Fame,*
> *From your destruction raise a nobler Name;*
> *To right their Sex's wrongs devote their mind,*
> *And future Millwoods prove to plague Mankind.*

ACT V. SCENE I

A Room in a Prison

THOROWGOOD, BLUNT, *and* LUCY

Thor. I have recommended to *Barnwell* a Reverend Divine, whose judgment & integrity I am well acquainted with; nor has *Millwood* been neglected, but she, unhappy Woman, still obstinate, refuses his assistance.

Lucy. This pious charity to the afflicted well becomes your character; yet pardon me, Sir, if I wonder you were not at their Trial.

Thor. I knew it was impossible to save him, and I and my Family bear so great a part in his distress, that to have been present wou'd have aggravated our sorrows without relieving his.

Blunt. It was mournful indeed. *Barnwell*'s youth & modest deportment, as he past, drew tears from every eye: When placed at the Bar, and arraigned before the Reverend Judges, with many tears and interrupting sobs he confess'd and aggravated his offences, without accusing, or once reflecting on *Millwood*, the shameless Author of his ruin, who dauntless and unconcern'd stood by his side, viewing with visible pride and contempt the vast Assembly, who all with sympathizing sorrow wept for the wretched Youth. *Millwood*, when called upon to answer, loudly insisted upon her innocence, and made an artful and a bold defence; but finding all in vain, the impartial Jury and the learned Bench concurring to find her guilty, how did she curse her self, poor *Barnwell*, us, her Judges, all Mankind; but what cou'd that avail? she was condemn'd, & is this day to suffer with him.

Thor. The time draws on, I am going to visit *Barnwell*, as you are *Millwood*.

Lucy. We have not wrong'd her, yet I dread this interview. She's proud, impatient, wrathful, & unforgiving. To be the branded instruments of vengeance, to suffer in her shame, and sympathize with her in all she suffers, is the tribute we must pay for our former ill spent lives, & long confederacy with her in wickedness.

Thor. Happy for you it ended when it did. What you have done against *Millwood* I know proceeded from a just abhorrence of her crimes, free from interest, malice, or revenge. Proselytes to Virtue shou'd be encourag'd. Pursue your proposed Reformation, & know me hereafter for your Friend.

Lucy. This is a blessing as unhop'd for as unmerited; but Heaven, that snatched us from impending ruin, sure intends you as its instrument to secure us from Apostacy.

Thor. With gratitude to impute your deliverance to Heaven is just. Many, less virtuously dispos'd than *Barnwell* was, have never fallen in the manner he has done;—may not such owe their safety rather to Providence than to themselves? With pity & compassion let us judge him. Great were his faults, but strong was the temptation. Let his ruin learn us diffidence, humanity & circumspection;—for we,—who wonder at his Fate,—perhaps had we like him, been tryed,—like him, we had fallen too.

SCENE II

A Dungeon, a Table and Lamp

Thorowgood, Barnwell *reading*

Thor. See there the bitter fruits of Passion's detested Reign, and sensual appetite indulg'd. Severe reflections, penitence & tears.

Barn. My honoured injured Master, whose goodness has covered me a thousand times with shame, forgive this last unwilling disrespect,—indeed I saw you not.

Thor. 'Tis well, I hope you were better imploy'd in viewing of your self;—your journey's long, your time for preparation almost spent.—I sent a Reverend Divine to teach you to improve it, and shou'd be glad to hear of his success.

Barn. The word of truth, which he recommended for my constant companion in this my sad retirement, has at length remov'd the doubts I labour'd under. From thence I've

learn'd the infinite extent of heavenly Mercy; that my
offences, tho' great, are not unpardonable; and that 'tis not
my interest only, but my duty to believe and to rejoice in that
hope,—So shall Heaven receive the glory, & future Penitents
the profit of my Example.

Thor. Go on.—How happy am I who live to see this!

Barn. 'Tis wonderful,—that Words shou'd charm Despair, speak Peace and Pardon to a Murderer's Conscience;—
but Truth and Mercy flow in every sentence, attended with
force and energy divine. How shall I describe my present state
of mind? I hope in doubt,—and trembling I rejoice.—I feel
my grief increase, even as my fears give way.—Joy & Gratitude now supply more tears, than the Horror & Anguish of
Despair before.

Thor. These are the genuine signs of true Repentance, the
only preparatory, certain way to everlasting Peace.—O the joy
it gives to see a Soul form'd & prepar'd for Heaven!—For this
the faithful Minister devotes himself to Meditation, Absti-
nence & Prayer, shuning the vain delights of sensual joys, and
daily dies that others may live for ever.—For this he turns the
sacred Volumes o'er, & spends his life in painful search of
Truth.—The love of Riches and the lust of Power he looks on
with just contempt & detestation, who only counts for wealth
the Souls he wins; and whose highest Ambition is to serve
Mankind.—If the reward of all his pains be to preserve one
Soul from wandering, or turn one from the error of his ways,
how does he then rejoice, & own his little labours over paid.

Barn. What do I owe for all your generous kindness? but
tho' I cannot, Heaven can & will reward you.

Thor. To see thee thus, is joy too great for words. Farewell,—Heaven strengthen thee.—Farewell.

Barn. O! Sir, there's something I cou'd say, if my sad
swelling heart would give me leave.

Thor. Give it vent a while, and try.

Barn. I had a Friend,—'tis true I am unworthy, yet methinks your generous example might perswade;—cou'd I not
see him once before I go from whence there's no return?

Thor. He's coming,—and as much thy Friend as ever;—

but I'll not anticipate his sorrow,—too soon he'll see the sad effect of this contagious ruin. This torrent of domestick misery bears too hard upon me;—I must retire to indulge a weakness I find impossible to overcome. (*Aside*.)—Much lov'd—and much lamented Youth—Farewell—Heaven strengthen thee—Eternally Farewell.

Barn. The best of Masters & of Men—Farewell—while I live let me not want your prayers.

Thor. Thou shalt not;—thy Peace being made with Heaven, Death's already vanquish'd;—bear a little longer the pains that attend this transitory life, and cease from pain for ever.   (*Exit.*

Barn. I find a Power within that bears my Soul above the fears of Death, and, spight of conscious shame and guilt, gives me a taste of pleasure more than mortal.

(*To him.*) TRUEMAN *and* KEEPER

Keep. Sir, there's the Prisoner.   (*Exit.*

Barn. Trueman!—My Friend, whom I so wisht to see, yet now he's here I dare not look upon him.   (*Weeps.*

Tr. O Barnwell! Barnwell!

Barn. Mercy! Mercy! gracious Heaven! for Death, but not for this, was I prepared.

Tr. What have I suffer'd since I saw you last?—what pain has absence given me?—But oh! to see thee thus!

Barn. I know it is dreadful! I feel the anguish of thy generous Soul,—but I was born to murder all who love me.
          (*Both weep.*

Tr. I came not to reproach you;—I thought to bring you comfort, but I'm deceiv'd, for I have none to give;—I came to share thy sorrow, but cannot bear my own.

Barn. My sense of guilt indeed you cannot know,—'tis what the Good and Innocent like you can ne'er conceive;—but other griefs at present I have none, but what I feel for you.—In your sorrow I read you love me still, but yet methinks 'tis strange—when I consider what I am.

Tr. No more of that.—I can remember nothing but thy Virtues,—thy honest, tender Friendship, our former happy state, & present misery.—O had you trusted me when first the fair Seducer tempted you, all might have been prevented.

Barn. Alas, thou know'st not what a Wretch I've been! Breach of Friendship was my first & least offence.—So far was I lost to goodness,—so devoted to the Author of my ruin,—that had she insisted on my murdering thee,—I think,—I shou'd have done it.

Tr. Prithee aggravate thy faults no more.

Barn. I think I shou'd!—thus good & generous as you are, I shou'd have murder'd you!

Tr. We have not yet embrac'd, and may be interrupted. Come to my arms.

Barn. Never, never will I taste such joys on Earth; never will I so sooth my just remorse. Are those honest arms, and faithful bosom, fit to embrace and to support a Murderer?—These iron fetters only shall clasp, and flinty pavement bear me; (*Throwing himself on the ground.*) even these too good for such a bloody Monster.

Tr. Shall Fortune sever those whom Friendship join'd?—Thy Miseries cannot lay thee so low, but Love will find thee. (*Lies down by him.*) Upon this rugged couch then let us lie, for well it suits our most deplorable condition.—Here will we offer to stern Calamity,—this earth the Altar, and our selves the Sacrifice.—Our mutual groans shall eccho to each other thro' the dreary vault.—Our sighs shall number the moments as they pass,—and mingling tears communicate such anguish, as words were never made to express.

Barn. Then be it so.—Since you propose an intercourse of woe, pour all your griefs into my breast,—and in exchange take mine. (*Embracing.*) Where's now the anguish that you promis'd?—You've taken mine, and make me no return.—Sure Peace and Comfort dwell within these arms, and sorrow can't approach me while I'm here.—This too is the work of Heaven, who, having before spoke peace and pardon to me, now sends thee to confirm it.—O take, take some of the joy that overflows my breast!

Tr. I do, I do. Almighty Power, how have you made us capable to bear, at once, the extreams of Pleasure and of Pain?

Enter KEEPER

Keeper. Sir.

Tr. I come.

Barn. Must you leave me?—Death would soon have parted us for ever.

Tr. O, my *Barnwell*, there's yet another task, behind:—Again your Heart must bleed for others' woes.

Barn. To meet and part with you, I thought was all I had to do on Earth! What is there more for me to do or suffer?

Tr. I dread to tell thee, yet it must be known.—*Maria*.

Barn. Our Master's fair & virtuous Daughter!

Tr. The same.

Barn. No misfortune, I hope, has reach'd that lovely Maid! Preserve her, Heaven, from every ill, to show Mankind that Goodness is your care.

Tr. Thy, thy misfortunes, my unhappy Friend, have reach'd her. Whatever you & I have felt, and more, if more be possible, she feels for you.

Barn. I know he doth abhor a lie, & would not trifle with his dying Friend.—This is, indeed, the bitterness of Death!
                                                      (*Aside.*

Tr. You must remember, for we all observ'd it, for some time past, a heavy melancholy weigh'd her down.—Disconsolate she seem'd, & pin'd & languish'd from a cause unknown;—till hearing of your dreadful fate,—the long stifled flame blaz'd out.—She wept, she wrung her hands, and tore her hair, &, in the transport of her grief, discover'd her own lost state, whilst she lamented yours.

Barn. Will all the pain I feel restore thy ease, lovely unhappy Maid? (*Weeping.*) Why didn't you let me die and never know it?

Tr. It was impossible,—she makes no secret of her passion for you, & is determin'd to see you e'er you die;—she waits for me to introduce her.—   (*Exit.*

Barn. Vain busy thoughts be still!—What avails it to think on what I might have been?—I now am—what I've made my self.

Enter TRUEMAN *and* MARIA

Tr. Madam, reluctant I lead you to the dismal Scene: This is the seat of Misery and Guilt.—Here awful Justice reserves her publick Victims.—This is the entrance to shameful Death.—

Ma. To this sad place then no improper Guest, the abandon'd lost *Maria* brings Despair. And see the subject and the cause of all this world of woe.—Silent and motionless he stands, as if his Soul had quitted her abode, & the lifeless form alone was left behind,—yet that so perfect, that Beauty & Death,—ever at enmity,—now seem united there.

Barn. I groan, but murmur not.—Just Heaven, I am your own, do with me what you please.

Ma. Why are your streaming eyes still fix'd below?—as tho' thoud'st give the greedy Earth thy sorrows, and rob me of my due.—Were happiness within your power, you should bestow it where you pleas'd;—but in your misery I must & will partake.

Barn. Oh! say not so, but fly, abhor, and leave me to my Fate.—Consider what you are:—How vast your Fortune, and how bright your Fame:—Have pity on your Youth, your Beauty, & unequalled Virtue,—for which so many noble Peers have sigh'd in vain. Bless with your charms some honourable Lord.—Adorn with your Beauty, and, by your Example, improve the *English* Court, that justly claims such merit; so shall I quickly be to you as though I had never been.—

Ma. When I forget you, I must be so indeed.—Reason, Choice, Virtue, all forbid it.—Let Women, like *Millwood*, if there be more such Women, smile in prosperity, and in adversity forsake. Be it the pride of Virtue to repair, or to partake, the ruin such have made.

Tr. Lovely, ill-fated Maid!—Was there ever such generous distress before?—How must this peirce his grateful heart, and aggravate his woes!

Barn. E'er I knew Guilt or Shame, when Fortune smil'd, & when my youthful hopes were at the highest; if then to have rais'd my thoughts to you, had been presumption in me, never to have been pardon'd,—think how much beneath your self you condescend to regard me now.

Ma. Let her blush, who, professing Love, invades the freedom of your Sex's choice, and meanly sues in hopes of a return.—Your inevitable Fate hath render'd hope impossible as vain.—Then why shou'd I fear to avow a Passion so just & so disinterested?

Tr. If any shou'd take occasion, from *Millwood*'s crimes, to libel the best and fairest part of the Creation, here let them see their error.—The most distant hopes of such a tender passion, from so bright a Maid, might add to the happiness of the most happy, & make the greatest proud.—Yet here 'tis lavish'd in vain:—Tho' by the rich present, the generous Donor is undone,—he, on whom it is bestow'd, receives no benefit.

Barn. So the aromatick Spices of the East, which all the living covet & esteem, are, with unavailing kindness, wasted on the dead.

Ma. Yes, fruitless is my love, and unavailing all my sighs and tears.—Can they save thee from approaching Death?—from such a death?—O terrible idea!—What is her misery, and distress, who sees the first last object of her love, for whom alone she'd live,—for whom she'd die a thousand, thousand deaths, if it were possible,—expiring in her arms?—Yet she is happy, when compar'd to me.—Were millions of Worlds mine, I'd gladly give them in exchange for her condition.—The most consummate woe is light to mine. The last of curses to other miserable Maids, is all I ask; & that's deny'd me.

Tr. Time and reflection cure all ills.

Ma. All but this;—his dreadful Catastrophe Virtue her self abhors.—To give a Holiday to suburb Slaves, and passing entertain the savage herd, who, elbowing each other for a sight, pursue, and press upon him like his Fate.—A mind with piety and resolution arm'd, may smile on death.—But publick ignominy, everlasting shame.—Shame, the death of souls;—to die a thousand times, and yet survive even death it. . . .

self, in never dying infamy, is this to be endured?—Can I, who live in him, and must, each hour of my devoted life, feel all these woes renew'd,—can I endure this?—

Tr. Grief has impair'd her Spirits; she pants, as in the agonies of death.—

Barn. Preserve her, Heaven, & restore her peace,—nor let her death be added to my crimes.—(*Bell tolls.*) I am summon'd to my fate.

SCENE III

(*To them.*) KEEPER

Keep. The Officers attend you, Sir.—Mrs. *Millwood* is already summon'd.

Barn. Tell 'em I'm ready.—And now, my Friend, farewell. (*Embracing.*) Support and comfort the best you can this mourning Fair.—No more.—Forget not to pray for me.—(*Turning to* Maria) Would you, bright Excellence, permit me the honour of a chaste embrace,—the last happiness this World cou'd give were mine. (*She enclines towards him; they embrace.*) Exalted Goodness!—O turn your eyes from Earth, and me, to Heaven,—where Virtue, like yours, is ever heard. —Pray for the peace of my departing Soul.—Early my race of wickedness began, & soon has reach'd the summit:—E'er Nature has finish'd her work, and stamp'd me Man,—just at the time that others begin to stray,—my course is finish'd; tho' short my span of life, and few my days. Yet count my crimes for years, and I have liv'd whole Ages.—Justice and Mercy are in Heaven the same: Its utmost severity is Mercy to the whole,—thereby to cure Man's folly & presumption, which else wou'd render even infinite mercy vain and ineffectual.—Thus Justice, in compassion to Mankind, cuts off a Wretch like me, by one such example to secure thousands from future ruin.

> If any Youth, like you,—in future times,
> Shall mourn my Fate,—tho' he abhor my crimes;

Or tender Maid, like you,—my tale shall hear,
And to my sorrows give a pitying tear :
To each such melting eye, and throbbing heart,
Would gracious Heaven this benefit impart,
Never to know my guilt,—nor feel my pain, ⎫
Then must you own, you ought not to complain ; ⎬
Since you nor weep,—nor shall I die in vain. ⎭

SCENE IV

TRUEMAN, BLUNT, *and* LUCY

Lucy. Heart-breaking sight!—O wretched, wretched *Millwood!*

Tr. You come from her, then:—How is she disposed to meet her fate?

Blunt. Who can describe unalterable woe?

Lucy. She goes to death encompassed with horror, loathing life, and yet afraid to die; no tongue can tell her anguish and despair.

Tr. Heaven be better to her than her fears; may she prove a warning to others, a monument of Mercy in her self.

Lucy. O sorrow insupportable! break, break my heart.

Tr. In vain,

> *With bleeding hearts, and weeping eyes we show*
> *A human gen'rous sense of others woe ;*
> *Unless we mark what drew their ruin on,*
> *And by avoiding that, prevent our own.*

FINIS

EPILOGUE

Written by COLLEY CIBBER, *Esq*;
and spoken by Mrs. CIBBER

SINCE Fate has robb'd me of the hapless Youth,
For whom my heart had hoarded up its truth;
By all the Laws of Love and Honour, now,
I'm free again to chuse,—and one of you.

But soft,—With caution first I'll round me peep;
Maids, in my case, shou'd look, before they leap:
Here's choice enough, of various sorts, and hue,
The Cit, the Wit, the Rake cock'd up in cue,
The fair spruce Mercer, and the tawney Jew.

Suppose I search the sober Gallery;—No,
There's none but Prentices,—& Cuckolds all a row:
And these, I doubt, are those that make 'em so.
                                    (Pointing to the Boxes.

'Tis very well, enjoy the jest:—But you,
Fine powder'd Sparks;—nay, I am told 'tis true,
Your happy Spouses—can make Cuckolds too.
'Twixt you and them, the diff'rence this perhaps,
The Cit's asham'd whene'er his Duck he traps;
But you, when Madam's tripping, let her fall,
Cock up your hats, and take no shame at all.

What if some favour'd Poet I cou'd meet,
Whose Love wou'd lay his Lawrels at my feet?
No,—Painted Passion real Love abhors;—
His flame wou'd prove the Suit of Creditors.

Not to detain you then with longer pause,
In short, my heart to this conclusion draws,
I yield it to the hand, that's loudest in applause.

IRENE:

A

TRAGEDY.

As it is Acted at the

THEATRE ROYAL

IN

DRURY-LANE.

By Mr. *SAMUEL JOHNSON*.

LONDON:

Printed for R. Dodsley at *Tully's*-head *Pall-mall*
and sold by M. Cooper in *Pater-noster-Row*.

MDCCXLIX.

PROLOGUE

YE glitt'ring Train! whom Lace and Velvet bless,
Suspend the soft Sollicitudes of Dress;
From grov'ling Business and superfluous Care,
Ye Sons of Avarice! a Moment spare:
Vot'ries of Fame and Worshippers of Pow'r!
Dismiss the pleasing Phantoms for an Hour.
Our daring Bard with Spirit unconfin'd,
Spreads wide the mighty Moral for Mankind.
Learn here how Heav'n supports the virtuous Mind,
Daring, tho' calm; and vigorous, tho' resign'd.
Learn here what Anguish racks the guilty Breast,
In Pow'r dependent, in Success deprest.
Learn here that Peace from Innocence must flow;
All else is empty Sound, and idle Show.

If Truths like these with pleasing Language join;
Ennobled, yet unchang'd, if Nature shine:
If no wild Draught depart from Reason's Rules,
Nor Gods his Heroes, nor his Lovers Fools:
Intriguing Wits! his artless Plot forgive;
And spare him, Beauties! tho' his Lovers live.

Be this at least his Praise; be this his Pride;
To force Applause no modern Arts are try'd.
Shou'd partial Cat-calls all his Hopes confound,
He bids no Trumpet quell the fatal Sound.
Shou'd welcome Sleep relieve the weary Wit,
He rolls no Thunders o'er the drowsy Pit.
No Snares to captivate the Judgment spreads;
Nor bribes your Eyes to prejudice your Heads.
Unmov'd tho' Witlings sneer and Rivals rail;
Studious to please, yet not asham'd to fail.
He scorns the meek Address, the suppliant Strain,
With Merit needless, and without it vain.
In Reason, Nature, Truth he dares to trust:
Ye Fops be silent! and ye Wits be just!

EPILOGUE

MARRY a Turk! a haughty, Tyrant King,
Who thinks us Women born to dress and sing
To please his Fancy,—see no other Man—
Let him persuade me to it—if he can:
Besides, he has fifty Wives; and who can bear
To have the fiftieth Part her paultry Share?

   'Tis true, the Fellow's handsome, strait and tall;
But how the Devil should he please us all!
My Swain is little—true—but be it known,
My Pride's to have that little all my own.
Men will be ever to their Errors blind,
Where Woman's not allow'd to speak her Mind;
I swear this Eastern Pageantry is Nonsense,
And for one Man—one Wife's enough in Conscience.

   In vain proud Man usurps what's Woman's Due;
For us alone, they Honour's Paths pursue:
Inspir'd by us, they Glory's Heights ascend;
Woman the Source, the Object, and the End.
Tho' Wealth, and Pow'r, and Glory they receive,
These all are Trifles, to what we can give.
For us the Statesman labours, Hero fights,
Bears toilsome Days, and wakes long tedious Nights:
And when blest Peace has silenc'd War's Alarms,
Receives his full Reward in Beauty's Arms.

The PERSONS

MEN

MAHOMET,	Emperor of the *Turks*,	Mr. *Barry*
CALI BASSA,	First Visier,	Mr. *Berry*
MUSTAPHA,	A *Turkish* Aga,	Mr. *Sowden*
ABDALLA,	An Officer,	Mr. *Havard*
HASAN, CARAZA, }	*Turkish* Captains,	Mr. *Usher* Mr. *Burton*
DEMETRIUS, LEONTIUS, }	*Greek* Noblemen,	Mr. *Garrick* Mr. *Blakes*
MURZA,	An Eunuch,	

WOMEN

ASPASIA, IRENE, }	*Greek* Ladies,	Mrs. *Cibber* Mrs. *Pritchard*

Attendants on IRENE

IRENE,

A

TRAGEDY

ACT I. SCENE I

DEMETRIUS *and* LEONTIUS *in* Turkish *Habits*

LEONTIUS

And is it thus DEMETRIUS meets his Friend,
Hid in the mean Disguise of *Turkish* Robes,
With servile Secrecy to lurk in Shades,
And vent our Suff'rings in clandestine Groans?

DEMETRIUS

Till breathless Fury rested from Destruction
These Groans were fatal, these Disguises vain:
But now our *Turkish* Conquerors have quench'd
Their Rage, and pall'd their Appetite of Murder;
No more the glutted Sabre thirsts for Blood,
And weary Cruelty remits her Tortures.

LEONTIUS

Yet *Greece* enjoys no Gleam of transient Hope,
No soothing Interval of peaceful Sorrow;
The Lust of Gold succeeds the Rage of Conquest,
The Lust of Gold, unfeeling and remorseless!
The last Corruption of degenerate Man!
Urg'd by th' imperious Soldier's fierce Command,
The groaning *Greeks* break up their golden Caverns
Pregnant with Stores, that *India*'s Mines might envy,
Th' accumulated Wealth of toiling Ages.

DEMETRIUS

That Wealth, too sacred for their Country's Use!
That Wealth, too pleasing to be lost for Freedom!
That Wealth, which granted to their weeping Prince,
Had rang'd embattled Nations at our Gates:
But thus reserv'd to lure the Wolves of *Turkey*,
Adds Shame to Grief, and Infamy to Ruin.
Lamenting Av'rice now too late discovers
Her own neglected, in the publick Safety.

LEONTIUS

Reproach not Misery.—The Sons of *Greece*,
Ill-fated Race! So oft besieg'd in vain,
With false Security beheld Invasion.
Why should they fear?—That Power that kindly spreads
The Clouds, a Signal of impending Show'rs,
To warn the wand'ring Linnet to the Shade,
Beheld without Concern expiring *Greece*,
And not one Prodigy foretold our Fate.

DEMETRIUS

A thousand horrid Prodigies foretold it.
A feeble Government, eluded Laws,
A factious Populace, luxurious Nobles,
And all the Maladies of sinking States.
When publick Villainy, too strong for Justice,
Shows his bold front, the Harbinger of Ruin,
Can brave LEONTIUS call for airy Wonders,
Which Cheats interpret, and which Fools regard?
When some neglected Fabrick nods beneath
The Weight of Years, and totters to the Tempest,
Must Heaven dispatch the Messengers of Light,
Or wake the Dead to warn us of its Fall?

LEONTIUS

Well might the Weakness of our Empire sink
Before such Foes of more than human Force;

Some Pow'r invisible, from Heav'n or Hell,
Conducts their Armies and asserts their Cause.

DEMETRIUS

And yet, my Friend, what Miracles were wrought
Beyond the Power of Constancy and Courage;
Did unresisted Lightning aid their Cannon,
Did roaring Whirlwinds sweep us from the Ramparts:
'Twas Vice that shook our Nerves, 'twas Vice, LEONTIUS,
That froze our Veins, and wither'd all our Powers.

LEONTIUS

What e'er our Crimes, our Woes demand Compassion.
Each Night protected by the friendly Darkness,
Quitting my close Retreat, I range the City,
And weeping, kiss the venerable Ruins:
With silent Pangs I view the tow'ring Domes,
Sacred to Prayer, and wander thro' the Streets;
Where Commerce lavish'd unexhausted Plenty,
And Jollity maintain'd eternal Revels.—

DEMETRIUS

—How chang'd alas!—Now ghastly Desolation
In Triumph sits upon our shatter'd Spires,
Now Superstition, Ignorance and Error,
Usurp our Temples, and profane our Altars.

LEONTIUS

From ev'ry Palace burst a mingled Clamour,
The dreadful Dissonance of barb'rous Triumph,
Shrieks of Affright, and Wailings of Distress.
Oft when the Cries of violated Beauty
Arose to Heav'n, and pierc'd my bleeding Breast,
I felt thy Pains, and trembled for ASPASIA.

DEMETRIUS

ASPASIA! spare that lov'd, that mournful Name:

Dear hapless Maid—tempestuous Grief o'erbears
My reasoning Pow'rs—Dear, hapless, lost ASPASIA!

LEONTIUS

Suspend the Thought.

DEMETRIUS

     All Thought on her is Madness:
Yet let me think—I see the helpless Maid,
Behold the Monsters gaze with savage Rapture,
Behold how Lust and Rapine struggle round her.

LEONTIUS

Awake, DEMETRIUS, from this dismal Dream,
Sink not beneath imaginary Sorrows:
Call to your Aid your Courage, and your Wisdom;
Think on the sudden Change of human Scenes;
Think on the various Accidents of War;
Think on the mighty Pow'r of awful Virtue;
Think on that Providence that guards the Good.

DEMETRIUS

O Providence! extend thy Care to me,
For Courage droops unequal to the Combat,
And weak Philosophy denies her Succours.
Sure some kind Sabre in the Heat of Battle,
Ere yet the Foe found Leisure to be cruel,
Dismiss'd her to the Sky.

LEONTIUS

     Some virgin Martyr,
Perhaps, enamour'd of resembling Virtue,
With gentle Hand restrain'd the Streams of Life,
And snatch'd her timely from her Country's Fate.

DEMETRIUS

From those bright Regions of eternal Day,
Where now thou shin'st among thy Fellow-Saints,

Array'd in purer Light, look down on me:
In pleasing Visions, and assuasive Dreams;
O! sooth my Soul, and teach me how to lose thee.

LEONTIUS

Enough of unavailing Tears, DEMETRIUS,
I came obedient to thy friendly Summons,
And hop'd to share thy Counsels, not thy Sorrows:
While thus we mourn the Fortune of ASPASIA,
To what are we reserv'd?

DEMETRIUS

                              To what I know not:
But hope, yet hope, to Happiness and Honour;
If Happiness can be without ASPASIA.

LEONTIUS

But whence this new sprung Hope?

DEMETRIUS

                              From CALI BASSA:
The Chief, whose Wisdom guides the *Turkish* Counsels.
He, tir'd of Slav'ry, tho' the highest Slave,
Projects at once our Freedom and his own;
And bids us thus disguis'd await him here.

LEONTIUS

Can he restore the State he could not save?
In vain, when *Turkey*'s troops assail'd our Walls,
His kind Intelligence betray'd their Measures;
Their Arms prevail'd, though CALI was our Friend.

DEMETRIUS

When the tenth Sun had set upon our Sorrows,
At Midnight's private Hour a Voice unknown
Sounds in my sleeping Ear, 'Awake DEMETRIUS,
'Awake, and follow me to better Fortunes;'
Surpriz'd I start, and bless the happy Dream;

Then rouzing know the firy Chief ABDALLA,
Whose quick Impatience seiz'd my doubtful Hand,
And led me to the Shore where CALI stood,
Pensive and listning to the beating Surge.
There in soft Hints and in ambiguous Phrase,
With all the Diffidence of long Experience,
That oft' had practis'd Fraud, and oft' detected,
The Vet'ran Courtier half reveal'd his Project.
By his Command, equipp'd for speedy Flight,
Deep in a winding Creek a Galley lies,
Mann'd with the bravest of our fellow Captives,
Selected by my Care, a hardy Band,
That long to hail thee Chief.

LEONTIUS

                           But what avails
So small a Force? or why should CALI fly?
Or how can CALI's Flight restore our Country?

DEMETRIUS

Reserve these Questions for a safer Hour,
Or hear himself, for see the Bassa comes.

SCENE II

DEMETRIUS, LEONTIUS, CALI BASSA

CALI

Now summon all thy Soul, illustrious Christian!
Awake each Faculty that sleeps within thee,
The Courtier's Policy, the Sage's Firmness,
The Warrior's Ardour, and the Patriot's Zeal;
If chasing past Events with vain Pursuit,
Or wand'ring in the Wilds of future Being,
A single Thought now rove, recall it home.
But can thy Friend sustain the glorious Cause,
The Cause of Liberty, the Cause of Nations?

Demetrius

Observe him closely with a Statesman's Eye,
Thou that hast long perus'd the Draughts of Nature,
And know'st the Characters of Vice and Virtue,
Left by the Hand of Heav'n on human Clay.

Cali

His Mien is lofty, his Demeanour great,
Nor sprightly Folly wantons in his Air,
Nor dull Serenity becalms his Eyes.
Such had I trusted once as soon as seen,
But cautious Age suspects the flatt'ring Form,
And only credits what Experience tells.
Has Silence press'd her Seal upon his Lips?
Does adamantine Faith invest his Heart?
Will he not bend beneath a Tyrant's Frown?
Will he not melt before Ambition's Fire?
Will he not soften in a Friend's Embrace?
Or flow dissolving in a Woman's Tears?

Demetrius

Sooner these trembling Leaves shall find a Voice,
And tell the Secrets of their conscious Walks;
Sooner the Breeze shall catch the flying Sounds,
And shock the Tyrant with a Tale of Treason.
Your slaughter'd Multitudes that swell the Shore,
With Monuments of Death proclaim his Courage;
Virtue and Liberty engross his Soul,
And leave no Place for Perfidy or Fear.

Leontius

I scorn a Trust unwillingly repos'd;
Demetrius will not lead me to Dishonour;
Consult in private, call me when your Scheme
Is ripe for Action, and demands the Sword.   [*Going.*

Demetrius

Leontius stay.

CALI

   Forgive an old Man's Weakness,
And share the deepest Secrets of my Soul,
My Wrongs, my Fears, my Motives, my Designs:—
When unsuccessful Wars, and civil Factions,
Embroil'd the *Turkish* State—our Sultan's Father
Great *Amurath*, at my Request, forsook
The Cloister's Ease, resum'd the tott'ring Throne,
And snatch'd the Reins of abdicated Pow'r
From giddy MAHOMET's unskilful Hand.
This fir'd the youthful King's ambitious Breast,
He murmurs Vengeance at the Name of CALI,
And dooms my rash Fidelity to Ruin.

DEMETRIUS

Unhappy Lot of all that shine in Courts;
For forc'd Compliance, or for zealous Virtue,
Still odious to the Monarch, or the People.

CALI

Such are the Woes when arbitrary Pow'r,
And lawless Passion, hold the Sword of Justice.
If there be any Land, as Fame reports,
Where common Laws restrain the Prince and Subject,
A happy Land, where circulating Pow'r
Flows through each Member of th' embodied State,
Sure, not unconscious of the mighty Blessing,
Her grateful Sons shine bright with ev'ry Virtue;
Untainted with the Lust of Innovation,
Sure all unite to hold her League of Rule
Unbroken as the sacred Chain of Nature,
That links the jarring Elements in Peace.

LEONTIUS

But say, great Bassa, why the Sultan's Anger,
Burning in vain, delays the Stroke of Death?

CALI

Young, and unsettled in his Father's Kingdoms,
Fierce as he was, he dreaded to destroy
The Empire's Darling, and the Soldier's Boast;
But now confirm'd, and swelling with his Conquests,
Secure he tramples my declining Fame,
Frowns unrestrain'd, and dooms me with his Eyes.

DEMETRIUS

What can reverse thy Doom?

CALI

                    The Tyrant's Death.

DEMETRIUS

But *Greece* is still forgot.

CALI

                    On *Asia*'s Coast,
Which lately bless'd my gentle Government,
Soon as the Sultan's unexpected Fate,
Fills all th' astonish'd Empire with Confusion,
My Policy shall raise an easy Throne;
The *Turkish* Pow'rs from *Europe* shall retreat,
And harrass *Greece* no more with wasteful War.
A Galley mann'd with *Greeks*, thy charge, LEONTIUS,
Attends to waft us to Repose and Safety.

DEMETRIUS

That Vessel, if observ'd, alarms the Court,
And gives a thousand fatal Questions Birth;
Why stor'd for Flight? and why prepar'd by CALI?

CALI

This Hour I'll beg, with unsuspecting Face,
Leave to perform my Pilgrimage to *Mecca*;
Which granted, hides my Purpose from the World,
And, though refus'd, conceals it from the Sultan.

LEONTIUS

How can a single Hand attempt a Life
Which Armies guard, and Citadels inclose?

CALI

Forgetful of Command, with captive Beauties,
Far from his Troops, he toys his Hours away.
A roving Soldier seiz'd in *Sophia*'s Temple
A Virgin shining with distinguish'd Charms,
And brought his beauteous Plunder to the Sultan.

DEMETRIUS

In *Sophia*'s Temple!—What Alarm!—Proceed.

CALI

The Sultan gaz'd, he wonder'd and he lov'd;
In Passion lost, he bad the conqu'ring Fair
Renounce her Faith, and be the Queen of *Turkey*;
The pious Maid, with modest Indignation,
Threw back the glitt'ring Bribe.

DEMETRIUS

                              Celestial Goodness!
It must, it must be She; her Name?

CALI

                    ASPASIA.

DEMETRIUS

What Hopes, what Terrors rush upon my Soul!
O lead me quickly to the Scene of Fate;
Break through the Politician's tedious Forms,
ASPASIA calls me, let me fly to save her.

LEONTIUS

Did MAHOMET reproach or praise her Virtue?

CALI

His Offers oft repeated, still refus'd,
At length rekindled his accustom'd Fury,
And chang'd th' endearing Smile and am'rous Whisper
To threats of Torture, Death and Violation.

DEMETRIUS

These tedious Narratives of frozen Age
Distract my Soul; dispatch thy lingring Tale;
Say, did a Voice from Heav'n restrain the Tyrant?
Did interposing Angels guard her from him?

CALI

Just in the Moment of impending Fate,
Another Plund'rer brought the bright IRENE;
Of equal Beauty, but of softer Mien,
Fear in her Eye, Submission on her Tongue,
Her mournful Charms attracted his Regards,
Disarm'd his Rage, and in repeated Visits
Gain'd all his Heart; at length his eager Love
To her transferr'd the Offer of a Crown.

LEONTIUS

Nor found again the bright Temptation fail?

CALI

Trembling to grant, nor daring to refuse,
While Heav'n and MAHOMET divide her Fears,
With coy Caresses and with pleasing Wiles
She feeds his Hopes, and sooths him to Delay.
For her, Repose is banish'd from the Night
And Business from the Day. In her Apartments
He lives—

LEONTIUS

            And there must fall.

CALI

But yet th' Attempt
Is hazardous.

LEONTIUS

Forbear to speak of Hazards,
What has the Wretch that has surviv'd his Country,
His Friends, his Liberty, to hazard?

CALI

Life.

DEMETRIUS

Th' inestimable Privilege of Breathing!
Important Hazard! What's that airy Bubble
When weigh'd with *Greece*, with Virtue, with ASPASIA?
A floating Atom, Dust that falls unheeded
Into the adverse Scale, nor shakes the Balance.

CALI

At least this Day be calm—If we succeed,
ASPASIA's thine, and all thy Life is Rapture—
See! MUSTAPHA, the Tyrant's Minion, comes;
Invest LEONTIUS with his new Command;
And wait ABDALLA's unsuspected Visits:
Remember Freedom, Glory, *Greece*, and Love.
                    [*Exeunt* Demetrius and Leontius.

SCENE III

CALI, MUSTAPHA

MUSTAPHA

By what Enchantment does this lovely *Greek*
Hold in her Chains the captivated Sultan?
He tires his Fav'rites with IRENE's Praise,
And seeks the Shades to muse upon IRENE;

IRENE steals unheeded from his Tongue,
And mingles unperceiv'd with ev'ry Thought.

CALI

Why should the Sultan shun the Joys of Beauty,
Or arm his Breast against the Force of Love?
Love, that with sweet Vicissitude relieves
The Warrior's Labours, and the Monarch's Cares.
But will she yet receive the Faith of *Mecca*?

MUSTAPHA

Those pow'rful Tyrants of the Female Breast
Fear and Ambition, urge her to Compliance;
Dress'd in each Charm of gay Magnificence,
Alluring Grandeur courts her to his Arms,
Religion calls her from the wish'd Embrace,
Paints future Joys, and points to distant Glories.

CALI

Soon will th'unequal Contest be decided,
Prospects obscur'd by Distance faintly strike.
Each Pleasure brightens at its near Approach,
And every Danger shocks with double Horror.

MUSTAPHA

How shall I scorn the beautiful Apostate!
How will the bright ASPASIA shine above her!

CALI

Should she, for Proselytes are always zealous,
With pious Warmth receive our Prophet's Law—

MUSTAPHA

Heav'n will contemn the mercenary Fervour,
Which Love of Greatness, not of Truth, inflames.

CALI

Cease, cease thy Censures, for the Sultan comes
Alone, with am'rous Haste to seek his Love.

SCENE IV

Mahomet, Cali Bassa, Mustapha

CALI

Hail, Terror of the Monarchs of the World,
Unshaken be thy Throne as Earth's firm Base,
Live till the Sun forgets to dart his Beams,
And weary Planets loiter in their Courses.

MAHOMET

But, CALI, let IRENE share thy Prayers;
For what is Length of Days without IRENE?
I come from empty Noise, and tasteless Pomp,
From Crouds that hide a Monarch from himself,
To prove the Sweets of Privacy and Friendship,
And dwell upon the Beauties of IRENE.

CALI

O may her Beauties last unchang'd by Time,
As those that bless the Mansions of the Good.

MAHOMET

Each Realm where Beauty turns the graceful Shape,
Swells the fair Breast or animates the Glance,
Adorns my Palace with its brightest Virgins;
Yet unacquainted with these soft Emotions
I walk'd superior through the Blaze of Charms,
Prais'd without Rapture, left without Regret.
Why rove I now, when absent from my Fair,
From Solitude to Crouds, from Crouds to Solitude,
Still restless, till I clasp the lovely Maid,
And ease my loaded Soul upon her Bosom?

MUSTAPHA

Forgive, great Sultan, that intrusive Duty
Enquires the final Doom of *Menodorus*,
The *Grecian* Counsellor.

MAHOMET

Go see him die;
His martial Rhet'rick taught the *Greeks* Resistance;
Had they prevail'd, I ne'er had known IRENE.

[*Exit* Mustapha.

SCENE V

MAHOMET, CALI

MAHOMET

Remote from Tumult, in th' adjoining Palace,
Thy Care shall guard this Treasure of my Soul;
There let ASPASIA, since my Fair entreats it,
With Converse chase the melancholy Moments.
Sure, chill'd with sixty winter Camps, thy Blood
At Sight of female Charms will glow no more.

CALI

These Years, unconquer'd MAHOMET, demand
Desires more pure, and other Cares than Love.
Long have I wish'd, before our Prophet's Tomb,
To pour my Prayers for thy successful Reign,
To quit the Tumults of the noisy Camp,
And sink into the silent Grave in Peace.

MAHOMET

What! Think of Peace while haughty *Scanderbeg*
Elate with Conquest, in his native Mountains,
Prowls o'er the wealthy Spoils of bleeding *Turkey*?
While fair *Hungaria*'s unexhausted Vallies
Pour forth their Legions, and the roaring *Danube*
Rolls half his Floods unheard through shouting Camps?
Nor couldst thou more support a Life of Sloth
Than *Amurath*—

CALI

Still full of *Amurath*!   [*Aside.*

MAHOMET

Than *Amurath*, accustom'd to Command,
Could bear his Son upon the *Turkish* Throne.

CALI

This Pilgrimage our Lawgiver ordain'd—

MAHOMET

For those who could not please by nobler Service.—
Our warlike Prophet loves an active Faith,
The holy Flame of enterprizing Virtue,
Mocks the dull Vows of Solitude and Penance,
And scorns the lazy Hermit's cheap Devotion;
Shine thou distinguish'd by superior Merit,
With wonted Zeal pursue the Task of War,
Till every Nation reverence the *Koran*,
And ev'ry Suppliant lift his Eyes to *Mecca*.

CALI

This Regal Confidence, this pious Ardour,
Let Prudence moderate, though not suppress.
Is not each Realm that smiles with kinder Suns,
Or boasts a happier Soil, already thine?
Extended Empire, like expanded Gold,
Exchanges solid Strength for feeble Splendor.

MAHOMET

Preach thy dull Politics to vulgar Kings,
Thou know'st not yet thy Master's future Greatness,
His vast Designs, his Plans of boundless Pow'r.
　　When ev'ry Storm in my Domain shall roar,
　　When ev'ry Wave shall beat a *Turkish* Shore,
　　Then, CALI, shall the Toils of Battle cease,
　　Then dream of Prayer, and Pilgrimage, and Peace.
　　　　　　　　　　　　　　　　　[*Exeunt.*

ACT II. SCENE I
ASPASIA, IRENE

IRENE

ASPASIA, yet pursue the sacred Theme;
Exhaust the Stores of pious Eloquence,
And teach me to repell the Sultan's Passion.
Still at ASPASIA's Voice a sudden Rapture
Exalts my Soul, and fortifies my Heart.
The glitt'ring Vanities of empty Greatness,
The Hopes and Fears, the Joys and Pains of Life,
Dissolve in Air, and vanish into Nothing.

ASPASIA

Let nobler Hopes and juster Fears succeed,
And bar the Passes of IRENE's Mind
Against returning Guilt.

IRENE

When thou art absent
Death rises to my View, with all his Terrors;
Then Visions horrid as a Murd'rer's Dreams
Chill my Resolves, and blast my blooming Virtue:
Stern Torture shakes his bloody Scourge before me,
And Anguish gnashes on the fatal Wheel.

ASPASIA

Since Fear predominates in every Thought,
And sways thy Breast with absolute Dominion,
Think on th' insulting Scorn, the conscious Pangs,
The future Miseries that wait th' Apostate;
So shall Timidity assist thy Reason,
And Wisdom into Virtue turn thy Frailty.

IRENE

Will not that Pow'r that form'd the Heart of Woman,

And wove the feeble Texture of her Nerves,
Forgive those Fears that shake the tender Frame?

ASPASIA

The Weakness we lament, our selves create.
Instructed from our infant Years to court
With counterfeited Fears the Aid of Man,
We learn to shudder at the rustling Breeze,
Start at the Light, and tremble in the Dark;
Till Affectation, rip'ning to Belief,
And Folly, frighted at her own Chimeras,
Habitual Cowardice usurps the Soul.

IRENE

Not all like thee can brave the Shocks of Fate,
Thy Soul by Nature great, enlarg'd by Knowledge,
Soars unencumber'd with our idle Cares,
And all ASPASIA but her Beauty's Man.

ASPASIA

Each generous Sentiment is thine, DEMETRIUS,
Whose Soul, perhaps, yet mindful of ASPASIA,
Now hovers o'er this melancholy Shade,
Well pleas'd to find thy Precepts not forgotten.
O! could the Grave restore the pious Hero,
Soon would his Art or Valour set us free,
And bear us far from Servitude and Crimes.

IRENE

He yet may live.

ASPASIA

Alas! delusive Dream!
Too well I know him, his immod'rate Courage,
Th' impetuous Sallies of excessive Virtue,
Too strong for Love, have hurried him on Death.

SCENE II

Aspasia, Irene, Cali, Abdalla

Cali *to* Abdalla, *as they advance*

Behold our future Sultaness, Abdalla;—
Let artful Flatt'ry now, to lull Suspicion,
Glide through Irene to the Sultan's Ear.
Wouldst thou subdue th' obdurate Cannibal
To tender Friendship, praise him to his Mistress.

To Irene

Well may those Eyes that view these heav'nly Charms,
Reject the Daughters of contending Kings;
For what are pompous Titles, proud Alliance,
Empire or Wealth, to Excellence like thine?

Abdalla

Receive th' impatient Sultan to thy Arms;
And may a long Posterity of Monarchs,
The Pride and Terror of succeeding Days,
Rise from the happy Bed; and future Queens
Diffuse Irene's Beauty through the World.

Irene

Can Mahomet's imperial Hand descend
To clasp a Slave? or, can a Soul like mine,
Unus'd to Power, and form'd for humbler Scenes,
Support the splendid Miseries of Greatness?

Cali

No regal Pageant deck'd with casual Honours,
Scorn'd by his Subjects, trampled by his Foes;
No feeble Tyrant of a petty State
Courts thee to shake on a dependent Throne;
Born to command, as thou to charm Mankind,
The Sultan from himself derives his Greatness.
Observe, bright Maid, as his resistless Voice

Drives on the Tempest of destructive War,
How Nation after Nation falls before him.

ABDALLA

At his dread Name the distant Mountains shake
Their cloudy Summits, and the Sons of Fierceness,
That range unciviliz'd from Rock to Rock,
Distrust th' eternal Fortresses of Nature,
And wish their gloomy Caverns more obscure.

ASPASIA

Forbear this lavish Pomp of dreadful Praise;
The horrid Images of War and Slaughter
Renew our Sorrows, and awake our Fears.

ABDALLA

CALI, methinks yon waving Trees afford
A doubtful Glimpse of our approaching Friends;
Just as I mark'd them, they forsook the Shore,
And turn'd their hasty Steps towards the Garden.

CALI

Conduct these Queens, ABDALLA, to the Palace:
Such heav'nly Beauty form'd for Adoration,
The Pride of Monarchs, the Reward of Conquest;
Such Beauty must not shine to vulgar Eyes.

SCENE III

CALI *solus*

How Heav'n in Scorn of human Arrogance,
Commits to trivial Chance the Fate of Nations!
While with incessant Thought laborious Man
Extends his mighty Schemes of Wealth and Pow'r,
And tow'rs and triumphs in ideal Greatness,
Some accidental Gust of Opposition
Blasts all the Beauties of his new Creation,

O'erturns the Fabrick of presumptuous Reason,
And whelms the swelling Architect beneath it.
Had not the Breeze untwin'd the meeting Boughs,
And through the parted Shade disclos'd the *Greeks*,
Th' important Hour had pass'd unheeded by,
In all the sweet Oblivion of Delight,
In all the Fopperies of meeting Lovers;
In Sighs and Tears, in Transports and Embraces,
In soft Complaints, and idle Protestations.

SCENE IV

CALI, DEMETRIUS, LEONTIUS

CALI

Could Omens fright the Resolute and Wise,
Well might we fear impending Disappointments.

LEONTIUS

Your artful Suit, your Monarch's fierce Denial,
The cruel Doom of hapless *Menodorus*—

DEMETRIUS

And your new Charge, that dear, that heav'nly Maid.—

LEONTIUS

All this we know already from ABDALLA.

DEMETRIUS

Such slight Defeats but animate the Brave
To stronger Efforts, and maturer Counsels.

CALI

My Doom confirm'd establishes my Purpose,
Calmly he heard, till *Amurath*'s Resumption
Rose to his Thought, and set his Soul on Fire:
When from his Lips the fatal Name burst out,

A sudden Pause th' imperfect Sense suspended,
Like the dread Stillness of condensing Storms.

DEMETRIUS

The loudest Cries of Nature urge us forward;
Despotick Rage pursues the Life of CALI;
His groaning Country claims LEONTIUS' Aid;
And yet another Voice, forgive me *Greece*,
The pow'rful Voice of Love inflames DEMETRIUS;
Each ling'ring Hour alarms me for ASPASIA.

CALI

What Passions reign among thy Crew, LEONTIUS?
Does chearless Diffidence oppress their Hearts?
Or sprightly Hope exalt their kindling Spirits?
Do they with Pain repress the struggling Shout,
And listen eager to the rising Wind?

LEONTIUS

All there is Hope, and Gaiety, and Courage,
No cloudy Doubts, or languishing Delays;
Ere I could range them on the crowded Deck,
At once a hundred Voices thunder'd round me,
And every Voice was Liberty and *Greece*.

DEMETRIUS

Swift let us rush upon the careless Tyrant,
Nor give him Leisure for another Crime.

LEONTIUS

Then let us now resolve, nor idly waste
Another Hour in dull Deliberation.

CALI

But see, where destin'd to protract our Counsels,
Comes MUSTAPHA.—Your *Turkish* Robes conceal you—
Retire with Speed, while I prepare to meet him
With artificial Smiles, and seeming Friendship.

SCENE V

CALI *and* MUSTAPHA

CALI

I see the Gloom that low'rs upon thy Brow,
These Days of Love and Pleasure charm not thee;
Too slow these gentle Constellations roll,
Thou long'st for Stars that frown on human Kind,
And scatter Discord from their baleful Beams.

MUSTAPHA

How blest art thou, still jocund and serene,
Beneath the Load of Business, and of Years.

CALI

Sure by some wond'rous Sympathy of Souls,
My Heart still beats responsive to the Sultan's;
I share, by secret Instinct, all his Joys,
And feel no Sorrow while my Sov'reign smiles.

MUSTAPHA

The Sultan comes, impatient for his Love;
Conduct her hither, let no rude Intrusion
Molest these private Walks, or Care invade
These Hours assign'd to Pleasure and IRENE.

SCENE VI

MAHOMET, MUSTAPHA

MAHOMET

Now, MUSTAPHA, pursue thy Tale of Horror.
Has Treason's dire Infection reach'd my Palace?
Can CALI dare the Stroke of heav'nly Justice,
In the dark Precincts of the gaping Grave,
And load with Perjuries his parting Soul?

Was it for this, that sick'ning in *Epirus*,
My Father call'd me to his Couch of Death,
Join'd CALI's Hand to mine, and falt'ring cry'd,
Restrain the Fervour of impetuous Youth
With venerable CALI's faithful Counsels?
Are these the Counsels? This the Faith of CALI?
Were all our Favours lavish'd on a Villain?
Confest?——

MUSTAPHA

Confest by dying *Menodorus*.
In his last Agonies the gasping Coward,
Amidst the Tortures of the burning Steel,
Still fond of Life, groan'd out the dreadful Secret,
Held forth this fatal Scroll, then sunk to nothing.

MAHOMET, *examining the Paper*

His Correspondence with our Foes of *Greece*!
His Hand! His Seal! The Secrets of my Soul
Conceal'd from all but him! All! all conspire
To banish Doubt, and brand him for a Villain.
Our Schemes for ever cross'd, our Mines discover'd,
Betray'd some Traytor lurking near my Bosom.
Oft have I rag'd, when their wide-wasting Cannon
Lay pointed at our Batt'ries yet unform'd,
And broke the meditated Lines of War.
Detested CALI too, with artful Wonder,
Would shake his wily Head, and closely whisper,
Beware of MUSTAPHA, beware of Treason.

MUSTAPHA

The Faith of MUSTAPHA disdains Suspicion;
But yet, great Emperor, beware of Treason;
Th' insidious Bassa fir'd by Disappointment—

MAHOMET

Shall feel the Vengeance of an injur'd King.
Go, seize him, load him with reproachful Chains;

Before th' assembled Troops proclaim his Crimes;
Then leave him stretch'd upon the ling'ring Rack,
Amidst the Camp to howl his Life away.

MUSTAPHA

Should we before the Troops proclaim his Crimes,
I dread his Arts of seeming Innocence,
His bland Address, and Sorcery of Tongue;
And should he fall unheard, by sudden Justice,
Th' adoring Soldiers would revenge their Idol.

MAHOMET

CALI, this Day with hypocritick Zeal,
Implor'd my Leave to visit *Mecca*'s Temple;
Struck with the Wonder of a Statesman's Goodness,
I rais'd his Thoughts to more sublime Devotion.
Now let him go, pursu'd by silent Wrath,
Meet unexpected Daggers in his Way,
And in some distant Land obscurely die.

MUSTAPHA

There will his boundless Wealth, the Spoil of *Asia*,
Heap'd by your Father's ill-plac'd Bounties on him,
Disperse Rebellion through the Eastern World;
Bribe to his Cause and lift beneath his Banners
Arabia's roving Troops, the Sons of Swiftness,
And arm the *Persian* Heretick against thee;
There shall he waste thy Frontiers, check thy Conquests,
And though at length subdued, elude thy Vengeance.

MAHOMET

Elude my Vengeance? no—My Troops shall range
Th' eternal Snows that freeze beyond *Meotis*,
And *Afric*'s torrid Sands in search of CALI.
Should the fierce North upon his frozen Wings
Bear him aloft above the wond'ring Clouds,
And seat him in the *Pleiad*'s golden Chariots,

Thence should my Fury drag him down to Tortures;
Wherever Guilt can fly, Revenge can follow.

MUSTAPHA

Wilt thou dismiss the Savage from the Toils
Only to hunt him round the ravag'd World?

MAHOMET

Suspend his Sentence—Empire and IRENE
Claim my divided Soul. This Wretch unworthy
To mix with nobler Cares, I'll throw aside
For idle Hours, and crush him at my Leisure.

MUSTAPHA

Let not th' unbounded Greatness of his Mind
Betray my King to negligence of Danger.
Perhaps the Clouds of dark Conspiracy
Now roll full fraught with Thunder o'er your Head.
Twice since the Morning rose I saw the Bassa,
Like a fell Adder swelling in a Brake,
Beneath the Covert of this verdant Arch
In private Conference; beside him stood
Two Men unknown, the Partners of his Bosom;
I mark'd them well, and trac'd in either Face
The gloomy Resolution, horrid Greatness,
And stern Composure of despairing Heroes;
And, to confirm my Thought, at sight of me,
As blasted by my Presence, they withdrew
With all the speed of Terror and of Guilt.

MAHOMET

The strong Emotions of my troubled Soul
Allow no pause for Art or for Contrivance;
And dark Perplexity distracts my Counsels.
Do thou resolve: For see IRENE comes!
At her approach each ruder Gust of Thought
Sinks like the sighing of a Tempest spent,
And Gales of softer Passion fan my Bosom.

[CALI *enters with* IRENE, *and exit with* MUSTAPHA.

SCENE VII

MAHOMET, IRENE

MAHOMET

Wilt thou descend, fair Daughter of Perfection,
To hear my Vows, and give Mankind a Queen?
Ah! cease, IRENE, cease those flowing Sorrows,
That melt a Heart, impregnable till now,
And turn thy Thoughts henceforth to Love and Empire.
How will the matchless Beauties of IRENE,
Thus bright in Tears, thus amiable in Ruin,
With all the graceful Pride of Greatness heighten'd.
Amidst the Blaze of Jewels and of Gold,
Adorn a Throne, and dignify Dominion.

IRENE

Why all this glare of splendid Eloquence,
To paint the Pageantries of guilty State?
Must I for these renounce the Hope of Heav'n,
Immortal Crowns and fulness of Enjoyment?

MAHOMET

Vain Raptures all—For your inferiour Natures
Form'd to delight, and happy by delighting,
Heav'n has reserv'd no future Paradise,
But bids you rove the Paths of Bliss, secure
Of total Death and careless of Hereafter;
While Heav'n's high Minister, whose awful Volume
Records each Act, each Thought of sov'reign Man,
Surveys your Plays with inattentive Glance,
And leaves the lovely Trifler unregarded.

IRENE

Why then has Nature's vain Munificence
Profusely pour'd her Bounties upon Woman?
Whence then those Charms thy Tongue has deign'd to flatter,
That Air resistless and enchanting Blush,

Unless the beauteous Fabrick was design'd
A Habitation for a fairer Soul?

MAHOMET

Too high, bright Maid, thou rat'st exteriour Grace
Not always do the fairest Flow'rs diffuse
The richest Odours, nor the speckled Shells
Conceal the Gem; let female Arrogance
Observe the feather'd Wand'rers of the Sky,
With Purple varied and bedrop'd with Gold,
They prune the Wing, and spread the glossy Plumes,
Ordain'd, like you, to flutter and to shine,
And chear the weary Passenger with Musick.

IRENE

Mean as we are, this Tyrant of the World
Implores our Smiles, and trembles at our Feet:
Whence flow the Hopes and Fears, Despair and Rapture,
Whence all the Bliss and Agonies of Love?

MAHOMET

Why, when the Balm of Sleep descends on Man,
Do gay Delusions, wand'ring o'er the Brain,
Sooth the delighted Soul with empty Bliss?
To Want give Affluence? and to Slav'ry Freedom?
Such are Love's Joys, the Lenitives of Life,
A fancy'd Treasure, and a waking Dream.

IRENE

Then let me once, in honour of our Sex,
Assume the boastful Arrogance of Man.
Th' attractive Softness, and th' indearing Smile,
And pow'rful Glance, 'tis granted, are our own;
Nor has impartial Nature's frugal Hand
Exhausted all her nobler Gifts on you;
Do not we share the comprehensive Thought,
Th' enlivening Wit, the penetrating Reason?

Beats not the female Breast with gen'rous Passions,
The thirst of Empire, and the Love of Glory?

MAHOMET

Illustrious Maid, new Wonders fix me thine,
Thy Soul compleats the Triumphs of thy Face.
I thought, forgive my Fair, the noblest Aim,
The strongest Effort of a female Soul,
Was but to chuse the Graces of the Day;
To tune the Tongue, to teach the Eyes to roll,
Dispose the Colours of the flowing Robe,
And add new Roses to the faded Cheek.
Will it not charm a Mind like thine exalted,
To shine the Goddess of applauding Nations,
To scatter Happiness and Plenty round thee,
To bid the prostrate Captive rise and live,
To see new Cities tow'r at thy Command,
And blasted Kingdoms flourish at thy Smile?

IRENE

Charm'd with the Thought of blessing human Kind,
Too calm I listen to the flatt'ring Sounds.

MAHOMET

O seize the Power to bless—IRENE's Nod
Shall break the Fetters of the groaning Christian;
Greece, in her lovely Patroness secure,
Shall mourn no more her plunder'd Palaces.

IRENE

Forbear—O do not urge me to my Ruin!

MAHOMET

To State and Pow'r I court thee, not to Ruin:
Smile on my Wishes, and command the Globe.
Security shall spread her Shield before thee,
And Love infold thee with his downy Wings.

If Greatness please thee, mount th' imperial Seat;
If Pleasure charm thee, view this soft Retreat;
Here ev'ry Warbler of the Sky shall sing;
Here ev'ry Fragrance breathe of ev'ry Spring:
To deck these Bow'rs each Region shall combine,
And ev'n our Prophet's Gardens envy thine:
Empire and Love shall share the blissful Day,
And varied Life steal unperceiv'd away.

ACT III. SCENE I

CALI, ABDALLA

CALI *enters with a discontented Air; to him enters* ABDALLA

CALI

Is this the fierce Conspirator ABDALLA?
Is this the restless Diligence of Treason?
Where hast thou linger'd while th' encumber'd Hours
Fly lab'ring with the Fate of future Nations,
And hungry Slaughter scents Imperial Blood?

ABDALLA

Important Cares detain'd me from your Counsels.

CALI

Some petty Passion! some domestick Trifle!
Some vain Amusement of a vacant Soul!
A weeping Wife perhaps, or dying Friend,
Hung on your Neck, and hinder'd your Departure.
Is this a Time for Softness or for Sorrow?
Unprofitable, peaceful, female Virtues!
When eager Vengeance shows a naked Foe,
And kind Ambition points the Way to Greatness.

ABDALLA

Must then Ambition's Votaries infringe

The Laws of Kindness, break the Bonds of Nature?
And quit the Names of Brother, Friend, and Father?

CALI

This sov'reign Passion, scornful of Restraint,
Ev'n from the Birth affects supreme Command,
Swells in the Breast, and with resistless Force,
O'erbears each gentler Motion of the Mind.
As when a Deluge overspreads the Plains,
The wand'ring Rivulet, and silver Lake,
Mix undistinguish'd with the gen'ral Roar.

ABDALLA

Yet can Ambition in ABDALLA's Breast
Claim but the second Place: there mighty Love
Has fix'd his Hopes, Inquietudes, and Fears,
His glowing Wishes, and his jealous Pangs.

CALI

Love is indeed the Privilege of Youth;
Yet, on a Day like this, when Expectation
Pants for the dread Event—But let us reason—

ABDALLA

Hast thou grown old amidst the Croud of Courts,
And turn'd th' instructive Page of Human Life,
To cant, at last, of Reason to a Lover?
Such ill-tim'd Gravity, such serious Folly,
Might well befit the solitary Student,
Th' unpractis'd Dervise, or sequester'd Faquir.
Know'st thou not yet, when Love invades the Soul,
That all her Faculties receive his Chains?
That Reason gives her Scepter to his Hand,
Or only struggles to be more enslav'd?
ASPASIA! who can look upon thy Beauties?
Who hear thee speak, and not abandon Reason?
Reason! the hoary Dotard's dull Directress,
That loses all because the hazards nothing:

Reason! the tim'rous Pilot, that to shun
The Rocks of Life, for ever flies the Port.

CALI

But why this sudden Warmth?

ABDALLA

             Because I love:
Because my slighted Passion burns in vain!
Why roars the Lioness distress'd by Hunger?
Why foam the swelling Waves when Tempests rise?
Why shakes the Ground, when subterraneous Fires
Fierce through the bursting Caverns rend their Way?

CALI

Not till this Day thou saw'st this fatal Fair;
Did ever Passion make so swift a Progress?
Once more reflect, suppress this infant Folly.

ABDALLA

Gross Fires, enkindled by a Mortal Hand,
Spread by Degrees, and dread th' oppressing Stream;
The subtler Flames emitted from the Sky,
Flash out at once, with Strength above Resistance.

CALI

How did ASPASIA welcome your Address?
Did you proclaim this unexpected Conquest?
Or pay with speaking Eyes a Lover's Homage?

ABDALLA

Confounded, aw'd, and lost in Admiration,
I gaz'd, I trembled; but I could not speak:
When ev'n as Love was breaking off from Wonder,
And tender Accents quiver'd on my Lips,
She mark'd my sparkling Eyes, and heaving Breast,
And smiling, conscious of her Charms, withdrew.

             Enter Demetrius *and* Leontius.

CALI

Now be some Moments Master of thyself,
Nor let DEMETRIUS know thee for a Rival.
Hence! or be calm—To disagree is Ruin.

SCENE II

CALI, DEMETRIUS, LEONTIUS, ABDALLA

DEMETRIUS

When will Occasion smile upon our Wishes,
And give the Tortures of Suspence a Period?
Still must we linger in uncertain Hope?
Still languish in our Chains, and dream of Freedom
Like thirsty Sailors gazing on the Clouds,
Till burning Death shoots through their wither'd Limbs?

CALI

Deliverance is at Hand; for *Turkey*'s Tyrant
Sunk in his Pleasures, confident and gay,
With all the Heroe's dull Security,
Trusts to my Care his Mistress and his Life,
And laughs and wantons in the Jaws of Death.

LEONTIUS

So weak is Man, when destin'd to Destruction,
The Watchful slumber, and the Crafty trust.

CALI

At my Command yon' Iron Gates unfold;
At my Command the Sentinels retire;
With all the Licence of Authority,
Through bowing Slaves, I range the private Rooms,
And of To-morrow's Action fix the Scene.

DEMETRIUS

To-morrow's Action? Can that hoary Wisdom

Born down with Years, still doat upon To-morrow?
That fatal Mistress of the Young, the Lazy,
The Coward, and the Fool, condemn'd to lose
An useless Life in waiting for To-morrow,
To gaze with longing Eyes upon To-morrow,
Till interposing Death destroys the Prospect!
Strange! that this gen'ral Fraud from Day to Day
Should fill the World with Wretches undetected.
The Soldier lab'ring through a Winter's March,
Still sees To-morrow drest in Robes of Triumph;
Still to the Lover's long-expecting Arms,
To-morrow brings the visionary Bride.
But thou, too old to bear another Cheat,
Learn, that the present Hour alone is Man's.

LEONTIUS

The present Hour with open Arms invites;
Seize the kind Fair, and press her to thy Bosom.

DEMETRIUS

Who knows, ere this important Morrow rise,
But Fear, or Mutiny may taint the *Greeks*?
Who knows if MAHOMET's awaking Anger
May spare the fatal Bow-string till To-morrow?

ABDALLA

Had our first *Asian* Foes but known this Ardour,
We still had wander'd on *Tartarian* Hills.
Rouse, CALI, shall the Sons of conquer'd *Greece*,
Lead us to Danger, and abash their Victors?
This Night with all her conscious Stars be witness,
Who merits most, DEMETRIUS or ABDALLA.

DEMETRIUS

Who merits most!—I knew not we were Rivals.

CALI

Young Man, forbear—The Heat of Youth, no more—

Well,—'tis decreed—This Night shall fix our Fate.
Soon as the Veil of Evening clouds the Sky,
With cautious Secrecy, LEONTIUS, steer
Th' appointed Vessel to yon' shaded Bay,
Form'd by this Garden jutting on the Deep;
There, with your Soldiers arm'd, and Sails expanded,
Await our coming, equally prepar'd
For speedy Flight, or obstinate Defence.   [*Exit* Leont.

SCENE III

CALI, ABDALLA, DEMETRIUS

DEMETRIUS

Now pause, great Bassa, from the Thoughts of Blood,
And kindly grant an Ear to gentler Sounds.
If e'er thy Youth has known the Pangs of Absence,
Or felt th' impatience of obstructed Love,
Give me, before th' approaching Hour of Fate,
Once to behold the Charms of bright ASPASIA,
And draw new Virtue from her heav'nly Tongue.

CALI

Let Prudence, ere the Suit be farther urg'd,
Impartial weigh the Pleasure with the Danger.
A little longer, and she's thine for ever.

DEMETRIUS

Prudence and Love conspire in this Request,
Lest unacquainted with our bold Attempt,
Surprize o'erwhelm her, and retard our Flight.

CALI

What I can grant, you cannot ask in vain—

DEMETRIUS

I go to wait thy Call; this kind Consent
Completes the Gift of Freedom and of Life.   [*Exit* Dem.

SCENE IV

CALI, ABDALLA

ABDALLA

And this is my Reward—to burn, to languish,
To rave unheeded, while the happy *Greek*,
The Refuse of our Swords, the Dross of Conquest,
Throws his fond Arms about ASPASIA's Neck,
Dwells on her Lips, and sighs upon her Breast;
Is't not enough, he lives by our Indulgence,
But he must live to make his Masters wretched?

CALI

What Claim hast thou to plead?

ABDALLA

                    The Claim of Pow'r,
Th' unquestion'd Claim of Conquerors, and Kings!

CALI

Yet in the Use of Pow'r remember Justice.

ABDALLA

Can then th' Assassin lift his treach'rous Hand
Against his King, and cry, Remember Justice?
Justice demands the forfeit Life of CALI;
Justice demands that I reveal your Crimes;
Justice demands—But see th' approaching Sultan.
Oppose my Wishes, and—Remember Justice.

CALI

Disorder sits upon thy Face—retire.
                              [*Exit* Abdalla, *Enter* Mahomet.

SCENE V

CALI, MAHOMET

CALI

Long be the Sultan bless'd with happy Love!
My Zeal marks Gladness dawning on thy Cheek,
With Raptures such as fire the Pagan Crouds,
When pale, and anxious for their Years to come,
They see the Sun surmount the dark Eclipse,
And hail unanimous their conqu'ring God.

MAHOMET

My Vows, 'tis true, she hears with less Aversion,
She sighs, she blushes, but she still denies.

CALI

With warmer Courtship press the yielding Fair,
Call to your Aid with boundless Promises
Each rebel Wish, each traitor Inclination
That raises Tumults in the female Breast,
The love of Pow'r, of Pleasure, and of Show.

MAHOMET

These Arts I try'd, and to inflame her more,
By hateful Business hurried from her sight,
I bad a hundred Virgins wait around her,
Sooth her with all the Pleasures of Command,
Applaud her Charms, and court her to be Great.

Exit MAHOMET.

SCENE VI

CALI *solus*

He's gone—Here rest, my Soul, thy fainting Wing,
Here recollect thy dissipated Pow'rs.—

Our distant Int'rests, and our different Passions
Now haste to mingle in one common Center,
And Fate lies crouded in a narrow Space.
Yet in that narrow Space what Dangers rise?—
Far more I dread ABDALLA's fiery Folly,
Than all the Wisdom of the grave Divan.
Reason with Reason fights on equal Terms,
The raging Madman's unconnected Schemes
We cannot obviate, for we cannot guess.
Deep in my Breast be treasured this Resolve,
When CALI mounts the Throne ABDALLA dies,
Too fierce, too faithless for Neglect or Trust.

> [*Enter* Irene *with Attendants.*

SCENE VII

CALI, IRENE, ASPASIA, &c.

CALI

Amidst the Splendor of encircling Beauty,
Superiour Majesty proclaims the Queen,
And Nature justifies our Monarch's Choice.

IRENE

Reserve this Homage for some other Fair;
Urge me not on to glittering Guilt, nor pour
In my weak Ear th' intoxicating sounds.

CALI

Make haste, bright Maid, to rule the willing World;
Aw'd by the Rigour of the Sultan's Justice,
We court thy gentleness.

ASPASIA

                    Can CALI's Voice
Concur to press a hapless Captive's Ruin?

CALI

Long would my Zeal for MAHOMET and Thee
Detain me here. But Nations call upon me,
And Duty bids me chuse a distant Walk,
Nor taint with Care the Privacies of Love.

SCENE VIII

IRENE, ASPASIA, Attendants

ASPASIA

If yet this shining Pomp, these sudden Honours,
Swell not thy Soul beyond Advice or Friendship,
Not yet inspire the Follies of a Queen,
Or tune thine Ear to soothing Adulation,
Suspend awhile the Privilege of Pow'r
To hear the Voice of Truth; dismiss thy Train,
Shake off th' Incumbrances of State a moment,
And lay the tow'ring Sultaness aside,
                    [Irene *signs to her Attendants to retire.*
While I foretell thy Fate; that Office done,—
No more I boast th' ambitious Name of Friend,
But sink among thy Slaves without a Murmur.

IRENE

Did regal Diadems invest my Brow,
Yet should my Soul, still faithful to her Choice,
Esteem ASPASIA's Breast the noblest Kingdom.

ASPASIA

The Soul once tainted with so foul a Crime,
No more shall glow with Friendship's hallow'd Ardour:
Those holy Beings, whose superiour Care
Guides erring Mortals to the Paths of Virtue,
Affrighted at Impiety like thine,
Resign their Charge to Baseness and to Ruin.

IRENE

Upbraid me not with fancy'd Wickedness,
I am not yet a Queen, or an Apostate.
But should I sin beyond the hope of Mercy,
If when Religion prompts me to refuse,
The dread of instant Death restrains my Tongue?

ASPASIA

Reflect that Life and Death, affecting sounds,
Are only varied Modes of endless Being;
Reflect that Life, like ev'ry other Blessing,
Derives its Value from its Use alone;
Not for itself but for a nobler End
Th'Eternal gave it, and that End is Virtue.
When inconsistent with a greater Good,
Reason commands to cast the less away;
Thus Life, with loss of Wealth, is well preserv'd,
And Virtue cheaply sav'd with loss of Life.

IRENE

If built on settled Thought, this Constancy
Not idly flutters on a boastful Tongue,
Why, when Destruction rag'd around our Walls,
Why fled this haughty Heroine from the Battle?
Why then did not this warlike Amazon
Mix in the War, and shine among the Heroes?

ASPASIA

Heav'n, when its Hand pour'd softness on our Limbs
Unfit for Toil, and polish'd into Weakness,
Made passive Fortitude the Praise of Woman:
Our only Arms are Innocence and Meekness.
Not then with raving Cries I fill'd the City,
But while DEMETRIUS, dear lamented Name,
Pour'd storms of Fire upon our fierce Invaders,
Implor'd th' eternal Power to shield my Country,
With silent Sorrows, and with calm Devotion.

IRENE

O! did IRENE shine the Queen of *Turkey*,
No more should *Greece* lament those Prayers rejected.
Again should golden Splendour grace her Cities,
Again her prostrate Palaces should rise,
Again her Temples found with holy Musick:
No more should Danger fright, or Want distress
The smiling Widows, and protected Orphans.

ASPASIA

Be virtuous Ends pursued by virtuous Means,
Nor think th' Intention sanctifies the Deed:
That Maxim publish'd in an impious Age,
Would loose the wild Enthusiast to destroy,
And fix the fierce Usurper's bloody Title.
Then Bigottry might send her Slaves to War,
And bid Success become the Test of Truth,
Unpitying Massacre might waste the World,
And Persecution boast the Call of Heav'n.

IRENE

Shall I not wish to chear afflicted Kings,
And plan the Happiness of mourning Millions?

ASPASIA

Dream not of Pow'r thou never can'st attain:
When social Laws first harmonis'd the World,
Superiour Man possess'd the Charge of Rule,
The Scale of Justice, and the Sword of Pow'r,
Nor left us aught but Flattery and State.

IRENE

To me my Lover's Fondness will restore,
Whate'er Man's Pride has ravish'd from our Sex.

ASPASIA

When soft Security shall prompt the Sultan,
Freed from the Tumults of unsettled Conquest,

To fix his Court, and regulate his Pleasures,
Soon shall the dire Seraglio's horrid Gates
Close like th' eternal Bars of Death upon thee,
Immur'd, and buried in perpetual Sloth,
That gloomy Slumber of the stagnant Soul;
There shalt thou view from far the quiet Cottage,
And sigh for chearful Poverty in vain:
There wear the tedious Hours of Life away,
Beneath each Curse of unrelenting Heav'n,
Despair, and Slav'ry, Solitude, and Guilt.

IRENE

There shall we find the yet untasted Bliss
Of Grandeur and Tranquillity combin'd.

ASPASIA

Tranquillity and Guilt, disjoin'd by Heav'n,
Still stretch in vain their longing Arms afar;
Nor dare to pass th' insuperable Bound,
Ah! let me rather seek the Convent's Cell;
There when my Thoughts, at interval of Pray'r,
Descend to range these Mansions of Misfortune,
Oft' shall I dwell on our disastrous Friendship,
And shed the pitying Tear for lost IRENE.

IRENE

Go, languish on in dull Obscurity;
Thy dazzled Soul with all its boasted Greatness,
Shrinks at th' o'erpow'ring Gleams of regal State,
Stoops from the Blaze like a degenerate Eagle,
And flies for Shelter to the Shades of Life.

ASPASIA

On me, should Providence, without a Crime,
The weighty Charge of Royalty confer;
Call me to civilize the *Russian* Wilds,
Or bid soft Science polish *Britain*'s Heroes:
Soon shouldst thou see, how false thy weak Reproach.

My Bosom feels, enkindled from the Sky,
The lambent Flames of mild Benevolence,
Untouch'd by fierce Ambition's raging Fires.

IRENE

Ambition is the Stamp, impress'd by Heav'n
To mark the noblest Minds, with active Heat
Inform'd they mount the Precipice of Pow'r,
Grasp at Command, and tow'r in quest of Empire;
While vulgar Souls compassionate their Cares,
Gaze at their Height and tremble at their Danger:
Thus meaner Spirits with Amazement mark
The varying Seasons, and revolving Skies,
And ask, what guilty Pow'r's rebellious Hand
Rolls with eternal Toil the pond'rous Orbs;
While some Archangel nearer to Perfection,
In easy State presides o'er all their Motions,
Directs the Planets with a careless Nod,
Conducts the Sun, and regulates the Spheres.

ASPASIA

Well may'st thou hide in Labyrinths of Sound
The Cause that shrinks from Reason's powerful Voice.
Stoop from thy Flight, trace back th'entangled Thought,
And set the glitt'ring Fallacy to view.
Not Pow'r I blame, but Pow'r obtain'd by Crime;
Angelic Greatness is Angelic Virtue.
Amidst the Glare of Courts, the Shout of Armies,
Will not th' Apostate feel the Pangs of Guilt,
And wish too late for Innocence and Peace?
Curst as the Tyrant of th' infernal Realms,
With gloomy State and agonizing Pomp.

SCENE IX

IRENE, ASPASIA, MAID

MAID

A *Turkish* Stranger of majestick Mien,
Asks at the Gate Admission to ASPASIA,
Commission'd, as he says, by CALI BASSA.

IRENE

Whoe'er thou art, or whatso'er thy Message,   [*Aside*
Thanks for this kind Relief—with Speed admit him.

ASPASIA

He comes, perhaps, to separate us for ever;
When I am gone remember, O! remember,
That none are great, or happy, but the Virtuous.

[*Exit* IRENE, *Enter* DEMETRIUS.

SCENE X

ASPASIA, DEMETRIUS

DEMETRIUS

'Tis she—My Hope, my Happiness, my Love!
ASPASIA! do I once again behold thee?
Still, still the same—unclouded by Misfortune!
Let my blest Eyes for ever gaze———

ASPASIA

DEMETRIUS!

DEMETRIUS

Why does the Blood forsake thy lovely Cheek?
Why shoots this Chilness through thy shaking Nerves?
Why does thy Soul retire into herself?
Recline upon my Breast thy sinking Beauties:
Revive—Revive to Freedom and to Love.

ASPASIA

What well known Voice pronounc'd the grateful Sounds
Freedom and Love? Alas! I'm all Confusion,
A sudden Mist o'ercasts my darken'd Soul,
The Present, Past, and Future swim before me,
Lost in a wild Perplexity of Joy.

DEMETRIUS

Such Ecstacy of Love! such pure Affection,
What Worth can merit? or what Faith reward?

ASPASIA

A thousand Thoughts imperfect and distracted,
Demand a Voice, and struggle into Birth;
A thousand Questions press upon my Tongue,
But all give way to Rapture and DEMETRIUS.

DEMETRIUS

O say, bright Being, in this Age of Absence,
What Fears, what Griefs, what Dangers hast thou known?
Say, how the Tyrant threaten'd, flatter'd, sigh'd,
Say, how he threaten'd, flatter'd, sigh'd in vain!
Say, how the Hand of Violence was rais'd,
Say, how thou call'dst in Tears upon DEMETRIUS!

ASPASIA

Inform me rather, how thy happy Courage
Stem'd in the Breach the Deluge of Destruction,
And pass'd uninjur'd through the Walks of Death?
Did savage Anger, and licentious Conquest
Behold the Hero with ASPASIA's Eyes?
And thus protected in the gen'ral Ruin,
O say, what guardian Pow'r convey'd thee hither.

DEMETRIUS

Such strange Events, such unexpected Chances,
Beyond my warmest Hope, or wildest Wishes,
Concur'd to give me to ASPASIA's Arms,
I stand amaz'd, and ask, if yet I clasp thee.

ASPASIA

Sure Heav'n, for Wonders are not wrought in vain,
That joins us thus, will never part us more.

SCENE XI

DEMETRIUS, ASPASIA, ABDALLA

ABDALLA

It parts you now—The hasty Sultan sign'd
The Laws unread, and flies to his IRENE.

DEMETRIUS

Fix'd and intent on his IRENE's Charms,
He envies none the Converse of ASPASIA.

ABDALLA

ASPASIA's Absence will inflame Suspicion;
She cannot, must not, shall not linger here,
Prudence and Friendship bid me force her from you.

DEMETRIUS

Force her! profane her with a Touch, and die.

ABDALLA

'Tis *Greece*, 'tis Freedom calls ASPASIA hence,
Your careless Love betrays your Country's Cause.

DEMETRIUS

If we must part—

ASPASIA

No! let us die together.

DEMETRIUS

If we must part—

ABDALLA

                    Dispatch; th' encreasing Danger
Will not admit a Lover's long Farewell,
The long-drawn Intercourse of Sighs and Kisses.

DEMETRIUS

Then—O my Fair, I cannot bid thee goe;
Receive her, and protect her, gracious Heav'n!
Yet let me watch her dear departing Steps,
If Fate persues me, let it find me here.
    Reproach not, *Greece*, a Lover's fond Delays,
Nor think thy Cause neglected while I gaze,
New Force, new Courage, from each Glance I gain,
And find our Passions not infus'd in vain.

ACT IV. SCENE I

DEMETRIUS, ASPASIA, *enter as talking*

ASPASIA

Enough—resistless Reason calms my Soul—
Approving Justice smiles upon your Cause,
And Nature's Rights entreat th' asserting Sword.
Yet when your Hand is lifted to destroy,
Think—but excuse a Woman's needless Caution,
Purge well thy Mind from ev'ry private Passion,
Drive Int'rest, Love, and Vengeance from thy Thoughts,
Fill all thy ardent Breast with *Greece* and Virtue,
Then strike secure, and Heav'n assist the Blow.

DEMETRIUS

Thou kind Assistant of my better Angel,
Propitious Guide of my bewilder'd Soul,
Calm of my Cares, and Guardian of my Virtue.

ASPASIA

My Soul first kindled by thy bright Example,
To noble Thought and gen'rous Emulation,
Now but reflects those Beams that flow'd from thee.

DEMETRIUS

With native Lustre and unborrow'd Greatness,
Thou shin'st, bright Maid, superior to Distress;
Unlike the trifling Race of vulgar Beauties,
Those glitt'ring Dew-drops of a vernal Morn,
That spread their Colours to the genial Beam,
And sparkling quiver to the Breath of *May*;
But when the Tempest with sonorous Wing
Sweeps o'er the Grove, forsake the lab'ring Bough,
Dispers'd in Air or mingled with the Dust.

ASPASIA

Forbear this Triumph—still new Conflicts wait us,
Foes unforeseen, and Dangers unsuspected.
Oft when the fierce Besiegers' eager Host
Beholds the fainting Garrison retire,
And rushes joyful to the naked Wall,
Destruction flashes from th' insidious Mine,
And sweeps th' exulting Conqueror away:
Perhaps in vain the Sultan's Anger spar'd me,
To find a meaner Fate from treach'rous Friendship—
ABDALLA—

DEMETRIUS

      Can ABDALLA then dissemble?
That firy Chief, renown'd for gen'rous Freedom,
For Zeal unguarded, undissembled Hate,
For daring Truth, and turbulence of Honour?

ASPASIA

This open Friend, this undesigning Hero,
With noisy Falshoods forc'd me from your Arms,
To shock my Virtue with a Tale of Love.

DEMETRIUS

Did not the Cause of *Greece* restrain my Sword,
ASPASIA should not fear a second Insult.

ASPASIA

His Pride and Love by Turns inspir'd his Tongue,
And intermix'd my Praises with his own;
His Wealth, his Rank, his Honours he recounted,
Till in the midst of Arrogance and Fondness,
Th' approaching Sultan forc'd me from the Palace;
Then while he gaz'd upon his yielding Mistress,
I stole unheeded from their ravish'd Eyes,
And sought this happy Grove in quest of Thee.

DEMETRIUS

Soon may the final Stroke decide our Fate,
Lest baneful Discord crush our infant Scheme,
And strangled Freedom perish in the Birth.

ASPASIA

My Bosom harrass'd with alternate Passions,
Now hopes, now fears—

DEMETRIUS

                    Th' Anxieties of Love.

ASPASIA

Think how the sov'reign Arbiter of Kingdoms
Detests thy false Associates' black Designs,
And frowns on Perjury, Revenge and Murder.
Embark'd with Treason on the Seas of Fate,
When Heav'n shall bid the swelling Billows rage,
And point vindictive Lightnings at Rebellion,
Will not the Patriot share the Traytor's Danger?
Oh could thy Hand unaided free thy Country,
Nor mingled Guilt pollute the sacred Cause!

DEMETRIUS

Permitted oft, though not inspir'd by Heav'n,
Successful Treasons punish impious Kings.

ASPASIA

Nor end my Terrors with the Sultan's Death;
Far as Futurity's untravell'd Waste
Lies open to Conjecture's dubious Ken,
On ev'ry Side Confusion, Rage and Death,
Perhaps the Phantoms of a Woman's Fear,
Beset the treacherous Way with fatal Ambush;
Each *Turkish* Bosom burns for thy Destruction,
Ambitious CALI dreads the Statesman's Arts,
And hot ABDALLA hates the happy Lover.

DEMETRIUS

Capricious Man! to Good and Ill inconstant,
Too much to fear or trust, is equal Weakness.
Sometimes the Wretch unaw'd by Heav'n or Hell,
With mad Devotion idolizes Honour.
The Bassa, reeking with his Master's Murder,
Perhaps may start at violated Friendship.

ASPASIA

How soon, alas! will Int'rest, Fear, or Envy,
O'erthrow such weak, such accidental Virtue,
Nor built on Faith, nor fortify'd by Conscience?

DEMETRIUS

When desp'rate Ills demand a speedy Cure,
Distrust is Cowardice, and Prudence Folly.

ASPASIA

Yet think a Moment, ere you court Destruction,
What Hand, when Death has snatch'd away DEMETRIUS,
Shall guard ASPASIA from triumphant Lust.

DEMETRIUS

Dismiss these needless Fears—a Troop of *Greeks*
Well known, long try'd, expect us on the Shore.
Borne on the Surface of the smiling Deep,
Soon shalt thou scorn, in Safety's Arms repos'd,
ABDALLA's Rage and CALI's Stratagems.

ASPASIA

Still, still Distrust sits heavy on my Heart.
Will e'er an happier Hour revisit *Greece*?

DEMETRIUS

Should Heav'n yet unappeas'd refuse its Aid,
Disperse our Hopes, and frustrate our Designs,
Yet shall the Conscience of the great Attempt
Diffuse a Brightness on our future Days;
Nor will his Country's Groans reproach DEMETRIUS.
But how can'st thou support the Woes of Exile?
Can'st thou forget hereditary Splendours,
To live obscure upon a foreign Coast,
Content with Science, Innocence and Love?

ASPASIA

Nor Wealth, nor Titles, make ASPASIA's Bliss.
O'erwhelm'd and lost amidst the publick Ruins
Unmov'd I saw the glitt'ring Trifles perish,
And thought the petty Dross beneath a Sigh.
Chearful I follow to the rural Cell,
Love be my Wealth, and my Distinction Virtue.

DEMETRIUS

Submissive and prepar'd for each Event,
Now let us wait the last Award of Heav'n,
Secure of Happiness from Flight or Conquest,
Nor fear the Fair and Learn'd can want Protection.
The mighty *Tuscan* courts the banish'd Arts
To kind *Italia*'s hospitable Shades;
There shall soft Leisure wing th' excursive Soul,

And Peace propitious smile on fond Desire;
There shall despotick Eloquence resume
Her ancient Empire o'er the yielding Heart;
There Poetry shall tune her sacred Voice,
And wake from Ignorance the Western World.

SCENE II

DEMETRIUS, ASPASIA, CALI

CALI

At length th' unwilling Sun resigns the World
To Silence and to Rest. The Hours of Darkness,
Propitious Hours to Stratagem and Death,
Pursue the last Remains of ling'ring Light.

DEMETRIUS

Count not these Hours as Parts of vulgar Time,
Think them a sacred Treasure lent by Heav'n,
Which squander'd by Neglect, or Fear, or Folly,
No Pray'r recals, no Diligence redeems;
To-morrow's Dawn shall see the *Turkish* King
Stretch'd in the Dust, or tow'ring on his Throne;
To-morrow's Dawn shall see the mighty CALI
The sport of Tyranny, or Lord of Nations.

CALI

Then waste no longer these important Moments
In soft Endearments, and in gentle Murmurs,
Nor lose in Love the Patriot and the Hero.

DEMETRIUS

'Tis Love combin'd with Guilt alone, that melts
The soften'd Soul to Cowardice and Sloth;
But virtuous Passion prompts the great Resolve,
And fans the slumb'ring Spark of heav'nly Fire.
Retire, my Fair, that Pow'r that smiles on Goodness

Guide all thy Steps, calm ev'ry stormy Thought,
And still thy Bosom with the Voice of Peace.

ASPASIA

Soon may we meet again, secure and free,
To feel no more the Pangs of Separation.   [*Exit.*

DEMETRIUS, CALI

DEMETRIUS

This Night alone is ours—Our mighty Foe,
No longer lost in am'rous Solitude,
Will now remount the slighted Seat of Empire,
And show IRENE to the shouting People:
ASPASIA left her sighing in his Arms,
And list'ning to the pleasing Tale of Pow'r,
With soften'd Voice she dropp'd the faint Refusal,
Smiling Consent she sat, and blushing Love.

CALI

Now, Tyrant, with Satiety of Beauty,
Now feast thine Eyes, thine Eyes that ne'er hereafter
Shall dart their am'rous Glances at the Fair,
Or glare on CALI with malignant Beams.

SCENE III

DEMETRIUS, CALI, LEONTIUS, ABDALLA

LEONTIUS

Our Bark unseen has reach'd th' appointed Bay,
And where yon Trees wave o'er the foaming Surge
Reclines against the Shore: Our *Grecian* Troop
Extends its Lines along the sandy Beach,
Elate with Hope, and panting for a Foe.

ABDALLA

The fav'ring Winds assist the great Design,
Sport in our Sails, and murmur o'er the Deep.

CALI

'Tis well—A single Blow compleats our Wishes:
Return with speed, LEONTIUS, to your Charge;
The *Greeks*, disorder'd by their Leader's Absence,
May droop dismay'd, or kindle into Madness.

LEONTIUS

Suspected still?—What Villain's pois'nous Tongue
Dares join LEONTIUS' Name with Fear or Falshood?
Have I for this preserv'd my guiltless Bosom,
Pure as the Thoughts of infant Innocence?
Have I for this defy'd the Chiefs of *Turkey*,
Intrepid in the flaming Front of War?

CALI

Hast thou not search'd my Soul's profoundest Thoughts?
Is not the Fate of *Greece* and CALI thine?

LEONTIUS

Why has thy Choice then pointed out LEONTIUS,
Unfit to share this Night's illustrious Toils?
To wait remote from Action, and from Honour,
An idle List'ner to the distant Cries
Of slaughter'd Infidels, and Clash of Swords!
Tell me the Cause, that while thy Name, DEMETRIUS,
Shall soar triumphant on the Wings of Glory,
Despis'd and curs'd, LEONTIUS must descend
Through hissing Ages, a proverbial Coward,
The Tale of Women, and the Scorn of Fools?

DEMETRIUS

Can brave LEONTIUS be the Slave of Glory?
Glory, the casual Gift of thoughtless Crouds!
Glory, the Bribe of avaricious Virtue!
Be but my Country free, be thine the Praise;
I ask no Witness, but attesting Conscience,
No Records, but the Records of the Sky.

LEONTIUS

Wilt thou then head the Troop upon the Shore,
While I destroy th' Oppressor of Mankind?

DEMETRIUS

What can'st thou boast superiour to DEMETRIUS?
Ask to whose Sword the *Greeks* will trust their Cause,
My Name shall echo through the shouting Field;
Demand whose Force yon *Turkish* Heroes dread,
The shudd'ring Camp shall murmur out DEMETRIUS.

CALI

Must *Greece*, still wretched by her Children's Folly,
For ever mourn their Avarice or Factions?
DEMETRIUS justly pleads a double Title,
The Lover's Int'rest aids the Patriot's claim.

LEONTIUS

My Pride shall ne'er protract my Country's Woes;
Succeed, my Friend, unenvied by LEONTIUS.

DEMETRIUS

I feel new Spirit shoot along my Nerves,
My Soul expands to meet approaching Freedom.
Now hover o'er us with propitious Wings,
Ye sacred Shades of Patriots and of Martyrs;
All ye, whose blood tyrannick Rage effus'd,
Or Persecution drank, attend our Call;
And from the Mansions of perpetual Peace
Descend, to sweeten Labours once your own.

CALI

Go then, and with united Eloquence
Confirm your Troops; and when the Moon's fair Beam
Plays on the quiv'ring Waves, to guide our Flight,
Return, DEMETRIUS, and be free for ever.

[*Exeunt* Dem. *and* Leon.

SCENE IV

CALI, ABDALLA

ABDALLA

How the new Monarch, swell'd with airy Rule,
Looks down, contemptuous, from his fancy'd Height,
And utters Fate, unmindful of ABDALLA.

CALI

Far be such black Ingratitude from CALI,
When *Asia*'s Nations own me for their Lord,
Wealth, and Command, and Grandeur shall be thine.

ABDALLA

Is this the Recompence reserv'd for me?
Dar'st thou thus dally with ABDALLA's Passion?
Henceforward hope no more my slighted Friendship,
Wake from thy Dream of Pow'r to Death and Tortures,
And bid thy visionary Throne farewell.

CALI

Name and enjoy thy Wish—

ABDALLA

I need not name it;
ASPASIA's Lovers know but one Desire,
Nor hope, nor wish, nor live but for ASPASIA.

CALI

That fatal Beauty plighted to DEMETRIUS
Heav'n makes not mine to give.

ABDALLA

Nor to deny.

CALI

Obtain her and possess, thou know'st thy Rival.

ABDALLA

Too well I know him, since on *Thracia*'s Plains
I felt the Force of his tempestuous Arm,
And saw my scatter'd Squadrons fly before him.
Nor will I trust th' uncertain Chance of Combat;
The Rights of Princes let the Sword decide,
The petty Claims of Empire and of Honour:
Revenge and subtle Jealousy shall teach
A surer Passage to his hated Heart.

CALI

O spare the gallant *Greek*, in him we lose
The Politician's Arts, and Heroe's Flame.

ABDALLA

When next we meet before we storm the Palace,
The Bowl shall circle to confirm our League,
Then shall these Juices taint DEMETRIUS' Draught,
                                        [*Shewing a Phial.*
And stream destructive through his freezing Veins:
Thus shall he live to strike th' important Blow,
And perish ere he tastes the Joys of Conquest.

SCENE V

MAHOMET, MUSTAPHA, CALI, ABDALLA

MAHOMET

Henceforth for ever happy be this Day,
Sacred to Love, to Pleasure, and IRENE:
The matchless Fair has bless'd me with Compliance;
Let every Tongue resound IRENE's Praise,
And spread the general Transport through Mankind.

CALI

Blest Prince, for whom indulgent Heav'n ordains
At once the Joys of Paradise and Empire,

Now join thy People's, and thy CALI's Prayers,
Suspend thy Passage to the Seats of Bliss,
Nor wish for Houries in IRENE's Arms.

MAHOMET

Forbear—I know the long try'd Faith of CALI.

CALI

O! could the Eyes of Kings, like those of Heav'n,
Search to the dark Recesses of the Soul,
Oft would they find Ingratitude and Treason,
By Smiles, and Oaths, and Praises ill disguis'd.
How rarely would they meet in crouded Courts,
Fidelity so firm, so pure, as mine!

MUSTAPHA

Yet ere we give our loosen'd Thoughts to Rapture,
Let Prudence obviate an impending Danger.
Tainted by Sloth, the Parent of Sedition,
The hungry Janizary burns for Plunder,
And growls in private o'er his idle Sabre.

MAHOMET

To still their Murmurs, ere the twentieth Sun
Shall shed his Beams upon the bridal Bed,
I rouse to War, and conquer for IRENE.
Then shall the *Rhodian* mourn his sinking Tow'rs,
And *Buda* fall, and proud *Vienna* tremble,
Then shall *Venetia* feel the *Turkish* Pow'r,
And subject Seas roar round their Queen in vain.

ABDALLA

Then seize fair *Italy*'s delightful Coast,
To fix your Standard in Imperial *Rome*.

MAHOMET

Her Sons malicious Clemency shall spare,
To form new Legends, sanctify new Crimes,

To canonize the Slaves of Superstition,
And fill the World with Follies and Impostures,
Till angry Heav'n shall mark them out for Ruin,
And War o'erwhelm them in their Dream of Vice.
O could her fabled Saints, and boasted Prayers
Call forth her ancient Heroes to the Field,
How should I joy, 'midst the fierce shock of Nations,
To cross the Tow'rings of an equal Soul,
And bid the master Genius rule the World.
ABDALLA, CALI, go—proclaim my Purpose.

                                   [*Exeunt* Cali *and* Abdalla.

SCENE VI

MAHOMET, MUSTAPHA

MAHOMET

Still CALI lives, and must he live To-morrow?
That fawning Villain's forc'd Congratulations
Will cloud my Triumphs, and pollute the Day.

MUSTAPHA

With cautious Vigilance, at my Command,
Two faithful Captains, HASAN and CARAZA,
Pursue him through his Labyrinths of Treason,
And wait your Summons to report his Conduct.

MAHOMET

Call them—but let them not prolong their Tale,
Nor press too much upon a Lover's Patience. [*Exit* Must.

SCENE VII

MAHOMET *solus*

Whome'er the Hope, still blasted, still renew'd,
Of Happiness, lures on from Toil to Toil,

Remember MAHOMET, and cease thy Labour.
Behold him here, in Love, in War successful,
Behold him wretched in his double Triumph;
His Fav'rite faithless, and his Mistress base.
Ambition only gave her to my Arms,
By Reason not convinc'd, nor won by Love.
Ambition was her Crime, but meaner Folly,
Dooms me to loath at once, and doat on Falshood,
And idolize th' Apostate I contemn.
If thou art more than the gay Dream of Fancy,
More than a pleasing Sound without a Meaning,
O Happiness! sure thou art all ASPASIA's.

SCENE VIII

MAHOMET, MUSTAPHA, HASAN *and* CARAZA

MAHOMET

CARAZA speak—have ye remark'd the BASSA?

CARAZA

Close, as we might unseen, we watch'd his Steps;
His Air disorder'd, and his Gait unequal,
Betray'd the wild Emotions of his Mind.
Sudden he stops, and inward turns his Eyes,
Absorb'd in Thought; then starting from his Trance,
Constrains a sullen Smile, and shoots away.
With him ABDALLA we beheld—

MUSTAPHA

                    ABDALLA!

MAHOMET

He wears of late Resentment on his Brow,
Deny'd the Government of *Servia*'s Province.

CARAZA

We mark'd him storming in Excess of Fury,

And heard within the Thicket that conceal'd us,
An undistinguish'd Sound of threat'ning Rage.

MUSTAPHA

How Guilt once harbour'd in the conscious Breast,
Intimidates the Brave, degrades the Great.
See CALI, Dread of Kings, and Pride of Armies,
By Treason levell'd with the Dregs of Men.
Ere guilty Fear depress'd the hoary Chief,
An angry Murmur, a rebellious Frown,
Had stretch'd the fiery Boaster in the Grave.

MAHOMET

Shall Monarchs fear to draw the Sword of Justice,
Aw'd by the Croud, and by their Slaves restrain'd?
Seize him this Night, and through the private Passage
Convey him to the Prison's inmost Depths,
Reserv'd to all the Pangs of tedious Death.

[*Exeunt* Mahomet *and* Mustapha.

SCENE IX

HASAN, CARAZA

HASAN

Shall then the *Greeks*, unpunish'd and conceal'd,
Contrive perhaps, the Ruin of our Empire,
League with our Chiefs, and propagate Sedition?

CARAZA

Whate'er their Scheme the BASSA's Death defeats it,
And Gratitude's strong Ties restrain my Tongue.

HASAN

What Ties to Slaves? what Gratitude to Foes?

CARAZA

In that black Day when slaughter'd Thousands fell

Around these fatal Walls, the Tide of War
Bore me victorious onward, where DEMETRIUS
Tore unresisted from the Giant Hand
Of stern *Sebalias* the triumphant Crescent,
And dash'd the Might of *Asem* from the Ramparts.
There I became, nor blush to make it known,
The Captive of his Sword. The coward *Greeks*,
Enrag'd by Wrongs, exulting with Success,
Doom'd me to die with all the *Turkish* Captains.
But brave DEMETRIUS scorn'd the mean Revenge,
And gave me Life—

HASAN

                    Do thou repay the Gift,
Lest, unrewarded, Mercy lose its Charms.
    Profuse of Wealth, or bounteous of Success,
    When Heav'n bestows the Privilege to bless,
    Let no weak Doubt the gen'rous Hand restrain,
    For when was Pow'r beneficent in vain?

ACT V. SCENE I

ASPASIA *solus*

In these dark Moments of suspended Fate,
While yet the future Fortune of my Country
Lies in the Womb of Providence conceal'd,
And anxious Angels wait the mighty Birth;
O grant thy sacred Influence, pow'rful Virtue!
Attention rise, survey the fair Creation,
Till conscious of th' incircling Deity,
Beyond the Mists of Care thy Pinion tow'rs.
This Calm, these Joys, dear Innocence! are thine,
Joys ill exchang'd for Gold, and Pride, and Empire.

                    [*Enter* Irene *and Attendants.*

SCENE II

ASPASIA, IRENE, *and Attendants*

IRENE

See how the Moon through all th'unclouded Sky
Spreads her mild Radiance, and descending Dews
Revive the languid Flow'rs; thus Nature shone
New from the Maker's Hand, and fair array'd
In the bright Colours of primæval Spring;
When Purity, while Fraud was yet unknown,
Play'd fearless in th' inviolated Shades.
This elemental joy, this gen'ral Calm,
Is sure the Smile of unoffended Heav'n.
Yet why—

MAID

      Behold, within th' embow'ring Grove
Aspasia stands——

IRENE

      With melancholy Mien,
Pensive, and envious of IRENE's Greatness.
Steal unperceiv'd upon her Meditations——
But see, the lofty Maid at our Approach,
Resumes th' imperious Air of haughty Virtue.
Are these th' unceasing Joys, th' unmingled Pleasures
For which ASPASIA scorn'd the *Turkish* Crown?   [*To* Asp.
Is this th' unshaken Confidence in Heav'n?
Is this the boasted Bliss of conscious Virtue?
When did Content sigh out her Cares in secret?
When did Felicity repine in Deserts?

ASPASIA

Ill suits with Guilt the Gaieties of Triumph;
When daring Vice insults eternal Justice,
The Ministers of Wrath forget Compassion,
And snatch the flaming Bolt with hasty Hand.

IRENE

Forbear thy Threats, proud Prophetess of ill,
Vers'd in the secret Counsels of the Sky.

ASPASIA

Forbear—But thou art sunk beneath Reproach;
In vain affected Raptures flush the Cheek,
And Songs of Pleasure warble from the Tongue,
When Fear and Anguish labour in the Breast,
And all within is Darkness and Confusion;
Thus on deceitful *Etna's* flow'ry Side,
Unfading Verdure glads the roving Eye,
While secret Flames, with unextinguish'd Rage,
Insatiate on her wasted Entrails prey,
And melt her treach'rous Beauties into Ruin. [*Enter* Dem.

SCENE III

ASPASIA, IRENE, DEMETRIUS

DEMETRIUS

Fly, fly, my Love, Destruction rushes on us,
The Rack expects us, and the Sword pursues.

ASPASIA

Is *Greece* deliver'd? is the Tyrant fall'n?

DEMETRIUS

Greece is no more, the prosp'rous Tyrant lives,
Reserv'd, for other Lands, the Scourge of Heav'n.

ASPASIA

Say, by what Fraud, what Force were you defeated?
Betray'd by Falshood, or by Crouds o'erborn?

DEMETRIUS

The pressing Exigence forbids Relation.
ABDALLA——

ASPASIA

Hated Name! his jealous Rage
Broke out in Perfidy—Oh curs'd ASPASIA,
Born to compleat the Ruin of her Country;
Hide me, oh hide me from upbraiding *Greece*,
Oh, hide me from myself!

DEMETRIUS

Be fruitless Grief
The Doom of Guilt alone, nor dare to seize
The Breast where Virtue guards the Throne of Peace.
Devolve, dear Maid thy Sorrows on the Wretch
Whose Fear, or Rage, or Treachery betray'd us.

IRENE *aside*

A private Station may discover more;
Then let me rid them of IRENE's Presence:
Proceed, and give a loose to Love and Treason. [*Withdraws.*

ASPASIA

Yet tell.

DEMETRIUS

To tell, or hear, were Waste of Life.

ASPASIA

The Life, which only this Design supported,
Were now well lost, in hearing how you fail'd.

DEMETRIUS

Or meanly fraudulent, or madly gay,
ABDALLA, while we waited near the Palace,
With ill-tim'd Mirth propos'd the Bowl of Love.
Just as it reach'd my Lips, a sudden Cry
Urg'd me to dash it to the Ground untouch'd,
And seize my Sword with disencumber'd Hand.

ASPASIA

What Cry? The Stratagem? Did then ABDALLA?—

DEMETRIUS

At once a Thousand Passions fir'd his Cheek:
Then all is past, he cried—and darted from us;
Nor at the Call of CALI deign'd to turn.

ASPASIA

Why did you stay? deserted and betray'd?
What more could Force attempt, or Art contrive?

DEMETRIUS

Amazement seiz'd us, and the hoary Bassa
Stood torpid in Suspence; but soon ABDALLA
Return'd with Force that made Resistance vain,
And bade his new Confederates seize the Traitors.
CALI disarm'd was born away to Death;
Myself escap'd, or favour'd or neglected.

ASPASIA

O *Greece*! renown'd for Science and for Wealth,
Behold thy boasted Honours snatch'd away.

DEMETRIUS

Though Disappointment blast our general Scheme,
Yet much remains to hope. I shall not call
The Day disast'rous that secures our Flight;
Nor think that Effort lost which rescues thee. [*Enter* Abd.

SCENE IV

IRENE, ASPASIA, DEMETRIUS, ABDALLA

ABDALLA

At length the Prize is mine—The haughty Maid
That bears the Fate of Empires in her Air,
Henceforth shall live for me; for me alone
Shall plume her Charms, and, with attentive Watch,
Steal from ABDALLA's Eye the Sign to smile.

DEMETRIUS

Cease this wild Roar of savage Exultation;
Advance, and perish in the frantic Boast.

ASPASIA

Forbear, DEMETRIUS, 'tis ASPASIA calls thee;
Thy Love, ASPASIA, calls; restrain thy Sword;
Nor rush on useless Wounds with idle Courage.

DEMETRIUS

What now remains?

ASPASIA

It now remains to fly.

DEMETRIUS

Shall then the Savage live, to boast his Insult;
Tell how DEMETRIUS shun'd his single Hand,
And stole his Life and Mistress from his Sabre?

ABDALLA

Infatuate Loiterer, has Fate, in vain,
Unclasp'd his Iron Gripe to set thee free?
Still dost thou flutter in the Jaws of Death,
Snar'd with thy Fears, and maz'd in Stupefaction.

DEMETRIUS

Forgive, my Fair, 'tis Life, 'tis Nature calls.
Now, Traytor, feel the Fear that chills my Hand.

ASPASIA

'Tis Madness to provoke superfluous Danger,
And Cowardice to dread the Boast of Folly.

ABDALLA

Fly, Wretch, while yet my Pity grants thee Flight;
The Power of *Turkey* waits upon my Call.
Leave but this Maid, resign a hopeless Claim,
And drag away thy Life in Scorn and Safety,
Thy Life, too mean a Prey to lure ABDALLA.

DEMETRIUS

Once more I dare thy Sword, behold the Prize,
Behold I quit her to the Chance of Battle. [*Quitting* Aspasia.

ABDALLA

Well mayst thou call thy Master to the Combat,
And try the Hazard that hast Nought to stake;
Alike my Death or thine is gain to thee,
But soon thou shalt repent: another Moment
Shall throw th' attending Janizaries round thee.

[*Exit hastily* ABDALLA.

SCENE V

ASPASIA, DEMETRIUS

IRENE

ABDALLA fails, now Fortune all is mine.   [*Aside.*
Haste, MURZA, to the Palace, let the Sultan
                    [*To one of her Attendants.*
Dispatch his Guards to stop the flying Traytors,
While I protract their Stay. Be swift and faithful.

[*Exit* MURZA.
This lucky Stratagem shall charm the Sultan,   [*Aside.*
Secure his Confidence, and fix his Love.

DEMETRIUS

Behold a Boaster's Worth. Now snatch, my Fair,
The happy Moment, hasten to the Shore,
Ere he return with Thousands at his Side.

ASPASIA

In vain I listen to th' inviting Call
Of Freedom and of Love: My trembling Joints
Relax'd with Fear, refuse to bear me forward.
Depart, DEMETRIUS, lest my Fate involve thee,
Forsake a Wretch abandon'd to Despair,
To share the Miseries herself has caus'd.

DEMETRIUS

Let us not struggle with th' eternal Will,
Nor languish o'er irreparable Ruins;
Come haste, and live—Thy Innocence and Truth
Shall bless our Wand'rings, and propitiate Heav'n.

IRENE

Press not her Flight, while yet her feeble Nerves
Refuse their Office, and uncertain Life
Still labours with imaginary Woe;
Here let me tend her with officious Care,
Watch each unquiet Flutter of the Breast,
And joy to feel the vital Warmth return,
To see the Cloud forsake her kindling Cheek,
And hail the rosy Dawn of rising Health.

ASPASIA

Oh! rather scornful of flagitious Greatness,
Resolve to share our Dangers and our Toils,
Companion of our Flight, illustrious Exile,
Leave Slav'ry, Guilt, and Infamy behind.

IRENE

My Soul attends thy Voice, and banish'd Virtue
Strives to regain her Empire of the Mind:
Assist her Efforts with thy strong Persuasion;
Sure 'tis the happy Hour ordain'd above,
When vanquish'd Vice shall tyrannize no more.

DEMETRIUS

Remember, Peace and Anguish are before thee,
And Honour and Reproach, and Heav'n and Hell.

ASPASIA

Content with Freedom, and precarious Greatness.

DEMETRIUS

Now make thy Choice, while yet the Pow'r of Choice

Kind Heaven affords thee, and inviting Mercy
Holds out her Hand to lead thee back to Truth.

IRENE

Stay—in this dubious Twilight of Conviction,
The Gleams of Reason, and the Clouds of Passion,
Irradiate and obscure my Breast by Turns:
Stay but a Moment, and prevailing Truth
Will spread resistless Light upon my Soul.

DEMETRIUS

But since none knows the Danger of a Moment,
And Heav'n forbids to lavish Life away,
Let kind Compulsion terminate the Contest.

[*Seizing her Hand.*

Ye Christian Captives, follow me to Freedom:
A Galley waits us, and the Winds invite.

IRENE

Whence is this Violence?

DEMETRIUS

Your calmer Thought
Will teach a gentler Term.

IRENE

Forbear this Rudeness,
And learn the Rev'rence due to *Turkey*'s Queen.
Fly, Slaves, and call the Sultan to my Rescue.

DEMETRIUS

Farewell, unhappy Maid, may ev'ry Joy
Be thine, that Wealth can give, or Guilt receive.

ASPASIA

And when, contemptuous of imperial Pow'r,
Disease shall chase the Phantoms of Ambition,
May Penitence attend thy mournful Bed,
And wing thy latest Pray'r to pitying Heav'n.

[*Exeunt* Demetrius, Aspasia, *with Part of the Attendants.*

SCENE VI

IRENE *walks at a Distance from her Attendants*

After a Pause

Against the Head which Innocence secures,
Insidious Malice aims her Darts in vain;
Turn'd backwards by the powerful Breath of Heav'n.
Perhaps ev'n now the Lovers unpursu'd
Bound o'er the sparkling Waves. Go, happy Bark,
Thy sacred Freight shall still the raging Main.
To guide thy Passage shall th' aerial Spirits
Fill all the starry Lamps with double Blaze;
Th' applauding Sky shall pour forth all its Beams
To grace the Triumph of victorious Virtue.
While I, not yet familiar to my Crimes,
Recoil from Thought, and shudder at myself.
How am I chang'd! How lately did IRENE
Fly from the busy Pleasures of her Sex,
Well pleas'd to search the Treasures of Remembrance,
And live her guiltless Moments o'er anew!
Come let us seek new Pleasures in the Palace,

> [*To her Attendants, going off.*

Till soft Fatigue invite us to repose.

SCENE VII

Enter MUSTAPHA, *meeting and stopping her*

MUSTAPHA

Fair Falshood, stay.

IRENE

What Dream of sudden Power
Has taught my Slave the Language of Command!
Henceforth be wise, nor hope a second Pardon.

MUSTAPHA

Who calls for Pardon from a Wretch condemn'd?

IRENE

Thy Look, thy Speech, thy Action, all is Wildness—
Who charges Guilt on me?

MUSTAPHA

                    Who charges Guilt?
Ask of thy Heart; attend the Voice of Conscience—
Who charges Guilt! lay by this proud Resentment
That fires thy Cheek, and elevates thy Mien,
Nor thus usurp the Dignity of Virtue.
Review this Day.

IRENE

              Whate'er thy Accusation,
The Sultan is my Judge.

MUSTAPHA

                That Hope is past;
Hard was the Strife of Justice and of Love;
But now 'tis o'er, and Justice has prevail'd.
Know'st thou not CALI? know'st thou not DEMETRIUS?

IRENE

Bold Slave, I know them both—I know them Traytors.

MUSTAPHA

Perfidious!—yes—too well thou know'st them Traytors.

IRENE

Their Treason throws no Stain upon IRENE.
This Day has prov'd my Fondness for the Sultan;
He knew IRENE's Truth.

MUSTAPHA

                The Sultan knows it,
He knows how near Apostacy to Treason—
But 'tis not mine to judge—I scorn and leave thee.

I go, lest Vengeance urge my Hand to Blood,
To Blood, too mean to stain a Soldier's Sabre.

[*Exit* Mustapha.

IRENE *to her Attendants*

Go, blust'ring Slave.—He has not heard of MURZA.
That dext'rous Message frees me from Suspicion.

SCENE VIII

Enter HASAN, CARAZA *with Mutes, who throw the black Robe
upon* IRENE, *and sign to her Attendants to withdraw*

HASAN

Forgive, fair Excellence, th' unwilling Tongue,
The Tongue, that, forc'd by strong Necessity,
Bids Beauty, such as thine, prepare to die.

IRENE

What wild Mistake is this? Take hence with speed
Your Robe of Mourning, and your Dogs of Death.
Quick from my Sight you inauspicious Monsters,
Nor dare henceforth to shock IRENE's Walks.

HASAN

Alas! they come, commanded by the Sultan,
Th' unpitying Ministers of *Turkish* Justice,
Nor dare to spare the Life his Frown condemns.

IRENE

Are these the rapid Thunderbolts of War,
That pour with sudden Violence on Kingdoms,
And spread their Flames resistless o'er the World?
What sleepy charms benumb these active Heroes,
Depress their Spirits, and retard their Speed?
Beyond the Fear of ling'ring Punishment,
ASPASIA now within her Lover's Arms

Securely sleeps, and, in delightful Dreams,
Smiles at the Threat'nings of defeated Rage.

CARAZA

We come, bright Virgin, tho' relenting Nature
Shrinks at the hated Task, for thy Destruction;
When, summon'd by the Sultan's clam'rous Fury,
We ask'd, with tim'rous Tongue, th' Offender's Name,
He struck his tortur'd Breast, and roar'd, IRENE:
We started at the Sound, again enquir'd,
Again his thund'ring Voice return'd, IRENE.

IRENE

Whence is this Rage? what barb'rous Tongue has wrong'd
    me?
What Fraud misleads him? or what Crimes incense?

HASAN

Expiring CALI nam'd IRENE's Chamber,
The Place appointed for his Master's Death.

IRENE

IRENE's Chamber! From my faithful Bosom
Far be the Thought—But hear my Protestation.

CARAZA

'Tis ours, alas! to punish, not to judge,
Not call'd to try the Cause, we heard the Sentence,
Ordain'd the mournful Messengers of Death.

IRENE

Some ill designing Statesman's base Intrigue!
Some cruel Stratagem of jealous Beauty!
Perhaps yourselves the Villains that defame me,
Now haste to murder, ere returning Thought
Recall th' extorted Doom.—It must be so,
Confess your Crime, or lead me to the Sultan,
There dauntless Truth shall blast the vile Accuser,

Then shall you feel what Language cannot utter,
Each piercing Torture, every Change of Pain,
That Vengeance can invent, or Pow'r inflict.

> [*Enter* ABDALLA, *he stops short and listens.*

SCENE IX

IRENE, HASAN, CARAZA, ABDALLA

ABDALLA *Aside*

All is not lost, ABDALLA, see the Queen,
See the last Witness of thy Guilt and Fear
Enrob'd in Death—Dispatch her and be great.

CARAZA

Unhappy Fair! Compassion calls upon me
To check this Torrent of imperious Rage.
While unavailing Anger crouds thy Tongue
With idle Threats and fruitless Exclamation,
The fraudful Moments ply their silent Wings,
And steal thy Life away. Death's horrid Angel
Already shakes his bloody Sabre o'er thee.
The raging Sultan burns till our Return,
Curses the dull Delays of ling'ring Mercy,
And thinks his fatal Mandates ill obey'd.

ABDALLA

Is then your Sov'reign's Life so cheaply rated,
That thus you parly with detected Treason?
Should she prevail to gain the Sultan's Presence,
Soon might her Tears engage a Lover's Credit;
Perhaps her Malice might transfer the Charge,
Perhaps her pois'nous Tongue might blast ABDALLA.

IRENE

O let me but be heard, nor fear from me
Or Flights of Pow'r, or Projects of Ambition.

My Hopes, my Wishes, terminate in Life,
A little Life for Grief, and for Repentance.

ABDALLA

I mark'd her wily Messenger afar,
And saw him skulking in the closest Walks:
I guess'd her dark Designs, and warn'd the Sultan,
And bring her former Sentence new confirm'd.

HASAN

Then call it not our Cruelty, nor Crime,
Deem us not deaf to Woe, nor blind to Beauty,
That thus constrain'd we speed the Stroke of Death.
                              [*Beckons the Mutes.*

IRENE

O name not Death! Distraction and Amazement,
Horror and Agony are in that Sound!
Let me but live, heap Woes on Woes upon me,
Hide me with Murd'rers in the Dungeon's Gloom,
Send me to wander on some pathless Shore,
Let Shame and hooting Infamy pursue me,
Let Slav'ry harrass, and let Hunger gripe.

CARAZA

Could we reverse the Sentence of the Sultan,
Our bleeding Bosoms plead IRENE's Cause.
But Cries and Tears are vain, prepare with Patience
To meet that Fate we can delay no longer.
                    [*The Mutes at the Sign lay hold of her.*

ABDALLA

Dispatch, ye ling'ring Slaves, or nimbler Hands
Quick at my Call shall execute your Charge;
Dispatch, and learn a fitter Time for Pity.

IRENE

Grant me one Hour, O grant me but a Moment,

And bounteous Heaven repay the mighty Mercy
With peaceful Death, and Happiness eternal.

CARAZA

The Prayer I cannot grant——I dare not hear.
Short be thy Pains.   [*Signs again to the Mutes.*

IRENE

Unutterable Anguish!
Guilt and Despair! pale Spectres, grin around me,
And stun me with the Yellings of Damnation!
O, hear my Pray'rs! accept, all-pitying Heaven,
These Tears, these Pangs, these last Remains of Life,
Nor let the Crimes of this detested Day
Be charg'd upon my Soul. O, Mercy! Mercy!
            [*Mutes force her out.*

SCENE X

ABDALLA, HASAN, CARAZA

ABDALLA *Aside*

Safe in her Death, and in DEMETRIUS' Flight,
ABDALLA, bid thy troubled Breast be calm;
Now shalt thou shine the Darling of the Sultan,
The Plot all CALI's, the Detection thine.

HASAN *to* CARAZA

Does not thy Bosom, for I know thee tender,
A Stranger to th' Oppressor's savage Joy,
Melt at IRENE's Fate, and share her Woes?

CARAZA

Her piercing Cries yet fill the loaded Air,
Dwell on my Ear, and sadden all my Soul;
But let us try to clear our clouded Brows,
And tell the horrid Tale with chearful Face;
The stormy Sultan rages at our stay.

ABDALLA

Frame your Report with circumspective Art,
Inflame her Crimes, exalt your own Obedience,
But let no thoughtless Hint involve ABDALLA.

CARAZA

What need of Caution to report the Fate
Of her the Sultan's Voice condemn'd to die?
Or why should he, whose Violence of Duty
Has serv'd his Prince so well, demand our Silence?

ABDALLA

Perhaps my Zeal too fierce betray'd my Prudence;
Perhaps my Warmth exceeded my Commission;
Perhaps I will not stoop to plead my Cause;
Or argue with the Slave that sav'd DEMETRIUS.

CARAZA

From his Escape learn thou the Pow'r of Virtue,
Nor hope his Fortune while thou want'st his Worth.

HASAN

The Sultan comes, still gloomy, still enrag'd.

SCENE XI

HASAN, CARAZA, MAHOMET, MUSTAPHA, ABDALLA

MAHOMET

Where's this fair Trait'ress? Where's this smiling Mischief?
Whom neither Vows could fix, nor Favours bind?

HASAN

Thine Orders, mighty Sultan! are perform'd,
And all IRENE now is breathless Clay.

MAHOMET

Your hasty Zeal defrauds the Claim of Justice,

And disappointed Vengeance burns in vain;
I came to heighten Tortures by Reproach,
And add new Terrors to the Face of Death.
Was this the Maid whose Love I bought with Empire!
True, she was fair; the Smile of Innocence
Play'd on her Cheek—So shone the first Apostate—
IRENE's Chamber! Did not roaring CALI,
Just as the Rack forc'd out his struggling Soul,
Name for the Scene of Death IRENE's Chamber?

MUSTAPHA

His Breath prolong'd but to detect her Treason,
Then in short Sighs forsook his broken Frame.

MAHOMET

Decreed to perish in IRENE's Chamber!
There had she lull'd me with endearing Falshoods,
Clasp'd in her Arms, or slumb'ring on her Breast,
And bar'd my Bosom to the Ruffian's Dagger.

SCENE XII

HASAN, CARAZA, MAHOMET, MUSTAPHA, MURZA, ABDALLA

MURZA

Forgive, great Sultan! that by Fate prevented,
I bring a tardy Message from IRENE.

MAHOMET

Some artful Wile of counterfeited Love!
Some soft Decoy to lure me to Destruction!
And thou, the curs'd Accomplice of her Treason,
Declare thy Message, and expect thy Doom.

MURZA

The Queen requested that a chosen Troop

Might intercept the Traitor *Greek*, DEMETRIUS,
Then ling'ring with his captive Mistress here.

MUSTAPHA

The *Greek*, DEMETRIUS! whom th' expiring Bassa
Declar'd the chief Associate of his Guilt.

MAHOMET

A chosen Troop—to intercept—DEMETRIUS—
The Queen requested—Wretch, repeat the Message;
And if one varied Accent prove thy Falshood,
Or but one Moment's Pause betray Confusion,
Those trembling Limbs—Speak out, thou shiv'ring Traitor.

MURZA

The Queen requested—

MAHOMET

                    Who? the dead IRENE?
Was she then guiltless! Has my thoughtless Rage
Destroy'd the fairest Workmanship of Heav'n!
Doom'd her to Death unpity'd and unheard,
Amidst her kind Solicitudes for me!
Ye Slaves of Cruelty, ye Tools of Rage,   [*To* Has. *and* Car.
Ye blind officious Ministers of Folly,
Could not her Charms repress your Zeal for Murder?
Could not her Prayers, her Innocence, her Tears,
Suspend the dreadful Sentence for an Hour?
One Hour had freed me from the fatal Error,
One Hour had sav'd me from Despair and Madness.

CARAZA

Your fierce Impatience forc'd us from your Presence,
Urg'd us to Speed, and bad us banish Pity,
Nor trust our Passions with her fatal Charms.

MAHOMET

What hadst thou lost by slighting those Commands?
Thy Life perhaps—Were but IRENE spar'd,

Well if a Thousand Lives like thine had perish'd;
Such Beauty, Sweetness, Love, were cheaply bought,
With half the grov'ling Slaves that load the Globe.

MUSTAPHA

Great is thy Woe! but think, illustrious Sultan,
Such Ills are sent for Souls like thine to conquer.
Shake off this Weight of unavailing Grief,
Rush to the War, display thy dreadful Banners,
And lead thy Troops victorious round the World.

MAHOMET

Robb'd of the Maid, with whom I wish'd to triumph,
No more I burn for Fame or for Dominion;
Success and Conquest now are empty Sounds,
Remorse and Anguish seize on all my Breast;
Those Groves, whose Shades embower'd the dear IRENE,
Heard her last Cries, and fann'd her dying Beauties,
Shall hide me from the tasteless World for ever.

[Mahomet *goes back and returns.*

Yet ere I quit the Scepter of Dominion,
Let one just Act conclude the hateful Day.
Hew down, ye Guards, those Vassals of Distraction,

[*Pointing to* Hasan *and* Caraza.

Those Hounds of Blood, that catch the Hint to kill,
Bear off with eager haste th' unfinish'd Sentence,
And speed the Stroke lest Mercy should o'ertake them.

CARAZA

Then hear, great MAHOMET, the Voice of Truth.

MAHOMET

Hear! shall I hear thee! did'st thou hear IRENE?

CARAZA

Hear but a Moment.

MAHOMET

Had'st thou heard a Moment,
Thou might'st have liv'd, for thou hadst spar'd IRENE.

CARAZA

I heard her, pitied her, and wish'd to save her.

MAHOMET

And wish'd—Be still thy Fate to wish in vain.

CARAZA

I heard, and soften'd, till ABDALLA brought
Her final Doom, and hurried her Destruction.

MAHOMET

ABDALLA brought her Doom! ABDALLA brought it!
The Wretch, whose Guilt declar'd by tortur'd CALI,
My Rage and Grief had hid from my remembrance,
ABDALLA brought her Doom!

HASAN

ABDALLA brought it,
While she yet beg'd to plead her Cause before thee.

MAHOMET

O seize me, Madness—Did she call on me!
I feel, I see the Ruffian's barb'rous Rage.
He seiz'd her melting in the fond Appeal,
And stopp'd the heav'nly Voice that call'd on me.
My Spirits fail, awhile support me, Vengeance—
Be just ye Slaves, and, to be just, be cruel,
Contrive new Racks, imbitter every Pang,
Inflict whatever Treason can deserve,
Which murder'd Innocence that call'd on me.

[*Exit* Mahomet.
[Abdalla *is dragg'd off.*

SCENE XIII

Hasan, Caraza, Mustapha, Murza

Mustapha *to* Murza

What Plagues, what Tortures, are in store for thee,
Thou sluggish Idler, dilatory Slave?
Behold the Model of consummate Beauty,
Torn from the mourning Earth by thy Neglect.

Murza

Such was the Will of Heav'n—A Band of *Greeks*
That mark'd my Course, suspicious of my Purpose,
Rush'd out and seiz'd me, thoughtless and unarm'd,
Breathless, amaz'd, and on the guarded Beach
Detain'd me till Demetrius set me free.

Mustapha

So sure the Fall of Greatness rais'd on Crimes,
So fix'd the Justice of all-conscious Heav'n.
    When haughty Guilt exults with impious Joy,
    Mistake shall blast, or Accident destroy;
    Weak Man with erring Rage may throw the Dart,
    But Heav'n shall guide it to the guilty Heart.

FINIS

THE
GAMESTER.
A
TRAGEDY.

As it is Acted at the

Theatre-Royal in *Drury-Lane.*

L O N D O N:

Printed for R. FRANCKLIN, in *Ruffel-Street,*
Covent-Garden; and Sold by R. DODSLEY,
in *Pall-Mall*, M.DCC.LIII.

[Price One Shilling and Six Pence.]

TO THE

RIGHT HONOURABLE

HENRY PELHAM

SIR,

IT was a very fine Piece of Oratory of a young Lawyer at the Bar, who as Council against a Highwayman, observed that the Prosecutor had been robbed of a certain Quantity of Ore, which being purified by Fire, cut into circular Pieces, and impressed with the Image of a King and the Arms of a State, brought with it the Necessaries, the Conveniences and the Luxuries of Life. I'll be hanged, says an honest Country Gentleman who was standing by, if this flourishing Fool does not mean Money. But if he had said it in one Word, would not all the rest have been implied?

Just such a Censure as this should I deserve, if in an Address to Mr. *Pelham* I endeavoured to enumerate the Qualities he possesses. The Characters of great Men are generally connected with their Names; and it is impossible for any one to read the Name of Mr. *Pelham*, without connecting with it, in his own Mind, the Virtues of Humanity.

It is therefore sufficient that I desire his Acceptance of this Play; that I acknowledge the Obligations I owe him, and that I subscribe myself

His most grateful, and
most obedient Servant,

EDW. MOORE

PROLOGUE

Written and Spoken by Mr. GARRICK

LIKE fam'd La Mancha's *Knight, who Launce in hand,*
Mounted his Steed to free th' enchanted Land,
Our Quixote Bard sets forth a Monster-taming,
*Arm'd at all Points, to fight that Hydra——*GAMING.
Aloft on Pegasus he waves his Pen,
And hurls Defiance at the Caitiff's Den.
The First on fancy'd Giants spent his Rage,
But This has more than Windmills to engage.
He combats Passion, rooted in the Soul,
Whose Powers at once delight ye and controul;
Whose Magic Bondage each lost Slave enjoys,
Nor wishes Freedom, tho' the Spell destroys.
To save our Land from this MAGICIAN's *Charms,*
And rescue Maids and Matrons from his Arms,
Our Knight Poetic comes——And Oh! ye Fair!
This black ENCHANTER's *wicked Arts beware!*
His subtle Poison dims the brightest Eyes,
And at his Touch, each Grace and Beauty dies.
Love, Gentleness and Joy to Rage give Way,
And the soft Dove becomes a Bird of Prey.
May this our bold Advent'rer break the Spell,
And drive the Dæmon to his native Hell.

Ye Slaves of Passion, and ye Dupes of Chance,
Wake all your Pow'rs from this destructive Trance!
Shake off the Shackles of this Tyrant Vice:
Hear other Calls than those of Cards and Dice:
Be learn'd in nobler Arts, than Arts of Play,
And other Debts than those of Honour pay.
No longer live insensible to Shame,
Lost to your Country, Families and Fame.

Cou'd our romantic Muse this Work atchieve,
Wou'd there one honest Heart in Britain *grieve?*
Th' Attempt, tho' wild, wou'd not in vain be made,
If ev'ry honest Hand wou'd lend its Aid.

EPILOGUE

Written by a FRIEND

And Spoken by Mrs. PRITCHARD

O N ev'ry Gamester in th' Arabian Nation,
'Tis said, that Mahomet denounc'd Damnation;
But in Return for wicked Cards and Dice,
He gave them black-ey'd Girls in Paradise.
Should he thus preach, good Countrymen, to You,
His Converts would, I fear, be mighty few.
So much your Hearts are set on sordid Gain,
The brightest Eyes around you shine in vain.
Shou'd the most heav'nly Beauty bid you take her,
You'd rather hold——two Aces and a Maker.
By your Example, our poor Sex drawn in,
Is guilty of the same unnat'ral Sin;
The Study now of every Girl of Parts
Is how to win your Money, not your Hearts.
O! in what sweet, what ravishing Delights,
Our Beaux and Belles together pass their Nights!
By ardent Perturbations kept awake,
Each views with longing Eyes the other's——Stake.
The Smiles and Graces are from Britain flown, ⎫
Our Cupid is an errant Sharper grown, ⎬
And Fortune sits on Cytherea's Throne. ⎭
In all these Things tho' Women may be blam'd,
Sure Men, the wiser Men shou'd be asham'd!
And 'tis a horrid Scandal I declare
That four strange Queens shou'd rival all the Fair.
Four Jilts with neither Beauty, Wit nor Parts,
O Shame! have got Possession of their Hearts;
And those bold Sluts, for all their Queenly Pride,
Have play'd loose Tricks, or else they're much bely'd.
Cards were at first for Benefits design'd,
Sent to amuse, and not enslave the Mind.
From Good to Bad how easy the Transition!
For what was Pleasure once, is now Perdition.
Fair Ladies then these wicked Gamesters shun,
Whoever weds one, is, you see, undone.

Dramatis Personæ

MEN

Beverley,	*Mr.* Garrick
Lewson,	*Mr.* Mossop
Stukely,	*Mr.* Davies
Jarvis,	*Mr.* Berry
Bates,	*Mr.* Burton
Dawson,	*Mr.* Blakes
Waiter,	*Mr.* Ackman

WOMEN

Mrs. Beverley,	*Mrs.* Pritchard
Charlotte,	*Miss* Haughton
Lucy,	*Mrs.* Price

The GAMESTER

A

TRAGEDY

ACT I. SCENE I

Enter Mrs. Beverley *and* Charlotte

Mrs. *Beverley.* Be comforted, my Dear; all may be well yet. And now, methinks, the Lodgings begin to look with another Face. O Sister! Sister! if these were all my Hardships; if all I had to complain of were no more than quitting my House, Servants, Equipage and Shew, your Pity would be Weakness.

Char. Is Poverty nothing then?

Mrs. *Bev.* Nothing in the World, if it affected only Me. While we had a Fortune, I was the happiest of the Rich: And now 'tis gone, give me but a bare Subsistence and my Husband's Smiles, and I'll be the happiest of the Poor. To me now these Lodgings want nothing but their Master. Why do you look so at me?

Char. That I may hate my Brother.

Mrs. *Bev.* Don't talk so, *Charlotte.*

Char. Has he not undone you?—Oh! this pernicious Vice of Gaming! But methinks his usual Hours of four or five in the Morning might have contented him; 'twas Misery enough to wake for him till then. Need he have staid out all Night? I shall learn to detest him.

Mrs. *Bev.* Not for the first Fault. He never slept from me before.

Char. Slept from you! no, no, his Nights have nothing to do with Sleep. How has this one Vice driven him from every Virtue! Nay, from his Affections too!—The Time was, Sister——

Mrs. Bev. And is. I have no fear of his Affections. Would I knew that he were safe!

Char. From Ruin and his Companions——But that's impossible. His poor little Boy too! What must become of him?

Mrs. Bev. Why, Want shall teach him Industry. From his Father's Mistakes he shall learn Prudence, and from his Mother's Resignation, Patience. Poverty has no such Terrors in it as you imagine. There's no Condition of Life, Sickness and Pain excepted, where Happiness is excluded. The Husbandman, who rises early to his Labour, enjoys more welcome Rest at Night for't. His Bread is sweeter to him; his Home happier; his Family dearer; his Enjoyments surer. The Sun that rouses him in the Morning, sets in the Evening to release him. All Situations have their Comforts, if sweet Contentment dwell in the Heart. But my poor *Beverley* has none. The Thought of having ruin'd those he loves, is Misery for ever to him. Would I could ease his Mind of that!

Char. If he alone were ruin'd, 'twere just he shou'd be punish'd. He is my Brother, 'tis true; but when I think of what he has done; of the Fortune you brought him; of his own large Estate too, squander'd away upon this vilest of Passions, and among the vilest of Wretches! O! I have no Patience! My own little Fortune is untouch'd, he says. Wou'd I were sure on't.

Mrs. Bev. And so you may——'twould be a Sin to doubt it.

Char. I will be sure on't——'Twas Madness in me to give it to his Management. But I'll demand it from him this Morning. I have a melancholy Occasion for't.

Mrs. Bev. What Occasion?

Char. To support a Sister.

Mrs. Bev. No; I have no Need on't. Take it, and reward a Lover with it. The generous *Lewson* deserves much more. Why won't you make him happy?

Char. Because my Sister's miserable.

Mrs. Bev. You must not think so. I have my Jewels left yet. I'll sell 'em to supply our Wants; and when all's gone these Hands shall toil for our Support. The Poor should be industrious——Why those Tears, *Charlotte*?

Char. They flow in Pity for you.

Mrs. *Bev.* All may be well yet. When he has nothing to lose I shall fetter him in these Arms again; and then what is it to be poor?

Char. Cure him but of this destructive Passion, and my Uncle's Death may retrieve all yet.

Mrs. *Bev.* Ay, *Charlotte*, could we cure him. But the Disease of Play admits no Cure but Poverty; and the Loss of another Fortune wou'd but encrease his Shame and his Affliction. Will Mr. *Lewson* call this Morning?

Char. He said so last Night. He gave me Hints too, that he had Suspicions of our Friend *Stukely*.

Mrs. *Bev.* Not of Treachery to my Husband? That he loves Play I know; but surely he's honest.

Char. He wou'd fain be thought so; therefore I doubt him. Honesty needs no Pains to set itself off.

Mrs. *Bev.* What now, *Lucy*?

Enter Lucy

Lucy. Your old Steward, Madam. I had not the Heart to deny him Admittance, the good old Man begg'd so hard for't.   (*Exit* Lucy.

Enter Jarvis

Mrs. *Bev.* Is this well, *Jarvis*? I desir'd you to avoid me.

Jar. Did you, Madam? I am an old Man, and had forgot. Perhaps too you forbad my Tears; but I am old, Madam, and Age will be forgetful.

Mrs. *Bev.* The faithful Creature! how he moves me.
                                        (*To* Char.

Char. Not to have seen him had been Cruelty.

Jar. I have forgot these Apartments too. I remember none such in my young Master's House; and yet I have liv'd in't these five and twenty Years. His good Father would not have dismiss'd me.

Mrs. *Bev.* He had no Reason, *Jarvis*.

Jar. I was faithful to him while he liv'd, and when he dy'd, he bequeath'd me to his Son. I have been faithful to Him too.

Mrs. *Bev.* I know it, I know it, *Jarvis*.

Char. We both know it.

Jar. I am an old Man, Madam, and have not a long Time to live. I ask'd but to have dy'd with him, and he dismiss'd me.

Mrs. *Bev.* Prithee no more of this! 'Twas his Poverty that dismiss'd you.

Jar. Is he indeed so poor then?——Oh! he was the Joy of my old Heart——But must his Creditors have all?—And have they sold his House too? His Father built it when He was but a prating Boy. The Times I have carry'd him in these Arms! And, *Jarvis*, says he, when a Beggar has ask'd Charity of me, why should People be poor? You shan't be poor, *Jarvis*; if I was a King, no-body should be poor. Yet He is poor. And then he was so brave!——O he was a brave little Boy! And yet so merciful he'd not have kill'd the Gnat that stung him.

Mrs. *Bev.* Speak to him *Charlotte*; for I cannot.

Char. When I have wip'd my Eyes.

Jar. I have a little Money, Madam; it might have been more, but I have lov'd the Poor. All that I have is yours.

Mrs. *Bev.* No, *Jarvis*; we have enough yet. I thank you tho', and will deserve your Goodness.

Jar. But shall I see my Master? And will he let me attend him in his Distresses? I'll be no Expence to him: and 'twill kill me to be refused. Where is he, Madam?

Mrs. *Bev.* Not at home, *Jarvis*. You shall see him another Time.

Char. To-morrow, or the next Day—O, *Jarvis*! what a Change is here!

Jar. A Change indeed, Madam! My old Heart akes at it. And yet methinks—But here's somebody coming.

Enter Lucy *with* Stukely

Lucy. Mr. *Stukely*, Madam.　　　　　　　　(*Exit* Lucy.

Stu. Good Morning to you, Ladies. Mr. *Jarvis*, your Servant. Where's my Friend, Madam?　　　　(*To* Mrs. *Bev.*

Mrs. *Bev.* I shou'd have ask'd that Question of You. Have not you seen him to-day?

Stu. No, Madam.

Char. Nor last Night?

Stu. Last Night! Did not he come home then?

Mrs. *Bev.* No. Were not you together?

Stu. At the Beginning of the Evening; but not since. Where can he have staid?

Char. You call yourself his Friend, Sir; why do you encourage him in this Madness of Gaming?

Stu. You have ask'd me that Question before, Madam; and I told you my Concern was that I could not save him. Mr. *Beverley* is a Man, Madam; and if the most friendly Entreaties have no Effect upon him, I have no other Means. My Purse has been his, even to the Injury of my Fortune. If That has been Encouragement, I deserve Censure; but I meant it to retrieve him.

Mrs. *Bev.* I don't doubt it, Sir; and I thank you—But where did you leave him last Night?

Stu. At *Wilson*'s, Madam, if I ought to tell; in Company I did not like. Possibly he may be there still. Mr. *Jarvis* knows the House, I believe.

Jar. Shall I go, Madam?

Mrs. *Bev.* No, he may take it ill.

Char. He may go as from himself.

Stu. And, if he pleases, Madam, without naming Me. I am faulty myself, and should conceal the Errors of a Friend. But I can refuse nothing here.   (*Bowing to the Ladies.*

Jar. I would fain see him methinks.

Mrs. *Bev.* Do so then. But take care how you upbraid him. I have never upbraided him.

Jar. Would I could bring him Comfort!   (*Exit* Jarvis.

Stu. Don't be too much alarm'd, Madam. All Men have their Errors, and their Times of seeing 'em. Perhaps my Friend's Time is not come yet. But he has an Uncle; and old Men don't live for ever. You shou'd look forward, Madam; we are taught how to value a second Fortune by the Loss of a first.   (*Knocking at the Door.*

Mrs. *Bev.* Hark!—No—that Knocking was too rude for Mr. *Beverley.* Pray Heaven he be well!

Stu. Never doubt it, Madam. You shall be well too——
Every Thing shall be well. (*Knocking again.*

Mrs. *Bev.* The knocking is a little loud tho'—Who waits
there? Will none of you answer?——None of you, did I say?
——Alas! what was I thinking of!——I had forgot myself.

Char. I'll go, Sister——But don't be alarm'd so.

(*Exit* Charlotte.

Stu. What extraordinary Accident have you to fear,
Madam?

Mrs. *Bev.* I beg your Pardon; but 'tis ever thus with me
in Mr. *Beverley*'s Absence. No one knocks at the Door,
but I fancy it is a Messenger of ill News.

Stu. You are too fearful, Madam; 'twas but one Night of
Absence; and if ill Thoughts intrude (as Love is always
doubtful) think of your Worth and Beauty, and drive 'em
from your Breast.

Mrs. *Bev.* What Thoughts? I have no Thoughts that
wrong my Husband.

Stu. Such Thoughts indeed would wrong him. The
World is full of Slander; and every Wretch that knows himself unjust, charges his Neighbour with like Passions; and by
the general Frailty hides his own——If you are wise, and
would be happy, turn a deaf Ear to such Reports. 'Tis Ruin
to believe 'em.

Mrs. *Bev.* Ay, worse than Ruin. 'Twou'd be to sin against
Conviction. Why was it mention'd?

Stu. To guard you against Rumour. The Sport of half
Mankind is Mischief; and for a single Error they make Men
Devils. If their Tales reach you, disbelieve 'em.

Mrs. *Bev.* What Tales? By whom? Why told? I have
heard nothing—or if I had, with all his Errors, my *Beverly*'s
firm Faith admits no Doubt——It is my Safety, my Seat of
Rest and Joy, while the Storm threatens round me. I'll not
forsake it. (Stukely *sighs and looks down*) Why turn you, Sir,
away? And why that Sigh?

Stu. I was attentive, Madam; and Sighs will come we
know not why. Perhaps I have been too busy——If it should
seem so, impute my Zeal to Friendship, that meant to guard

you against evil Tongues. Your *Beverley* is wrong'd, slander'd most vilely——My Life upon his Truth.

Mrs. Bev. And mine too. Who is't that doubts it? But no Matter——I am prepar'd, Sir——Yet why this Caution? ——You are my Husband's Friend; I think you mine too; the common Friend of both. (*pauses*) I had been unconcern'd else.

Stu. For Heaven's Sake, Madam, be so still! I meant to guard you against Suspicion, not to alarm it.

Mrs. Bev. Nor have you, Sir. Who told you of Suspicion? I have a Heart it cannot reach.

Stu. Then I am happy—I wou'd say more—but am prevented.

Enter Charlotte

Mrs. Bev. Who was it *Charlotte*?

Char. What a Heart has that *Jarvis*!—A Creditor, Sister. But the good old Man has taken him away——Don't distress his Wife! Don't distress his Sister! I cou'd hear him say. 'Tis cruel to distress the afflicted——And when he saw me at the Door, he begg'd Pardon that his Friend had knock'd so loud.

Stu. I wish I had known of this. Was it a large Demand, Madam?

Char. I heard not that; but Visits such as these, we must expect often.—Why so distress'd, Sister? This is no new Affliction.

Mrs. Bev. No, *Charlotte*; but I am faint with watching—— quite sunk and spiritless——Will you excuse me, Sir? I'll to my Chamber, and try to rest a little.

Stu. Good Thoughts go with you, Madam.

                                        (*Exit Mrs.* Bev.
My Bait is taken then. (*Aside.*) Poor Mrs. *Beverley*! How my Heart grieves to see her thus!

Char. Cure her, and be a Friend then.

Stu. How cure her, Madam?

Char. Reclaim my Brother.

Stu. Ay; give him a new Creation; or breathe another

Soul into him. I'll think on't, Madam. Advice I see is thankless.

Char. Useless I am sure it is, if thro' mistaken Friendship, or other Motives, you feed his Passion with your Purse, and sooth it by Example. Physicians to cure Fevers keep from the Patient's thirsty Lip the Cup that wou'd enflame him; You give it to his Hands—(*a Knocking.*) Hark! Sir— These are my Brother's desperate Symptoms——Another Creditor.

Stu. One not so easily got rid of——What, *Lewson*!

Enter Lewson

Lew. Madam, your Servant——Yours, Sir. I was enquiring for you at your Lodgings.

Stu. This Morning? You had Business then?

Lew. You'll call it by another Name, perhaps. Where's Mr. *Beverley*, Madam?

Char. We have sent to enquire for him.

Lew. Is he abroad then? He did not use to go out so early.

Char. No; nor to stay out so late.

Lew. Is that the Case? I am sorry for it. But Mr. *Stukely*, perhaps, may direct you to him.

Stu. I have already, Sir.——But what was your Business with Me?

Lew. To congratulate you upon your late Successes at Play. Poor *Beverley*! But You are his Friend; and there's a Comfort in having successful Friends.

Stu. And what am I to understand by this?

Lew. That *Beverley*'s a poor Man, with a rich Friend— that's all.

Stu. Your Words wou'd mean something, I suppose. Another Time, Sir, I shall desire an Explanation.

Lew. And why not now? I am no Dealer in long Sentences. A Minute or two will do for me.

Stu. But not for Me, Sir. I am slow of Apprehension, and must have Time and Privacy. A Lady's Presence engages my Attention——Another Morning I may be found at Home.

Lew. Another Morning then, I'll wait upon you.

Stu. I shall expect you, Sir. Madam, your Servant. (*Exit* Stu.

Char. What mean you by this?

Lew. To hint to him that I know him.

Char. How know him? Mere Doubt and Supposition!

Lew. I shall have Proof soon.

Char. And what then? Wou'd you risk your Life to be his Punisher?

Lew. My Life, Madam! Don't be afraid. And yet I am happy in your Concern for me. But let it content you that I know this *Stukely*——'Twou'd be as easy to make him honest as brave.

Char. And what do you intend to do?

Lew. Nothing, 'till I have Proof. Yet my Suspicions are well grounded——But methinks, Madam, I am acting here without Authority, Cou'd I have leave to call Mr. *Beverley* Brother, his Concerns would be my own. Why will you make my Services appear officious?

Char. You know my Reasons, and shou'd not press me. But I am cold, you say; and cold I will be, while a poor Sister's destitute——My Heart bleeds for her! and 'till I see her Sorrows moderated, Love has no Joys for me.

Lew. Can I be less a Friend by being a Brother? I wou'd not say an unkind Thing——But the Pillar of your House is shaken. Prop it with another, and it shall stand firm again—— You must comply.

Char. And will——when I have Peace within myself. But let us change the Subject.——Your Business here this Morning is with my Sister. Misfortunes press too hard upon her: Yet till to Day she has borne 'em nobly.

Lew. Where is she?

Char. Gone to her Chamber——Her Spirits fail'd her.

Lew. I hear her coming——Let what has pass'd with *Stukely* be a Secret—She has already too much to trouble her.

Enter Mrs. Beverley

Mrs. *Bev*. Good Morning, Sir; I heard your Voice, and as I thought, enquiring for Me——Where's Mr. *Stukely*, *Charlotte*?

Char. This Moment gone——You have been in Tears, Sister; but here's a Friend shall comfort you.

Lew. Or if I add to your Distresses, I'll beg your Pardon, Madam. The Sale of your House and Furniture was finish'd Yesterday.

Mrs. Bev. I know it, Sir. I know too your generous Reason for putting me in Mind of it. But you have obliged me too much already.

Lew. There are Trifles, Madam, which I know you have set a Value on: Those I have purchas'd, and will deliver. I have a Friend too that esteems you——He has bought largely; and will call nothing his, till he has seen you. If a Visit to him would not be painful, he has begg'd it may be this Morning.

Mrs. Bev. Not painful in the least. My Pain is from the Kindness of my Friends. Why am I to be oblig'd beyond the Power of Return?

Lew. You shall repay us at your own Time. I have a Coach waiting at the Door——Shall we have your Company, Madam?   (*To* Char.

Char. No. My Brother may return soon; I'll stay and receive him.

Mrs. Bev. He may want a Comforter, perhaps. But don't upbraid him, *Charlotte*. We shan't be absent long——Come, Sir, since I must be so oblig'd.

Lew. 'Tis I that am oblig'd. An Hour or less will be sufficient for us. We shall find you at Home, Madam?   (*To* Char.

(*Exit* Lew. & *Mrs.* Bev.

Char. Certainly. I have but little Inclination to appear abroad——O! this Brother! this Brother! To what Wretchedness has he reduc'd us.   (*Exit* Char.

SCENE *changes to* Stukely's *Lodgings*

Enter Stukely

Stu. That *Lewson* suspects me, 'tis too plain. Yet why shou'd he suspect me?——I appear the Friend of *Beverley* as much as he.—But I am rich it seems—and so I am; Thanks to another's Folly and my own Wisdom. To what Use is Wisdom, but to take Advantage of the weak? This *Beverley*'s my Fool; I cheat him, and he calls me Friend——But more Business must be done yet. His Wife's Jewels are unsold; so is the Reversion of his Uncle's Estate. I must have these too—— And then there's a Treasure above all——I love his Wife ——Before she knew this *Beverley* I lov'd her; but like a cringing Fool, bow'd at a Distance, while he stept in and won her——Never, never will I forgive him for't. My Pride, as well as Love, is wounded by this Conquest. I must have Vengeance. Those Hints, this Morning, were well thrown in ——Already they have fasten'd on her. If Jealousy shou'd weaken her Affections, Want may corrupt her Virtue——My Hate rejoyces in the Hope——These Jewels may do much. He shall demand 'em of her; which, when mine, shall be converted to special Purposes——What now, *Bates*?

Enter Bates

Bates. Is it a Wonder then to see me? The Forces are in readiness, and only wait for Orders. Where's *Beverley*?

Stu. At last Night's Rendezvous, waiting for Me. Is *Dawson* with you?

Bates. Dress'd like a Nobleman; with Money in his Pocket, and a Set of Dice that shall deceive the Devil.

Stu. That Fellow has a Head to undo a Nation. But for the rest, they are such low-manner'd, ill-looking Dogs, I wonder *Beverley* has not suspected 'em.

Bates. No Matter for Manners and Looks. Do You supply 'em with Money and they are Gentlemen by Profession—— The Passion of Gaming casts such a Mist before the Eyes, that the Nobleman shall be surrounded with Sharpers, and imagine himself in the best Company.

Stu. There's that *Williams* too——It was He, I suppose, that call'd at *Beverley*'s with the Note this Morning. What Directions did you give him?

Bates. To knock loud, and be clamorous. Did not you see him?

Stu. No. The Fool sneak'd off with *Jarvis*. Had he appear'd within Doors, as directed, the Note had been discharg'd. I waited there on Purpose. I want the Women to think well of me; for *Lewson*'s grown suspicious; he told me so himself.

Bates. What Answer did you make him?

Stu. A short one——That I wou'd see him soon, for farther Explanation.

Bates. We must take care of him. But what have we to do with *Beverley*? *Dawson* and the rest are wondering at you.

Stu. Why let 'em wonder. I have Designs above their narrow Reach. They see me lend him Money; and they stare at me. But they are Fools. I want him to believe me beggar'd by him.

Bates. And what then?

Stu. Ay, there's the Question; but no Matter. At Night you may know more. He waits for me at *Wilson*'s. I told the Women where to find him.

Bates. To what Purpose?

Stu. To save Suspicion. It look'd friendly; and they thank'd me. Old *Jarvis* was dispatch'd to him.

Bates. And may intreat him Home.

Stu. No; he expects Money from me: But I'll have none. His Wife's Jewels must go——Women are easy Creatures, and refuse nothing where they love——Follow to *Wilson*'s; but be sure he sees you not. You are a Man of Character, you know; of Prudence and Discretion. Wait for me in an outer Room; I shall have Business for you presently. Come, Sir——

> *Let drudging Fools by Honesty grow great.*
> *The shorter Road to Riches is Deceit.* (*Exeunt.*)

End of the first ACT

ACT II

SCENE *a Gaming House, with a Table, Box, Dice, &c.*

BEVERLEY *is discover'd sitting*

Bev. Why, what a World is this! The Slave that digs for Gold, receives his daily Pittance, and sleeps contented; while those, for whom he labours, convert their Good to Mischief; making Abundance the Means of Want. O Shame! Shame! ——Had Fortune given me but a little, that little had been still my own. But Plenty leads to Waste; and shallow Streams maintain their Currents, while swelling Rivers beat down their Banks, and leave their Channels empty. What had I to do with Play? I wanted nothing. My Wishes and my Means were equal. The Poor follow'd me with Blessings; Love scatter'd Roses on my Pillow, and Morning wak'd me to Delight——O, bitter Thought! that leads to what I was, by what I am! I wou'd forget both——Who's there?

Enter a Waiter

Wait. A Gentleman, Sir, enquires for you.

Bev. He might have us'd less Ceremony. *Stukely* I suppose?

Wait. No, Sir, a Stranger.

Bev. Well, shew him in.   (*Exit* Waiter.

A Messenger from *Stukely* then! From Him that has undone me!——Yet all in Friendship; and now he lends me from his Little, to bring back Fortune to me.

Enter Jarvis

Jarvis! Why this Intrusion?———Your Absence had been kinder.

Jar. I came in Duty, Sir. If it be troublesome———

Bev. It is——I wou'd be private——hid even from myself. Who sent you hither?

Jar. One that wou'd persuade you Home again. My Mistress is not well; her Tears told me so.

Bev. Go with thy Duty there then——But does she weep? I am to blame to let her weep. Prithee begone; I have no Business for thee.

Jar. Yes, Sir; to lead you from this Place. I am your Servant still. Your prosperous Fortune bless'd my old Age. If That has left you, I must not leave you.

Bev. Not leave me! Recall past Time then; or through this Sea of Storms and Darkness, shew me a Star to guide me——But what can'st Thou?

Jar. The little that I can, I will. You have been generous to me——I wou'd not offend you, Sir——but——

Bev. No. Think'st thou I'd ruin Thee too! I have enough of Shame already——My Wife! my Wife! Wou'd'st thou believe it, *Jarvis*? I have not seen her all this long Night—— I, who have lov'd her so, that every Hour of Absence seem'd as a Gap in Life. But other Bonds have held me——O! I have play'd the Boy, dropping my Counters in the Stream, and reaching to redeem 'em, have lost myself. Why wilt Thou follow Misery? Or if thou wilt, go to thy Mistress. She has no Guilt to sting her, and therefore may be comforted.

Jar. For Pity's Sake, Sir!——I have no Heart to see this Change.

Bev. Nor I to bear it——How speaks the World of me, *Jarvis*?

Jar. As of a good Man dead. Of one, who walking in a Dream, fell down a Precipice. The World is sorry for you.

Bev. Ay, and pities me. Says it not so? But I was born to Infamy——I'll tell thee what it says. It calls me Villain; a treacherous Husband; a cruel Father; a false Brother; one lost to Nature and her Charities. Or to say all in one short Word, it calls me—Gamester. Go to thy Mistress——I'll see her presently.

Jar. And why not now? Rude People press upon her; loud, bawling Creditors; Wretches, who know no Pity—— I met one at the Door; he wou'd have seen my Mistress. I wanted Means of present Payment, so promis'd it To-morrow. But others may be pressing; and she has Grief enough already. Your Absence hangs too heavy on her.

Bev. Tell her I'll come then. I have a Moment's Business. But what hast Thou to do with My Distresses? Thy Honesty has left thee poor; and Age wants Comfort. Keep what thou hast for Cordials; lest between thee and the Grave, Misery steal in. I have a Friend shall counsel me——This is that Friend.

Enter Stukely

Stu. How fares it, *Beverley*? Honest Mr. *Jarvis*, well met; I hop'd to find you here. That Viper *Williams*! Was it not He that troubled you this Morning?

Jar. My Mistress heard him then?——I am sorry that she heard him.

Bev. And *Jarvis* promis'd Payment.

Stu. That must not be. Tell him I'll satisfy him.

Jar. Will you, Sir? Heaven will reward you for't.

Bev. Generous *Stukely*! Friendship like yours, had it Ability like Will, wou'd more than ballance the Wrongs of Fortune.

Stu. You think too kindly of me—Make haste to *Williams*; his Clamours may be rude else.   (*to* Jar.

Jar. And my Master will go Home again—Alas! Sir, we know of Hearts there breaking for his Absence.   (*Exit.*

Bev. Wou'd I were dead!

Stu. Or turn'd Hermit; counting a String of Beads in a dark Cave; or under a weeping Willow, praying for Mercy on the Wicked. Ha! ha! ha!—Prithee be a Man, and leave dying to Disease and old Age. Fortune may be ours again; at least we'll try for't.

Bev. No; it has fool'd us on too far.

Stu. Ay, ruin'd us; and therefore we'll sit down contented. These are the Despondings of Men without Money; but let the shining Ore chink in the Pocket, and Folly turns to Wisdom. We are Fortune's Children—True, she's a fickle Mother; but shall We droop because She's peevish?—No; she has Smiles in Store. And these her frowns are meant to brighten 'em.

Bev. Is this a Time for Levity? But You are single in the

Ruin, and therefore may talk lightly of it. With Me 'tis com-
plicated Misery.

Stu. You censure me unjustly——I but assum'd these
Spirits to cheer my Friend. Heaven knows he wants a Comforter.

Bev. What new Misfortune?

Stu. I wou'd have brought you Money; but Lenders want
Securities. What's to be done? All that was mine is yours
already.

Bev. And there's the double Weight that sinks me. I have
undone my Friend too; one, who to save a drowning Wretch,
reach'd out his Hand, and perish'd with him.

Stu. Have better Thoughts.

Bev. Whence are they to proceed?——I have nothing left.

Stu. (*Sighing*) Then we're indeed undone. What Nothing?
No Moveables? Nor useless Trinkets? Bawbles lock'd up in
Caskets to starve their Owners?——I have ventur'd deeply
for you.

Bev. Therefore this Heart-ake; for I am lost beyond all
Hope.

Stu. No; Means may be found to save us. *Jarvis* is rich.
Who made him so? This is no Time for Ceremony.

Bev. And is it for Dishonesty? The good old Man! Shall
I rob Him too? My Friend wou'd grieve for't. No; lèt the
little that he has, buy Food and Cloathing for him.

Stu. Good Morning then.   (*Going.*

Bev. So hasty! Why, then good Morning.

Stu. And when we meet again, upbraid me. Say it was I
that tempted you. Tell *Lewson* so; and tell him I have wrong'd
you——He has Suspicions of me, and will thank you.

Bev. No; we have been Companions in a rash Voyage,
and the same Storm has wreck'd us both. Mine shall be Self-
Upbraidings.

Stu. And will they feed us? You deal unkindly by me. I
have sold and borrow'd for you, while Land or Credit lasted;
and now, when Fortune shou'd be try'd, and my Heart whis-
pers me Success, I am deserted; turn'd loose to Beggary,
while You have Hoards.

Bev. What Hoards? Name 'em, and take 'em.

Stu. Jewels.

Bev. And shall this thriftless Hand seize Them too? My poor, poor Wife! Must she lose all? I wou'd not wound her so.

Stu. Nor I, but from Necessity. One Effort more, and Fortune may grow kind. I have unusual Hopes.

Bev. Think of some other Means then.

Stu. I have; and you rejected 'em.

Bev. Prythee let me be a Man.

Stu. Ay, and your Friend a poor one. But I have done. And for these Trinkets of a Woman, why, let her keep 'em to deck out Pride with, and shew a laughing World that she has Finery to starve in.

Bev. No; she shall yield up all. My Friend demands it. But need he have talk'd lightly of her? The Jewels that She values are Truth and Innocence———Those will adorn her ever; and for the rest, she wore 'em for a Husband's Pride, and to his Wants will give 'em. Alas! you know her not. Where shall we meet?

Stu. No Matter. I have chang'd my Mind. Leave me to a Prison; 'tis the Reward of Friendship.

Bev. Perish Mankind first—Leave you to a Prison! No; fallen as you see me, I'm not that Wretch. Nor wou'd I change this Heart, o'ercharg'd as 'tis with Folly and Misfortune, for one most prudent and most happy, if callous to a Friend's Distresses.

Stu. You are too warm.

Bev. In such a Cause, not to be warm is to be frozen. Farewel. I'll meet you at your Lodgings.

Stu. Reflect a little. The Jewels may be lost. Better not hazard 'em———I was too pressing.

Bev. And I ungrateful. Reflection takes up Time. I have no Leisure for't. Within an Hour expect me.   (*Exit.*

Stu. The thoughtless, shallow Prodigal! We shall have Sport at Night then———But hold—The Jewels are not ours yet———The Lady may refuse 'em———The Husband may relent too———'Tis more than probable———I'll write a Note to *Beverley*, and the Contents shall spur him to demand

'em——But am I grown this Rogue thro' Avarice? No; I
have warmer Motives, Love and Revenge——Ruin the Hus-
band, and the Wife's Virtue may be bid for. 'Tis of uncertain
Value, and sinks, or rises in the Purchase, as Want, or Wealth,
or Passion governs. The Poor part cheaply with it; rich
Dames, tho' pleas'd with selling, will have high Prices for't.
Your Love-sick Girls give it for Oaths and Lying. But tender
Wives, who boast of Honour and Affections, keep it against a
Famine——Why, let the Famine come then; I am in haste to
purchase.

Enter Bates

Look to your Men, *Bates*; there's Money stirring. We meet
To-night upon this Spot. Hasten and tell 'em so. *Beverley*
calls upon me at my Lodgings, and we return together.
Hasten, I say, the Rogues will scatter else.

Bates. Not 'till their Leader bids 'em.

Stu. Come on then. Give 'em the Word and follow me; I
must advise with you——This is a Day of Business. (*Exeunt.*)

SCENE changes to Beverley's Lodgings

Enter Beverley and Charlotte

Char. Your Looks are chang'd too; there's Wildness in 'em.
My wretched Sister! How will it grieve her to see you thus!

Bev. No, no—a little Rest will ease me. And for your *Lewson*'s Kindness to her, it has my Thanks; I have no more to
give him.

Char. Yes; a Sister and her Fortune. I trifle with him and
he complains.—My Looks, he says, are cold upon him. He
thinks too——

Bev. That I have lost your Fortune—He dares not think so.

Char. Nor does he—You are too quick at guessing. He
cares not if you had. That Care is mine—I lent it you to husband, and now I claim it.

Bev. You have Suspicions then.

Char. Cure 'em, and give it me.

Bev. To stop a Sister's Chiding.

Char. To vindicate her Brother.

Bev. How if he needs no Vindication?

Char. I would fain hope so.

Bev. Ay, wou'd and cannot. Leave it to Time then; 'twill satisfy all Doubts.

Char. Mine are already satisfy'd.

Bev. 'Tis well. And when the Subject is renew'd, speak to me like a Sister, and I will answer like a Brother.

Char. To tell me I'm a Beggar.—Why, tell it now. I that can bear the Ruin of those dearer to me, the Ruin of a Sister and her Infant, can bear That too.

Bev. No more of this—you wring my Heart.

Cha. Wou'd that the Misery were all your own! But Innocence must suffer—Unthinking Rioter! whose Home was Heaven to him; an Angel dwelt there, and a little Cherub, that crown'd his Days with Blessings—How has he lost this Heaven, to league with Devils!

Bev. Forbear, I say; Reproaches come too late; they search, but cure not: And for the Fortune you demand, we'll talk To-morrow on't; our Tempers may be milder.

Cha. Or if 'tis gone, why farewell all. I claim'd it for a Sister. She holds my Heart in hers; and every Pang she feels tears it in Pieces—But I'll upbraid no more. What Heaven permits, perhaps, it may ordain; and Sorrow then is sinful. Yet that the Husband! Father! Brother! should be its Instrument of Vengeance!——'Tis grievous to know that.

Bev. If you're my Sister, spare the Remembrance—it wounds too deeply. To-morrow shall clear all; and when the worst is known, it may be better than your Fears. Comfort my Wife; and for the Pains of Absence, I'll make Atonement. The World may yet go well with us.

Cha. See where she comes!—Look chearfully upon her— Afflictions such as hers are prying, and lend those Eyes that read the Soul.

Enter Mrs. Beverley *and* Lewson

Mrs. *Bev.* My Life!

Bev. My Love! How fares it? I have been a truant Husband.

Mrs. Bev. But we meet now, and that heals all—Doubts and Alarms I have had; but in this dear Embrace I bury and forget 'em—My Friend here [*pointing to* Lewson] has been indeed a Friend. *Charlotte*, 'tis you must thank him: Your Brother's Thanks and mine are of too little Value.

Bev. Yet what we have we'll pay. I thank you, Sir, and am oblig'd. I wou'd say more, but that your Goodness to the Wife upbraids the Husband's Follies. Had I been wise, She had not trespass'd on your Bounty.

Lew. Nor has she trespass'd. The little I have done, Acceptance over-pays.

Cha. So Friendship thinks——

Mrs. Bev. And doubles Obligations by striving to conceal 'em—We'll talk another Time on't.—You are too thoughtful, Love.

Bev. No, I have Reason for these Thoughts.

Cha. And hatred for the Cause—Wou'd you had that too!

Bev. I have—The Cause was Avarice.

Cha. And who the Tempter?

Bev. A ruin'd Friend—ruin'd by too much Kindness.

Lew. Ay, worse than ruin'd; stabb'd in his Fame, mortally stabb'd—Riches can't cure him.

Bev. Or if they cou'd, those I have drain'd him of. Something of this he hinted in the Morning—That *Lewson* had Suspicions of him—Why these Suspicions?   [*angrily*.

Lew. At School we knew this *Stukely*. A cunning plodding Boy he was, sordid and cruel. Slow at his Task, but quick at Shifts and Tricking. He schem'd out Mischief, that others might be punish'd; and wou'd tell his Tale with so much Art, that for the Lash he merited, Rewards and Praise were given him. Shew me a Boy with such a Mind, and Time that ripens Manhood in him, shall ripen Vice too—I'll prove him, and lay him open t'you—'Till then be warn'd—I know him, and therefore shun him.

Bev. As I wou'd those that wrong him—You are too busy, Sir.

Mrs. Bev. No, not too busy—Mistaken perhaps—That had been milder.

Lew. No matter, Madam. I can bear this, and praise the Heart that prompts it—Pity such Friendship shou'd be so plac'd!

Bev. Again, Sir! But I'll bear too—You wrong him, *Lewson*, and will be sorry for't.

Cha. Ay, when 'tis prov'd he wrongs him. The World is full of Hypocrites.

Bev. And *Stukely* one—so you'd infer I think—I'll hear no more of this—my Heart akes for him—I have undone him.

Lew. The World says otherwise.

Bev. The World is false then—I have Business with you, Love. [*to Mrs*. Bev.] We'll leave 'em to their Rancour. [*going*.

Cha. No. We shall find Room within for't—Come this way, Sir.   [*to Lewson*.

Lew. Another Time my Friend will thank me; that Time is hastening too.   [*Ex*. Lew. *and* Char.

Bev. They hurt me beyond bearing—Is *Stukely* false? Then Honesty has left us! 'Twere sinning against Heav'n to think so.

Mrs. *Bev*. I never doubted him.

Bev. No; You are Charity. Meekness and ever-during Patience live in that Heart, and Love that knows no Change—Why did I ruin you?

Mrs. *Bev*. You have not ruin'd me. I have no Wants when You are present, nor Wishes in your Absence but to be blest with your Return. Be but resign'd to what has happen'd, and I am rich beyond the Dreams of Avarice.

Bev. My generous Girl!—But Memory will be busy; still crouding on my Thoughts, to sour the Present by the Past. I have another Pang too.

Mrs. *Bev*. Tell it, and let me cure it.

Bev. That Friend——that generous Friend, whose Fame they have traduc'd—I have undone Him too. While he had Means he lent me largely; and now a Prison must be his Portion.

Mrs. *Bev*. No; I hope otherwise.

Bev. To hope must be to act. The charitable Wish feeds not the Hungry—Something must be done.

Mrs. *Bev*. What?

Bev. In Bitterness of Heart he told me, just now he told me, I had undone him. Cou'd I hear that, and think of Happiness? No; I have disclaim'd it, while He is miserable.

Mrs. Bev. The World may mend with us, and then we may be grateful. There's Comfort in that Hope.

Bev. Ay; 'tis the sick Man's Cordial, his promis'd Cure; while in preparing it the Patient dies.——What now?

Enter Lucy

Lucy. A Letter, Sir.   [*delivers it and Ex.*

Bev. The Hand is *Stukely*'s. [*opens and reads it to himself.*

Mrs. Bev. And brings good News——at least I'll hope so ——What says he, Love?

Bev. Why this——too much for Patience. Yet he directs me to conceal it from you.   [*reads.*

'Let your Haste to see me be the only Proof of your Esteem 'for me. I have determin'd, since we parted, to bid Adieu 'to *England*; chusing rather to forsake my Country than 'owe my Freedom in it to the Means we talk'd of. Keep 'this a Secret at Home, and hasten to the ruin'd

'*R. Stukely.*'

Ruin'd by Friendship! I must relieve or follow him.

Mrs. Bev. Follow him, did you say? Then I am lost indeed!

Bev. O this infernal Vice! how has it sunk me! A Vice, whose highest Joy was poor to my domestic Happiness. Yet how have I pursu'd it! turn'd all my Comforts to bitterest Pangs! and all thy Smiles to Tears. Damn'd, damn'd Infatuation!

Mrs. Bev. Be cool, my Life! What are the Means the Letter talks of? Have you——have I those Means? Tell me, and ease me. I have no Life while you are wretched.

Bev. No, no; it must not be. 'Tis I alone have sinn'd; 'tis I alone must suffer. You shall reserve those Means to keep my Child and his wrong'd Mother from Want and Wretchedness.

Mrs. Bev. What Means?

Bev. I came to rob you of 'em—but cannot—dare not— Those Jewels are your sole Support—I shou'd be more than Monster to request 'em.

Mrs. Bev. My Jewels! Trifles, not worth the speaking of, if weigh'd against a Husband's Peace; but let 'em purchase That, and the World's Wealth is of less Value.

Bev. Amazing Goodness! How little do I seem before such Virtues!

Mrs. Bev. No more, my Love. I kept 'em 'till Occasion call'd to use 'em; now is the Occasion, and I'll resign 'em chearfully.

Bev. Why we'll be rich in Love then. But this Excess of Kindness melts me. Yet for a Friend one wou'd do much—— He has deny'd Me nothing.

Mrs. Bev. Come to my Closet——But let him manage wisely. We have no more to give him.

Bev. Where learn'd my Love this Excellence?—'Tis Heaven's own teaching: That Heaven, which to an Angel's Form has given a Mind more lovely. I am unworthy of you, but will deserve you better.

> *Henceforth my Follies and Neglects shall cease,*
> *And all to come be Penitence and Peace;*
> *Vice shall no more attract me with her Charms,*
> *Nor Pleasure reach me, but in these dear Arms.*

[Exeunt.

End of the Second ACT

ACT III

SCENE Stukely's *Lodgings*

Enter Stukely *and* Bates

Stu. So runs the World, *Bates.* Fools are the natural Prey of Knaves; Nature design'd them so, when she made Lambs for Wolves. The Laws that Fear and Policy have fram'd, Nature disclaims: She knows but two; and those are Force and Cunning. The nobler Law is Force; but then there's

Danger in't; while Cunning, like a skillful Miner, works safely and unseen.

Bat. And therefore wisely. Force must have Nerves and Sinews; Cunning wants neither. The Dwarf that has it shall trip the Giant's Heels up.

Stu. And bind him to the Ground. Why, we'll erect a Shrine for Nature, and be her Oracles. Conscience is Weakness; Fear made it, and Fear maintains it. The Dread of Shame, inward Reproaches, and fictitious Burnings swell out the Phantom. Nature knows none of this; Her Laws are Freedom.

Bat. Sound Doctrine, and well deliver'd!

Stu. We are sincere too, and practice what we teach. Let the grave Pedant say as much.——But now to Business. The Jewels are dispos'd of; and *Beverley* again worth Money. He waits to count his Gold out, and then comes hither. If my Design succeeds, this Night we finish with him. Go to your Lodgings and be busy—You understand Conveyances, and can make Ruin sure.

Bat. Better stop here. The Sale of this Reversion may be talk'd of—There's Danger in't.

Stu. No, 'tis the Mark I aim at. We'll thrive and laugh. You are the Purchaser, and there's the Payment. [*giving a Pocket Book.*] He thinks you rich; and so you shall be. Enquire for Titles, and deal hardly; 'twill look like Honesty.

Bat. How if he suspects us?

Stu. Leave it to me. I study Hearts, and when to work upon 'em. Go to your Lodgings; and if we come, be busy over Papers. Talk of a thoughtless Age, of Gaming and Extravagance; you have a Face for't.

Bat. A Feeling too that wou'd avoid it. We push too far; but I have caution'd you. If it ends ill, you'll think of me— and so adieu.   [*Exit* Bates.

Stu. This Fellow sins by halves; his Fears are Conscience to him. I'll turn these Fears to Use. Rogues that dread Shame will still be greater Rogues to hide their Guilt——This shall be thought of. *Lewson* grows troublesome——We must get rid of him.—He knows too much. I have a Tale for *Beverley*; Part of it Truth too—He shall call *Lewson* to Account—If it succeeds, 'tis well; if not, we must try other Means—But here he comes—I must dissemble.

Enter Beverley

Look to the Door there! [*in a seeming Fright*]—My Friend! —I thought of other Visitors.

Bev. No: These shall guard you from 'em—[*offering Notes*] Take 'em, and use 'em cautiously—The World deals hardly by us.

Stu. And shall I leave you destitute? No Your Wants are greatest. Another Climate may treat me kinder. The Shelter of To-night takes me from this.

Bev. Let these be your Support then—Yet is there need of Parting? I may have Means again; we'll share 'em, and live wisely.

Stu. No. I shou'd tempt you on. Habit is Nature in me; Ruin can't cure it. Even now I wou'd be gaming. Taught by Experience as I am, and knowing this poor Sum is all that's left us, I am for venturing still—And say I am to blame—Yet will this little supply our Wants? No; we must put it out to Usury. Whether 'tis Madness in me, or some resistless Impulse of good Fortune, I yet am Ignorant; but——

Bev. Take it, and succeed then. I'll try no more.

Stu. 'Tis surely Impulse; it pleads so strongly—But you are cold—We'll e'en part here then. And for this last Reserve keep it for better uses; I'll have none on't. I thank you tho', and will seek Fortune singly—One Thing I had forgot—

Bev. What is it?

Stu. Perhaps, 'twere best forgotten. But I am open in my Nature, and zealous for the Honour of my Friend—*Lewson* speaks freely of you.

Bev. Of You I know he does.

Stu. I can forgive him for't; but for my Friend I'm angry.

Bev. What says he of Me?

Stu. That *Charlotte*'s Fortune is embezzled—He talks on't loudly.

Bev. He shall be silenc'd then—How heard you of it?

Stu. From many. He question'd *Bates* about it. You must account with Him, he says.

Bev. Or He with Me—and soon too.

Stu. Speak mildly to him. Cautions are best.

Bev. I'll think on't—But whither go you?

Stu. From Poverty and Prisons—No matter whither. If Fortune changes you may hear from me.

Bev. May these be prosperous then. [*offering the Notes, which he refuses*] Nay, they are yours—I have sworn it, and will have nothing—take 'em and use 'em.

Stu. Singly I will not. My Cares are for my Friend; for his lost Fortune, and ruin'd Family. All separate Interests I disclaim. Together we have fall'n: together we must rise. My Heart, my Honour and Affections, all will have it so.

Bev. I am weary of being fool'd.

Stu. And so am I—Here let us part then—These Bodings of Good-fortune shall all be stifled; I'll call 'em Folly, and forget 'em—This one Embrace, and then farewell.

[*offering to Embrace.*

Bev. No; Stay a Moment—How my poor Heart's distracted! I have these Bodings too; but whether caught from You, or prompted by my good or evil Genius, I know not—The Trial shall determine—And yet, my Wife———

Stu. Ay, ay, she'll chide.

Bev. No; My Chidings are all here.

[*pointing to his Heart.*

Stu. I'll not perswade you.

Bev. I am perswaded; by Reason too; the strongest Reason; Necessity. Oh! cou'd I but regain the Height I have fallen from, Heaven shou'd forsake me in my latest Hour, if I again mix'd in these Scenes, or sacrific'd the Husband's Peace, his Joy and best Affections to Avarice and Infamy!

Stu. I have resolv'd like You; and since our Motives are so honest, why shou'd we fear Success?

Bev. Come on then—where shall we meet?

Stu. At *Wilson's*—Yet if it hurts you, leave me: I have misled you often.

Bev. We have misled each other—But come!—Fortune

is fickle, and may be tir'd with plaguing us—There let us rest our Hopes.

Stu. Yet think a little——

Bev. I cannot—thinking but distracts me.

> *When Desperation leads all Thoughts are vain;*
> *Reason wou'd lose, what Rashness may obtain.*

[*Exeunt.*

SCENE *changes to* Beverley's *Lodgings*

Enter Mrs. Beverley *and* Charlotte

Cha. 'Twas all a Scheme, a mean one; unworthy of my Brother.

Mrs. Bev. No, I am sure it was not—*Stukely* is honest too; I know he is—This Madness has undone 'em both.

Cha. My Brother irrecoverably—You are too spiritless a Wife—A mournful Tale, mixt with a few kind Words, will steal away your Soul. The World's too subtle for such Goodness. Had I been by, he shou'd have ask'd your Life sooner than those Jewels.

Mrs. Bev. He shou'd have had it then. [*warmly*] I live but to oblige him. She who can love, and is belov'd like Me, will do as much. Men have done more for Mistresses, and Women for a base Deluder. And shall a Wife do less? Your Chidings hurt me, *Charlotte*.

Cha. And come too late; they might have sav'd you else. How cou'd he use you so?

Mrs. Bev. 'Twas Friendship did it. His Heart was breaking for a Friend.

Cha. The Friend that has betray'd him.

Mrs. Bev. Prithee don't think so.

Cha. To-morrow he Accounts with Me.

Mrs. Bev. And fairly—I will not doubt it.

Cha. Unless a Friend has wanted—I have no Patience—Sister! Sister! we are bound to curse this Friend.

Mrs. Bev. My *Beverley* speaks nobly of him.

Cha. And *Lewson* truly—But I displease you with this Talk—To-morrow will instruct us.

Mrs. *Bev.* Stay till it comes then—I wou'd not think so hardly.

Cha. Nor I, but from Conviction—Yet we have Hope of better Days. My Uncle is infirm, and of an Age that threatens hourly—Or if he lives, you never have offended him; and for Distresses so unmerited he will have Pity.

Mrs. *Bev.* I know it, and am chearful. We have no more to lose; and for what's gone, if it brings Prudence Home, the Purchase was well made.

Cha. My *Lewson* will be kind too. While he and I have Life and Means, You shall divide with us—And see, he's here.

Enter Lewson

We were just speaking of you.

Lew. 'Tis best to interrupt you then. Few Characters will bear a Scrutiny; and where the Bad out-weighs the Good, he's safest that's least talk'd of. What say you, Madam?

[*To* Charlotte.

Cha. That I hate Scandal, tho' a Woman——therefore talk seldom of you.

Mrs. *Bev.* Or, with more Truth, that, tho' a Woman, she loves to Praise—Therefore talks always of you. I'll leave you to decide it.   [*Exit Mrs.* Bev.

Lew. How good and amiable! I came to talk in private with you; of Matters that concern you.

Cha. What Matters?

Lew. First answer me sincerely to what I ask.

Cha. I will—But you alarm me.

Lew. I am too grave, perhaps; but be assur'd of this, I have no News that troubles Me, and therefore shou'd not You.

Cha. I am easy then—Propose your Question.

Lew. 'Tis now a tedious Twelve-month, since with an open and kind Heart you said you lov'd me.

Cha. So tedious, did you say?

Lew. And when in Consequence of such sweet Words, I

press'd for Marriage, you gave a voluntary Promise that you
wou'd live for Me.

Cha. You think me chang'd then?   [*angrily.*

Lew. I did not say so. A thousand times I have press'd
for the Performance of this Promise; but private Cares, a
Brother's and a Sister's Ruin, were Reasons for delaying it.

Cha. I had no other Reasons—Where will this end?

Lew. It shall end presently.

Cha. Go on, Sir.

Lew. A Promise, such as this, given freely, not extorted,
The World thinks binding; but I think otherwise.

Cha. And wou'd release me from it?

Lew. You are too impatient, Madam.

Cha. Cool, Sir—quite cool—Pray go on.

Lew. Time and a near Acquaintance with my Faults may
have brought Change—if it be so; or for a Moment, if you
have wish'd this Promise were unmade, here I acquit you of
it—This is my Question then; and with such Plainness as I
ask it, I shall entreat an Answer. Have you repented of this
Promise?

Cha. Stay, Sir. The Man that can Suspect me, shall Find
me chang'd—Why am I doubted?

Lew. My Doubts are of myself. I have my Faults, and
You have Observation. If from my Temper, my Words or
Actions, you have conceiv'd a Thought against me, or even
a Wish for Separation, all that has pass'd is Nothing.

Cha. You startle me—But tell me—I must be answer'd
first. Is it from Honour you speak this? or do you wish me
chang'd?

Lew. Heaven knows I do not. Life and my *Charlotte* are so
connected, that to lose one, were Loss of both. Yet for a
Promise, tho' given in Love, and meant for binding; if Time,
or Accident, or Reason shou'd change Opinion——with Me
that Promise has no Force.

Cha. Why, now I'll answer you. Your Doubts are Pro-
phecies—I am really chang'd.

Lew. Indeed!

Cha. I cou'd torment you now, as you have Me; but 'tis

not in my Nature—That I am chang'd I own; for what at first was Inclination, is now grown Reason in me; and from that Reason, had I the World! nay, were I poorer than the poorest, and you too wanting Bread; with but a Hovel to invite me to—I wou'd be yours, and happy.

Lew. My kindest *Charlotte*! [*taking her Hand*] Thanks are too poor for this—and Words too weak! But if we love so, why shou'd our Union be delay'd?

Cha. For happier Times. The present are too wretched.

Lew. I may have Reasons that press it now.

Cha. What Reasons?

Lew. The strongest Reasons; unanswerable ones.

Cha. Be quick and name 'em.

Lew. No, Madam; I am bound in Honour to make Conditions first—I am bound by Inclination too. This sweet Profusion of kind Words pains while it pleases. I dread the losing you.

Cha. Astonishment! What mean you?

Lew. First promise, that To-morrow, or next Day, you will be mine for ever.

Cha. I do—tho' Misery shou'd succeed.

Lew. Thus then I seize you! And with you every Joy on this side Heaven!

Cha. And thus I seal my Promise. [*embracing him*] Now, Sir, your Secret?

Lew. Your Fortune's lost.

Cha. My Fortune lost!—I'll study to be humble then. But was my Promise claim'd for this? How nobly generous! Where learnt you this sad News?

Lew. From *Bates*, *Stukely*'s prime Agent. I have oblig'd him, and he's grateful—He told it me in Friendship, to warn me from my *Charlotte*.

Cha. 'Twas honest in him, and I'll esteem him for't.

Lew. He knows much more than he has told.

Cha. For Me it is enough. And for your generous Love, I thank you from my Soul. If you'd oblige me more, give me a little Time.

Lew. Why Time? It robs us of our Happiness.

Cha. I have a Task to learn first. The little Pride this

Fortune gave me must be subdu'd. Once we were equal; and might have met obliging and oblig'd. But now 'tis otherwise; and for a Life of Obligations, I have not learnt to bear it.

Lew. Mine is that Life, You are too noble.

Cha. Leave me to think on't.

Lew. To-morrow then you'll fix my Happiness?

Cha. All that I can, I will.

Lew. It must be so, we live but for each other. Keep what you know a Secret; and when we meet To-morrow, more may be known.—Farewell.   [*Exit* Lewson.

Cha. My poor, poor Sister! how wou'd this wound her! But I'll conceal it, and speak Comfort to her.   [*Exit.*

Scene changes to a Room in the Gaming-House

Enter Beverley *and* Stukely

Bev. Whither wou'd you lead me?   (*Angrily.*

Stu. Where we may vent our Curses.

Bev. Ay, on yourself, and those damn'd Counsels that have destroy'd me. A thousand Fiends were in that Bosom, and all let loose to tempt me—I had resisted else.

Stu. Go on, Sir—I have deserv'd this from you.

Bev. And Curses everlasting—Time is too scanty for 'em—

Stu. What have I done?

Bev. What the Arch-Devil of old did——sooth'd with false Hopes, for certain Ruin.

Stu. Myself unhurt; nay, pleas'd at your Destruction—So your Words mean. Why; tell it to the World. I am too poor to find a Friend in't.

Bev. A Friend! what's he? I had a Friend.

Stu. And have one still.

Bev. Ay; I'll tell you of this Friend. He found me happiest of the Happy. Fortune and Honour crown'd me; and Love and Peace liv'd in my Heart. One Spark of Folly lurk'd there; That too he found; and by deceitful Breath blew it to Flames that have consum'd me. This Friend were You to Me.

Stu. A little more perhaps—The Friend who gave his All to save you; and not succeeding, chose Ruin with you. But no matter, I have undone you, and am a Villain.

Bev. No; I think not——The Villains are within.

Stu. What Villains?

Bev. *Dawson* and the rest—We have been Dupes to Sharpers.

Stu. How know you this? I have had Doubts as well as you; yet still as Fortune chang'd I blush'd at my own Thoughts—But You have Proofs, perhaps.

Bev. Ay, damn'd ones. Repeated Losses—Night after Night, and no Reverse—Chance has no Hand in this.

Stu. I think more charitably; yet I am peevish in my Nature, and apt to doubt——The World speaks fairly of this *Dawson*, so does it of the rest. We have watch'd 'em closely too. But 'tis a Right usurp'd by Losers, to think the Winners Knaves—We'll have more Manhood in us.

Bev. I know not what to think. This Night has stung me to the quick—Blasted my Reputation too——I have bound my Honour to these Vipers; play'd meanly upon Credit, 'till I tir'd 'em; and now they shun me to rifle one another. What's to be done?

Stu. Nothing. My Counsels have been fatal.

Bev. By Heaven I'll not survive this Shame—Traitor! 'tis you have brought it on me. (*taking hold of him.*) Shew me the Means to save me, or I'll commit a Murder here, and next upon myself.

Stu. Why, do it then, and rid me of Ingratitude.

Bev. Prithee forgive this Language—I speak I know not what—Rage and Despair are in my Heart, and hurry me to Madness. My Home is Horror to me——I'll not return to't. Speak quickly; tell me, if in this Wreck of Fortune, one Hope remains? Name it, and be my Oracle.

Stu. To vent your Curses on—You have bestow'd 'em liberally. Take your own Counsel: and shou'd a desperate Hope present itself, 'twill suit your desperate Fortune. I'll not advise you.

Bev. What Hope? By Heaven I'll catch at it, however desperate. I am so sunk in Misery, it cannot lay me lower.

Stu. You have an Uncle.

Bev. Ay. What of Him?

Stu. Old Men live long by Temperance; while their Heirs starve on Expectation.

Bev. What mean you?

Stu. That the Reversion of his Estate is yours; and will bring Money to pay Debts with—Nay more, it may retrieve what's past.

Bev. Or leave my Child a Beggar.

Stu. And what's his Father? A dishonourable one; engag'd for Sums he cannot pay—That shou'd be thought of.

Bev. It is my Shame—the Poison that enflames me. Where shall we go? To whom? I am impatient 'till all's lost.

Stu. All may be yours again—Your Man is *Bates*——He has large Funds at his Command, and will deal justly by you.

Bev. I am resolv'd——Tell 'em within we'll meet 'em presently; and with full Purses too—Come, follow me.

Stu. No. I'll have no hand in this; nor do I counsel it—Use your Discretion, and act from that. You'll find me at my Lodgings.

Bev. Succeed what will, this Night I'll dare the worst. 'Tis loss of Fear, to be compleatly curs'd.   (*Exit* Bev.

Stu. Why, lose it then for ever—Fear is the Mind's worst Evil; and 'tis a friendly Office to drive it from the Bosom—Thus far has Fortune crown'd me—Yet *Beverley* is rich; rich in his Wife's best Treasure, her Honour and Affections. I wou'd supplant him there too. But 'tis the Curse of thinking Minds to raise up Difficulties. Fools only conquer Women. Fearless of Dangers which they see not, they press on boldly, and by persisting, prosper. Yet may a Tale of Art do much—*Charlotte* is sometimes absent. The Seeds of Jealousy are sown already. If I mistake not, they have taken Root too. Now is the Time to ripen 'em, and reap the Harvest. The softest of her Sex, if wrong'd in Love, or thinking that she's wrong'd, becomes a Tygress in Revenge——I'll instantly to *Beverley*'s—No Matter for the Danger—When Beauty leads us on, 'tis Indiscretion to reflect, and Cowardice to doubt.   (*Exit.*

Scene changes to Beverley's Lodgings

Enter Mrs. Beverley and Lucy

Mrs. *Bev.* Did *Charlotte* tell you any Thing?

Lu. No, Madam.

Mrs. *Bev.* She look'd confus'd methought; said she had Business with her *Lewson*; which, when I press'd to know, Tears only were her Answer.

Lu. She seem'd in haste too—Yet her Return may bring you Comfort.

Mrs. *Bev.* No, my kind Girl; I was not born for't—But why do I distress thee? Thy sympathizing Heart bleeds for the Ills of others—What Pity that thy Mistress can't reward thee! But there's a Power above, that sees, and will remember all. Prithee sooth me with the Song thou sung'st last Night. It suits this Change of Fortune; and there's a Melancholy in't that pleases me.

Lu. I fear it hurts you, Madam—Your Goodness too draws Tears from me—But I'll dry 'em, and obey you.

SONG

When Damon *languish'd at my Feet,*
　　And I believ'd him true,
The Moments of Delight how sweet!
　　But ah! how swift they flew!
The sunny Hill, the flow'ry Vale,
　　The Garden and the Grove,
Have echo'd to his ardent Tale,
　　And Vows of endless Love.

2

The Conquest gain'd, he left his Prize,
　　He left her to complain;
To talk of Joy with weeping Eyes,
　　And measure Time by Pain.
But Heav'n will take the Mourner's Part,
　　In pity to Despair;
And the last Sigh that rends the Heart,
　　Shall waft the Spirit there.

Mrs. *Bev.* I thank thee, *Lucy*——I thank Heaven too my Griefs are none of these. Yet *Stukely* deals in Hints—He talks of Rumours—I'll urge him to speak plainly—Hark! there's some one entering.

Lu. Perhaps my Master, Madam.   (*Exit.*

Mrs. *Bev.* Let him be well too, and I am satisfy'd. (*Goes to the Door, and listens.*) No; 'tis another's Voice; his had been Music to me. Who is it *Lucy*?

Re-enter Lucy *with* Stukely

Lu. Mr. *Stukely*, Madam.   (*Exit.*

Stu. To meet you thus alone, Madam, was what I wish'd. Unseasonable Visits, when Friendship warrants 'em, need no Excuse—Therefore I make none.

Mrs. *Bev.* What mean you, Sir? And where's your Friend?

Stu. Men may have Secrets, Madam, which their best Friends are not admitted to. We parted in the Morning, not soon to meet again.

Mrs. *Bev.* You mean to leave us then? To leave your Country too? I am no Stranger to your Reasons, and pity your Misfortunes.

Stu. Your Pity has undone you. Cou'd *Beverley* do this? That Letter was a false one; a mean Contrivance to rob you of your Jewels—I wrote it not.

Mrs. *Bev.* Impossible! whence came it then?

Stu. Wrong'd as I am, Madam, I must speak plainly—

Mrs. *Bev.* Do so, and ease me. Your Hints have troubled me. Reports, you say, are stirring—Reports of whom? You wish'd me not to credit 'em. What, Sir, are these Reports?

Stu. I thought 'em Slander, Madam; and caution'd you in Friendship; lest from officious Tongues the Tale had reach'd you, with double Aggravation.

Mrs. *Bev.* Proceed, Sir.

Stu. It is a Debt due to my Fame, due to an injur'd Wife too—We both are injur'd.

Mrs. *Bev.* How injur'd? And who has injur'd us?

Stu. My Friend, your Husband.

Mrs. Bev. You wou'd resent for both then? But know, Sir, My Injuries are my own, and do not need a Champion.

Stu. Be not too hasty, Madam. I come not in Resentment, but for Acquittance——You thought me poor; and to the feign'd Distresses of a Friend gave up your Jewels.

Mrs. Bev. I gave 'em to a Husband.

Stu. Who gave 'em to a ——

Mrs. Bev. What? Whom did he give 'em to?

Stu. A Mistress.

Mrs. Bev. No; on my Life he did not.

Stu. Himself confess'd it, with Curses on her Avarice.

Mrs. Bev. I'll not believe it——He has no Mistress—or if he has, why is it told to Me?

Stu. To guard you against Insults. He told me, that to move you to Compliance, he forg'd that Letter; pretending I was ruin'd; ruin'd by Him too. The Fraud succeeded; and what a trusting Wife bestow'd in Pity, was lavish'd on a Wanton.

Mrs. Bev. Then I am lost indeed; and my Afflictions are too powerful for me—His Follies I have borne without upbraiding, and saw the Approach of Poverty without a Tear— my Affections, my strong Affections supported me through every Trial.

Stu. Be patient, Madam.

Mrs. Bev. Patient! The barbarous, ungrateful Man! And does he think that the Tenderness of my Heart is his best Security for wounding it? But he shall find that Injuries such as these, can arm my Weakness for Vengeance and Redress.

Stu. Ha! then I may succeed—(*Aside.*) Redress is in your Power.

Mrs. Bev. What Redress?

Stu. Forgive me, Madam, if in my Zeal to serve you, I hazard your Displeasure.—Think of your wretched State. Already Want surrounds you. Is it in Patience to bear That? To see your helpless little one robb'd of his Birthright? A Sister too, with unavailing Tears, lamenting her lost Fortune? No Comfort left you, but ineffectual Pity from the Few, out-weigh'd by Insults from the Many?

Mrs. Bev. Am I so lost a Creature? Well, Sir, my Redress?

Stu. To be resolv'd is to secure it. The marriage Vow, once violated, is in the Sight of Heaven dissolv'd—Start not, but hear me! 'Tis now the Summer of your Youth; Time has not cropt the Roses from your Cheek, tho' Sorrow long has wash'd 'em—Then use your Beauty wisely; and freed by Injuries, fly from the cruelest of Men, for Shelter with the kindest.

Mrs. Bev. And who is He?

Stu. A Friend to the Unfortunate; a bold one too; who while the Storm is bursting on your Brow, and Lightening flashing from your Eyes, dares tell you that he loves you.

Mrs. Bev. Wou'd that these Eyes had Heaven's own Lightening! that with a Look, thus I might blast thee! Am I then fallen so low? Has Poverty so humbled me, that I shou'd listen to a hellish Offer, and sell my Soul for Bread? O Villain! Villain!———But now I know thee, and thank thee for the Knowledge.

Stu. If you are wise, you shall have Cause to thank me.

Mrs. Bev. An injur'd Husband too shall thank thee.

Stu. Yet know, proud Woman, I have a Heart as stubborn as your own; as haughty and imperious; and as it loves, so can it hate.

Mrs. Bev. Mean despicable Villain! I scorn thee and thy Threats. Was it for this that *Beverley* was false? That his too credulous Wife shou'd in Despair and Vengeance give up her Honour to a Wretch? But he shall know it, and Vengeance shall be his.

Stu. Why send him for Defiance then. Tell him I love his Wife; but that a worthless Husband forbids our Union. I'll make a Widow of you, and court you honourably.

Mrs. Bev. O Coward! Coward! thy Soul will shrink at him. Yet in the Thought of what may happen, I feel a Woman's Fears. Keep thy own Secret, and begone. Who's there?

Enter Lucy

Your Absence, Sir, wou'd please me.

Stu. I'll not offend you, Madam. (*Ex.* Stu. *with* Lucy.

Mrs. *Bev.* Why opens not the Earth to swallow such a Monster? Be Conscience then his Punisher, 'till Heaven in Mercy gives him Penitence, or dooms him in his Justice.

Re enter Lucy

Come to my Chamber, *Lucy*; I have a Tale to tell thee, shall make thee weep for thy poor Mistress.

> *Yet Heav'n the guiltless Sufferer regards,*
> *And whom it most afflicts, it most rewards.*

(*Exeunt.*

End of the THIRD ACT

ACT IV

SCENE Beverley's *Lodgings*

Enter Mrs. Beverley, Charlotte, *and* Lewson

Char. The smooth-tongu'd Hypocrite!

Lew. But we have found him, and will requite him—Be chearful, Madam; (*to Mrs.* Bev.) and for the Insults of this Ruffian, you shall have ample Retribution.

Mrs. *Bev.* But not by Violence—Remember you have sworn it; I had been silent else.

Lew. You need not doubt me; I shall be cool as Patience.

Mrs. *Bev.* See him To-morrow then.

Lew. And why not now? By Heaven the veriest Worm that crawls is made of braver Spirit than this *Stukely*—Yet for my Promise, I'll deal gently with him—I mean to watch his Looks—From those, and from his Answers to my Charge, much may be learnt. Next I'll to *Bates*, and sift him to the Bottom. If I fail there, the Gang is numerous, and for a Bribe will each betray the other—Good Night; I'll lose no Time.

(*Ex.* Lewson.

Mrs. *Bev.* These boisterous Spirits! how they wound me!

But Reasoning is in vain. Come, *Charlotte*; we'll to our usual Watch. The Night grows late.

Cha. I am fearful of Events; yet pleas'd——To-morrow may relieve us.   (*Going.*

Enter Jarvis

Cha. How now, good *Jarvis*?

Jar. I have heard ill News, Madam.

Mrs. Bev. What News? Speak quickly.

Jar. Men are not what they seem. I fear me Mr. *Stukely* is dishonest.

Char. We know it, *Jarvis*. But what's your News?

Jar. That there's an Action against my Master, at his Friend's Suit.

Mrs. Bev. O Villain! Villain! 'twas this he threaten'd then. Run to that Den of Robbers, *Wilson*'s—Your Master may be there. Entreat him Home, good *Jarvis*. Say I have Business with him—But tell him not of *Stukely*—It may provoke him to Revenge—Haste! haste! good *Jarvis*.

(*Exit* Jarvis.

Cha. This Minister of Hell! O I cou'd tear him Piece-meal!——

Mrs. Bev. I am sick of such a World—Yet Heaven is just; and in its own good Time, will hurl Destruction on such Monsters.   (*Exeunt.*

SCENE *changes to* Stukely's *Lodgings*

Enter Stukely *and* Bates *meeting*

Bates. Where have you been?

Stu. Fooling my Time away—Playing my Tricks, like a tame Monkey, to entertain a Woman—No Matter where—I have been vext and disappointed. Tell me of *Beverley*—How bore he his last Shock?

Bat. Like one (so *Dawson* says) whose Senses had been numb'd with Misery. When all was lost, he fixt his Eyes upon the Ground, and stood some Time, with folded Arms, stupid and motionless. Then snatching his Sword, that hung against the Wainscot, he sat him down; and with a Look of fixt Attention, drew Figures on the Floor—At last he started up, look'd wild, and trembled; and like a Woman, seiz'd with her Sex's Fits, laugh'd out aloud, while the Tears trickled down his Face—so left the Room.

Stu. Why, this was Madness.

Bat. The Madness of Despair.

Stu. We must confine him then. A Prison wou'd do well. (*a Knocking at the Door*) Hark! that Knocking may be his. Go that Way down.   (*Ex.* Bates. Who's there?

Enter Lewson

Lew. An Enemy—an open and avow'd one.

Stu. Why am I thus broke in upon? This House is mine, Sir; and shou'd protect me from Insult and Ill-manners.

Lew. Guilt has no Place of Sanctuary; wherever found, 'tis Virtue's lawful Game. The Fox's Hold, and Tyger's Den are no Security against the Hunter.

Stu. Your Business, Sir?

Lew. To tell you that I know you—Why this Confusion? That Look of Guilt and Terror?—Is *Beverley* awake? Or has his Wife told Tales? The Man that dares like You, shou'd have a Soul to justify his Deeds, and Courage to confront Accusers. Not with a Coward's Fear to shrink beneath Reproof.

Stu. Who waits there?   (*Aloud, and in Confusion.*

Lew. By Heaven he dies that interrupts us. (*shutting the Door.*) You shou'd have weigh'd your Strength, Sir; and then, instead of climbing to high Fortune, the World had mark'd you for what you are, a little paultry Villain.

Stu. You think I fear you.

Lew. I know you fear me. This is to prove it. (*pulls him by the Sleeve.*) You wanted Privacy! A Lady's Presence took up your Attention! Now we are alone, Sir. Why, what a Wretch! (*flings him from him.*) The vilest Insect in Creation will turn when trampled on; yet has this Thing undone a Man—by Cunning and mean Arts undone him. But we have found you,

Sir, trac'd you thro' all your Labyrinths. If you wou'd save yourself, fall to Confession. No Mercy will be shewn else.

Stu. First prove me what you think me—'Till then your Threatenings are in vain—And for this Insult, Vengeance may yet be mine.

Lew. Infamous Coward! why, take it now then—(*draws, and* Stukely *retires.*) Alas! I pity thee—Yet that a Wretch like this shou'd overcome a *Beverley*! it fills me with Astonishment!—A Wretch, so mean of Soul, that even Desperation cannot animate him to look upon an Enemy—You shou'd not thus have soar'd, Sir, unless, like others of your black Profession, you had a Sword to keep the Fools in Awe, your Villany has ruined.

Stu. Villany! 'Twere best to curb this Licence of your Tongue; for know, Sir, while there are Laws, this Outrage on my Reputation will not be borne with.

Lew. Laws! dar'st Thou seek Shelter from the Laws? Those Laws, which thou and thy infernal Crew live in the constant Violation of? Talk'st thou of Reputation too? when under Friendship's sacred Name, thou hast betray'd, robb'd, and destroy'd?

Stu. Ay, rail at Gaming; 'tis a rich Topic, and affords noble Declamation—Go, preach against it in the City: You'll find a Congregation in every Tavern. If they shou'd laugh at you, fly to my Lord, and sermonize it there. He'll thank you and reform.

Lew. And will Example sanctify a Vice? No, Wretch; the Custom of my Lord, or of the Cit that apes him, cannot excuse a Breach of Law, or make the Gamester's Calling reputable.

Stu. Rail on, I say—But is this Zeal for beggar'd *Beverley*? Is it for Him that I am treated thus? No; he and his Wife might both have groan'd in Prison, had but the Sister's Fortune escap'd the Wreck, to have rewarded the disinterested Love of honest Mr. *Lewson*.

Lew. How I detest thee for the Thought! But thou art lost to every human Feeling. Yet let me tell thee, and may it wring thy Heart! that tho' my Friend is ruin'd by thy Snares, thou hast unknowingly been kind to Me.

Stu. Have I? It was indeed unknowingly.

Lew. Thou hast assisted me in Love; given me the Merit that I wanted; since but for Thee, my *Charlotte* had not known 'twas her dear self I sigh'd for, and not her Fortune.

Stu. Thank me, and take her then.

Lew. And as a Brother to poor *Beverley*, I will pursue the Robber that has stript him, and snatch him from his Gripe.

Stu. Then know, imprudent Man, he *is* within my Gripe; and shou'd my Friendship for him be slander'd once again, the Hand that has supply'd him, shall fall and crush him.

Lew. Why, now there's Spirit in thee! This is indeed to be a Villain! But I shall reach thee yet—Fly where thou wilt, my Vengeance shall pursue thee—And *Beverley* shall yet be sav'd, be sav'd from Thee, thou Monster; nor owe his Rescue to his Wife's Dishonour.   (*Exit.*

Stu. (*pausing*) Then Ruin has enclos'd me. Curse on my coward Heart! I wou'd be bravely villanous; but 'tis my Nature to shrink at Danger, and he has found me. Yet Fear brings Caution, and That Security—More Mischief must be done to hide the past—Look to yourself, officious *Lewson*— there may be Danger stirring—How now, *Bates*?

Enter Bates

Bat. What is the Matter? 'Twas *Lewson* and not *Beverley* that left you—I heard him loud—You seem alarm'd too.

Stu. Ay, and with Reason—We are discover'd.

Bat. I fear'd as much, and therefore caution'd you—But You were peremptory.

Stu. Thus Fools talk ever; spending their idle Breath on what is past, and trembling at the future. We must be active. *Beverley*, at worst, is but suspicious; but *Lewson*'s Genius, and his Hate to Me, will lay all open. Means must be found to stop him.

Bat. What Means?

Stu. Dispatch him—Nay, start not——Desperate Occasions call for desperate Deeds—We live but by his Death.

Bat. You cannot mean it?

Stu. I do, by Heaven.

Bat. Good Night then.   (*Going.*

Stu. Stay. I must be heard, then answer'd. Perhaps the Motion was too sudden; and human Weakness starts at Murder, tho' strong Necessity compels it. I have thought long of this; and my first Feelings were like yours; a foolish Conscience aw'd me, which soon I conquer'd. The Man that wou'd undo me, Nature cries out, undo. Brutes know their Foes by Instinct; and where superior Force is given, they use it for Destruction. Shall Man do less? *Lewson* pursues us to our Ruin; and shall we, with the Means to crush him, fly from our Hunter, or turn and tear him? 'Tis Folly even to hesitate.

Bat. He has oblig'd me, and I dare not.

Stu. Why, live to Shame then, to Beggary and Punishment. You wou'd be privy to the Deed, yet want the Soul to act it. Nay more; had my Designs been levell'd at his Fortune, you had stept in the foremost——And what is Life without its Comforts? Those you wou'd rob him of; and by a lingring Death, add Cruelty to Murder. Henceforth adieu to half-made Villains—There's Danger in 'em. What you have got is yours; keep it, and hide with it—I'll deal my future Bounty to those who merit it.

Bat. What's the Reward?

Stu. Equal Division of our Gains. I swear it, and will be just.

Bat. Think of the Means then.

Stu. He's gone to *Beverley*'s—Wait for him in the Street—'Tis a dark Night, and fit for Mischief. A Dagger would be useful.

Bat. He sleeps no more.

Stu. Consider the Reward! When the Deed's done, I have farther Business with you. Send *Dawson* to me.

Bat. Think it already done—and so farewel.   (*Exit.*

Stu. Why, farewel *Lewson* then; and farewel to my Fears —This Night secures me. I'll wait the Event within. (*Exit.*

Scene changes to the Street. Stage darken'd

Enter Beverley

Bev. How like an Out-cast do I wander? Loaded with every Curse, that drives the Soul to Desperation——The Midnight Robber, as he walks his Rounds, sees by the glimmering Lamp my frantic Looks, and dreads to meet me.—— Whither am I going?——My Home lies there; all that is dear on Earth it holds too; yet are the Gates of Death more welcome to me—I'll enter it no more—Who passes there? 'Tis *Lewson*—He meets me in a gloomy Hour; and Memory tells me he has been meddling with my Fame.

Enter Lewson

Lew. Beverley! Well met. I have been busy in your Affairs.

Bev. So I have heard, Sir; and now must thank you as I ought.

Lew. To-morrow I may deserve your Thanks. Late as it is, I go to *Bates*. Discoveries are making that an arch Villain trembles at.

Bev. Discoveries are made, Sir, that You shall tremble at. Where is this boasted Spirit? this high Demeanour, that was to call me to Account? You say I have wrong'd my Sister——Now say as much. But first be ready for Defence, as I am for Resentment.   (*Draws.*

Lew. What mean you? I understand you not.

Bev. The Coward's stale Acquittance. Who, when he spreads foul Calumny abroad, and dreads just Vengeance on him, cries out, What mean you, I understand you not.

Lew. Coward, and Calumny! Whence are those Words? But I forgive, and pity you.

Bev. Your Pity had been kinder to my Fame. But you have traduc'd it; told a vile Story to the public Ear, that I have wrong'd my Sister.

Lew. 'Tis false. Shew me the Man that dares accuse me.

Bev. I thought you brave, and of a Soul superior to low Malice; but I have found you, and will have Vengeance. This is no Place for Argument.

Lew. Nor shall it be for Violence. Imprudent Man! who in Revenge for fancy'd Injuries, wou'd pierce the Heart that loves him. But honest Friendship acts from itself, unmov'd by Slander or Ingratitude. The Life you thirst for, shall be employ'd to serve you.

Bev. 'Tis thus you wou'd compound then—First do a Wrong beyond Forgiveness, and to redress it, load me with Kindness unsolicited. I'll not receive it. Your Zeal is troublesome.

Lew. No Matter. It shall be useful.

Bev. It will not be accepted.

Lew. It must. You know me not.

Bev. Yes; for the Slanderer of my Fame. Who under shew of Friendship, arraigns me of Injustice. Buzzing in every Ear foul Breach of Trust, and Family Dishonour.

Lew. Have I done this? Who told you so?

Bev. The World—'Tis talk'd of every where. It pleas'd you to add Threats too. You were to call me to Account ——Why, do it now then; I shall be proud of such an Arbiter.

Lew. Put up your Sword, and know me better. I never injur'd you. The base Suggestion comes from *Stukely*; I see him and his Aims.

Bev. What Aims? I'll not conceal it; 'twas *Stukely* that accus'd you.

Lew. To rid him of an Enemy——Perhaps of two—— He fears Discovery, and frames a Tale of Falsehood, to ground Revenge and Murder on.

Bev. I must have Proof of this.

Lew. Wait till To-morrow then.

Bev. I will.

Lew. Good Night—I go to serve you—Forget what's past as I do; and chear your Family with Smiles. To-morrow may confirm 'em, and make all happy.   (*Exit.*

Bev. (*Pausing.*) How vile, and how absurd is Man! His boasted Honour is but another Name for Pride; which easier bears the Consciousness of Guilt, than the World's just Reproofs. But 'tis the Fashion of the Times; and in defence of

Falsehood and false Honour, Men die Martyrs. I knew not
that my Nature was so bad.   (*stands musing.*

Enter Bates *and* Jarvis

Jar. This Way the Noise was—and yonder's my poor
Master.

Bat. I heard him at high Words with *Lewson.* The Cause I
know not.

Jar. I heard him too. Misfortunes vex him.

Bat. Go to him, and lead him Home—But he comes this
Way—I'll not be seen by him.   (*Ex.* Bates.

Bev. (*starting*) What Fellow's that? (*seeing* Jarvis) Art
thou a Murderer, Friend? Come, lead the Way; I have a
Hand as mischievous as thine; a Heart as desperate too——
Jarvis!—To Bed, old Man, the Cold will chill thee.

Jar. Why are you wandering at this late Hour?—Your
Sword drawn too!—For Heav'n's Sake sheath it, Sir—the
Sight distracts me.

Bev. Whose Voice was that?   (*wildly.*

Jar. 'Twas mine, Sir. Let me intreat you to give the Sword
to Me.

Bev. Ay, take it—quickly take it—Perhaps I am not so
curs'd, but Heav'n may have sent thee at this Moment to
snatch me from Perdition.

Jar. Then I am bless'd.

Bev. Continue so, and leave me. My Sorrows are contagious. No one is blest that's near me.

Jar. I came to seek you, Sir.

Bev. And now thou hast found me, leave me—My
Thoughts are wild and will not be disturb'd.

Jar. Such Thoughts are best disturb'd.

Bev. I tell thee that they will not—Who sent thee hither?

Jar. My weeping Mistress.

Bev. Am I so meek a Husband then? that a commanding
Wife prescribes my Hours, and sends to chide me for my
Absence?—Tell her, I'll not return.

Jar. Those Words wou'd kill her.

Bev. Kill her! Wou'd they not be kind then? But she shall

live to curse me—I have deserv'd it of her. Does she not hate me, *Jarvis*?

Jar. Alas, Sir! Forget your Griefs, and let me lead you to her. The Streets are dangerous.

Bev. Be wise, and leave me then. The Night's black Horrors are suited to my Thoughts———These Stones shall be my Resting-place. (*lies down.*) Here shall my Soul brood o'er its Miseries; 'till with the Fiends of Hell, and Guilty of the Earth, I start and tremble at the Morning's Light.

Jar. For Pity's Sake, Sir!—Upon my Knees I beg you to quit this Place, and these sad Thoughts. Let Patience, not Despair, possess you—Rise, I beseech you—There's not a Moment of your Absence, that my poor Mistress does not groan for.

Bev. Have I undone her, and is she still so kind? (*starting up*) It is too much—My Brain can't hold it—O, *Jarvis*! how desperate is that Wretch's State, which only Death or Madness can relieve.

Jar. Appease his Mind, good Heaven! and give him Resignation! Alas, Sir, cou'd Beings in the other World perceive the Events of this, how wou'd your Parents blessed Spirits grieve for you, even in Heaven!—Let me conjure you by their honour'd Memories; by the sweet Innocence of your yet helpless Child, and by the ceaseless Sorrows of my poor Mistress, to rouze your Manhood, and struggle with these Griefs.

Bev. Thou virtuous, good old Man! thy Tears and thy Entreaties have reach'd my Heart, thro' all its Miseries. O! had I listen'd to thy honest Warnings, no earthly Blessing had been wanting to me!—I was so happy, that even a Wish for more than I possess'd, was arrogant Presumption. But I have warr'd against the Power that bless'd me, and now am sentenc'd to the Hell I merit.

Jar. Be but resign'd, Sir, and Happiness may yet be yours.

Bev. Prithee be honest, and do not flatter Misery.

Jar. I do not, Sir—Hark! I hear voices—Come this Way; we may reach Home un-notic'd.

Bev. Well, lead me then—Un-notic'd did'st thou say? Alas! I dread no Looks, but of those Wretches I have made at Home.   (*Exeunt.*

SCENE *changes to* Stukely's

Enter Stukely *and* Dawson

Stu. Come hither *Dawson*. My Limbs are on the Rack, and my Soul shivers in me, 'till this Night's Business be complete. Tell me thy Thoughts: Is *Bates* determin'd, or does he waver?

Daw. At first he seem'd irresolute; wish'd the Employment had been mine; and mutter'd Curses on his Coward Hand, that trembled at the Deed.

Stu. And did he leave you so?

Daw. No. We walk'd together; and shelter'd by the Darkness, saw *Beverley* and *Lewson* in warm Debate. But soon they cool'd; and then I left 'em to hasten hither; but not 'till 'twas resolv'd *Lewson* shou'd die.

Stu. Thy Words have given me Life—That Quarrel too was fortunate; for if my Hopes deceive me not, it promises a Grave to *Beverley*.

Daw. You misconceive me. *Lewson* and he were Friends.

Stu. But my prolific Brain shall make 'em Enemies. If *Lewson* falls, he falls by *Beverley*. An upright Jury shall decree it. Ask me no Questions, but do as I direct. This Writ *(takes out a Pocket Book)* for some Days past, I have treasur'd here, 'till a convenient Time call'd for its Use. That Time is come. Take it, and give it to an Officer. It must be serv'd this Instant.   *(Gives a Paper.*

Daw. On *Beverley*?

Bev. Look at it. 'Tis for the Sums that I have lent him.

Daw. Must he to Prison then?

Stu. I ask'd Obedience; not Replies. This Night a Jail must be his Lodging. 'Tis probable he's not gone Home yet. Wait at his Door, and see it executed.

Daw. Upon a Beggar? He has no Means of Payment.

Stu. Dull and insensible! If *Lewson* dies, who was it kill'd him? Why, he that was seen quarreling with him; and I that knew of *Beverley*'s Intents, arrested him in Friendship—A little late, perhaps; but 'twas a virtuous Act, and Men will thank me for't. Now, Sir, you understand me?

Daw. Most perfectly—And will about it.

Stu. Haste then; and when 'tis done, come back and tell me.

Daw. 'Till then farewell.   [*Exit.*

Stu. Now tell thy Tale, fond Wife! And *Lewson*, if again thou can'st insult me, I'll kneel and own thee for my Master.

> *Not Avarice now, but Vengeance fires my Breast,*
> *And one short Hour must make me curst or blest.*
>
>   [*Exit.*

End of the Fourth ACT

ACT V. Scene continues

Enter Stukely, Bates, *and* Dawson

Bat. Poor *Lewson!*—But I told you enough last Night— The Thought of him is horrible to me.

Stu. In the Street, did you say? And no one near him?

Bat. By his own Door; he was leading me to his House. I pretended Business with him, and stabb'd him to the Heart, while he was reaching at the Bell.

Stu. And did he fall so suddenly?

Bat. The Repetition pleases you, I see. I told you, he fell without a Groan.

Stu. What heard you of him this Morning?

Bat. That the Watch found him in their Rounds, and alarm'd the Servants. I mingled with the Croud just now, and saw him dead in his own House.—The Sight terrify'd me.

Stu. Away with Terrors, 'till his Ghost rise and accuse us —We have no living Enemy to fear—unless 'tis *Beverley*; and him we have lodg'd safe in Prison.

Bat. Must He be murder'd too?

Stu. No; I have a Scheme to make the Law his Murderer —At what Hour did *Lewson* fall?

Bat. The Clock struck Twelve as I turn'd to leave him. 'Twas a melancholy Bell, I thought, tolling for his Death.

Stu. The Time was lucky for us—*Beverley* was arrested at
One, you say?   [*to* Dawson.

Daw. Exactly.

Stu. Good. We'll talk of this presently——The Women
were with him, I think?

Daw. And old *Jarvis.* I wou'd have told you of 'em, last
Night, but your Thoughts were too busy. 'Tis well you have
a Heart of Stone, the Tale wou'd melt it else.

Stu. Out with it then.

Daw. I trac'd him to his Lodgings; and pretended Pity
for his Misfortunes, kept the Door open, while the Officers
seiz'd him. 'Twas a damn'd Deed—but no Matter—I follow'd my Instructions.

Stu. And what said he?

Daw. He upbraided me with Treachery; call'd You a
Villain; acknowledg'd the Sums you had lent him, and submitted to his Fortune.

Stu. And the Women——

Daw. For a few Minutes Astonishment kept 'em silent—
They look'd wildly at one another, while the Tears stream'd
down their Cheeks. But Rage and Fury soon gave 'em Words;
and then, in the very Bitterness of Despair, they curs'd me,
and the Monster that had employ'd me.

Stu. And you bore it with Philosophy?

Daw. 'Till the Scene chang'd, and then I melted. I order'd
the Officers to take away their Prisoner. The Women shriek'd,
and wou'd have follow'd him; but we forbad 'em. 'Twas then
they fell upon their Knees, the Wife fainting, the Sister raving,
and both with all the Eloquence of Misery endeavouring to
soften us. I never felt Compassion 'till that Moment; and had
the Officers been mov'd like Me, we had left the Business undone, and fled with Curses on ourselves. But their Hearts were
steel'd by Custom. The Tears of Beauty and the Pangs of Affection were beneath their Pity. They tore him from their Arms,
and lodg'd him in Prison, with only *Jarvis* to comfort him.

Stu. There let him lie, 'till we have farther Business with
him—And for You, Sir, let me hear no more of your Compassion—A Fellow nurs'd in Villany, and employ'd from

Childhood in the Business of Hell, shou'd have no Dealings with Compassion.

Daw. Say you so, Sir?——You shou'd have nam'd the Devil that tempted me——

Stu. 'Tis false. I found you a Villain, and therefore employ'd you—But no more of this—We have embark'd too far in Mischief to recede. *Lewson* is dead, and we are all Principals in his Murder. Think of that—There's Time enough for Pity, when ourselves are out of Danger——*Beverley* still lives, tho' in a Jail—His Ruin will sit heavy on him; and Discoveries may be made to undo us all. Something must be done, and speedily——You saw him quarrelling with *Lewson* in the Street last Night?   [*To* Bates.

Bat. I did; his Steward, *Jarvis*, saw him too.

Stu. And shall attest it. Here's Matter to work upon—— An unwilling Evidence carries weight with him. Something of my Design I have hinted t'you before——*Beverley* must be the Author of this Murder; and we the Parties to convict him—But how to proceed will require Time and Thought— Come along with Me; the Room within is fitter for Privacy— But no Compassion, Sir—[*to* Dawson] We want Leisure for't——This Way.   [*Exeunt.*

SCENE *changes to* Beverley's *Lodgings*

Enter Mrs. Beverley *and* Charlotte

Mrs. *Bev.* No News of *Lewson* yet?

Char. None. He went out early, and knows not what has happen'd.

Mrs. *Bev.* The Clock strikes Eight—I'll wait no longer.

Cha. Stay but 'till *Jarvis* comes. He has sent twice to stop us 'till we see him.

Mrs. *Bev.* I have no Life in this Separation—O! What a Night was last Night! I wou'd not pass another such to purchase Worlds by it——My poor *Beverley* too! What must He have felt! The very Thought distracts me!——To have him torn at Midnight from me!—A loathsome Prison his

Habitation! A cold damp Room his Lodging! The bleak Winds perhaps blowing upon his Pillow! No fond Wife to lull him to his Rest! and no Reflections but to wound and tear him!—'Tis too horrible—I wanted Love for him, or they had not forc'd him from me. They shou'd have parted Soul and Body first—I was too tame.

Cha. You must not Talk so. All that we cou'd we did; and *Jarvis* did the rest—The faithful Creature will give him Comfort. Why does he delay coming?

Mrs. *Bev.* And there's another Fear. His poor Master may be claiming the last kind Office from him—His Heart perhaps is breaking.

Cha. See where he comes—His Looks are chearful too.

Enter Jarvis

Mrs. *Bev.* Are Tears then chearful? Alas, he weeps! Speak to him *Charlotte*——I have no Tongue to ask him Questions.

Char. How does your Master, *Jarvis*?

Jar. I am old and foolish, Madam; and Tears will come before my Words—But don't You weep. [*to Mrs.* Bev.] I have a Tale of Joy for you.

Mrs. *Bev.* What Tale?—Say but he's well, and I have Joy enough.

Jar. His Mind too shall be well—all shall be well—I have News for him that shall make his poor Heart bound again— Fie upon old Age—How childish it makes me! I have a Tale of Joy for you, and my Tears drown it.

Cha. Shed 'em in Showers then, and make Haste to tell it.

Mrs. *Bev.* What is it, *Jarvis*?

Jar. Yet why shou'd I rejoice when a good Man dies? Your Uncle, Madam, dy'd Yesterday.

Mrs. *Bev.* My Uncle!—O Heavens!

Cha. How heard you of his Death?

Jar. His Steward came Express, Madam—I met him in the Street, enquiring for your Lodgings—I shou'd not rejoice perhaps—but he was old, and my poor Master a Prisoner—Now he shall live again—O 'tis a brave Fortune! and 'twas Death to me to see him a Prisoner.

Cha. Where left you the Steward?

Jar. I wou'd not bring him hither, to be a Witness of your Distresses; and besides, I wanted once before I die, to be the Messenger of Joy t'you. My good Master will be a Man again.

Mrs. *Bev.* Haste, haste then; and let us fly to him—we are delaying our own Happiness.

Jar. I had forgot a Coach, Madam; and *Lucy* has order'd one.

Mrs. *Bev.* Where was the Need of that? The News has given me Wings.

Cha. I have no Joy, 'till my poor Brother shares it with me. How did he pass the Night, *Jarvis*?

Jar. Why now, Madam, I can tell you. Like a Man dreaming of Death and Horrors. When they led him to his Cell—For 'twas a poor Apartment for my Master—He flung himself upon a wretched Bed, and lay speechless 'till Day-break. A Sigh now and then, and a few Tears that follow'd those Sighs, were all that told me he was alive. I spoke to him, but he wou'd not hear me; and when I persisted, he rais'd his Hand at me, and knit his Brow so——I thought he wou'd have struck me.

Mrs. *Bev.* O Miserable! But what said he, *Jarvis*? Or was he silent all Night?

Jar. At Day-break he started from the Bed, and looking wildly at me, ask'd who I was. I told him, and bid him be of Comfort—Begone old Wretch, says he—I have sworn never to know Comfort—My Wife! my Child! my Sister! I have undone 'em all, and will know no Comfort—Then letting go his Hold, and falling upon his Knees, he imprecated Curses upon himself.

Mrs. *Bev.* This is too horrible!—But you did not leave him so?

Cha. No, I am sure he did not.

Jar. I had not the Heart, Madam. By Degrees I brought him to himself. A Shower of Tears came to his Relief; and then he call'd me his kindest Friend, and begg'd Forgiveness of me like a Child—I was a Child too, when he begg'd

Forgiveness of me. My Heart throbb'd so, I could not speak to him. He turn'd from me for a Minute or two, and suppressing a few bitter Sighs, enquir'd after his wretched Family—Wretched was his Word, Madam—Ask'd how you bore the Misery of last Night—If you had Goodness enough to see him in Prison—And then begg'd me to hasten to you. I told him he must be more himself first—He promis'd me he wou'd; and bating a few sullen Intervals, he became compos'd and easy—And then I left him; but not without an Attendant—A Servant in the Prison, whom I hir'd to wait upon him—'Tis an Hour since we parted—I was prevented in my Haste to be the Messenger of Joy t'you.

Mrs. Bev. What a Tale is this?—But we have staid too long—A Coach is needless.

Cha. Hark! I hear one at the Door.

Jar. And *Lucy* comes to tell us—We'll away this Moment.

Mrs. Bev. To comfort him or die with him. [*Exeunt.*

SCENE *changes to* Stukely's *Lodgings*

Enter Stukely, Bates *and* Dawson

Stu. Here's presumptive Evidence at least—or if we want more, why, we must swear more. But all unwillingly—We gain Credit by Reluctance—I have told you how to proceed. *Beverley* must die—We hunt him in View now, and must not slacken in the Chace. 'Tis either Death for Him, or Shame and Punishment for Us. Think of that, and remember your Instructions—You, *Bates*, must to the Prison immediately. I wou'd be there but a few Minutes before you. And you, *Dawson*, must follow in a few Minutes after. So here we divide————But answer me; are you resolv'd upon this Business like Men?

Bates. Like Villains rather—But you may depend upon us.

Stu. Like what we are then—You make no Answer, *Dawson*—Compassion, I suppose, has seiz'd you.

Daw. No; I have disclaim'd it—My Answer is *Bates*'s— You may depend upon me.

Stu. Consider the Reward! Riches and Security! I have sworn to divide with you to the last Shilling—So here we separate 'till we meet in Prison————Remember your Instructions and be Men.   (*Exeunt.*

SCENE *changes to a Prison*

Beverley *is discover'd sitting. After a short Pause he starts up, and comes forward*

Bev. Why, there's an End then. I have judg'd deliberately, and the Result is Death. How the Self-Murderer's Account may stand, I know not. But this I know—the Load of hateful Life oppresses me too much—The Horrors of my Soul are more than I can bear—(*Offers to kneel*) Father of Mercy!—— I cannot pray—Despair has laid his iron Hand upon me, and seal'd me for Perdition—Conscience! Conscience! thy Clamours are too loud——Here's that shall silence thee. (*Takes a Vial out of his Pocket, and looks at it.*) Thou art most friendly to the Miserable. Come then, thou Cordial for sick Minds ——Come to my Heart. (*Drinks.*) O, that the Grave wou'd bury Memory as well as Body! For if the Soul sees and feels the Sufferings of those dear Ones it leaves behind, the Everlasting has no Vengeance to torment it deeper——I'll think no more on't——Reflection comes too late——Once there was a Time for't—but now 'tis past.——Who's there?

Enter Jarvis

Jar. One that hop'd to see you with better Looks—— Why d'you turn so from me? I have brought Comfort with me—And see who comes to give it welcome.

Bev. My Wife and Sister! Why, 'tis but one Pang then, and farewel World.   (*Aside.*

Enter Mrs. Beverley *and* Charlotte

Mrs. *Bev.* Where is he? (*Runs and embraces him*) O I have him! I have him! And now they shall never part us more—I have News, Love, to make you happy for ever.—But don't look coldly on me.

Char. How is it, Brother?

Mrs. Bev. Alas! he hears us not—Speak to me, Love. I have no Heart to see you thus.

Bev. Nor I to bear the Sense of so much Shame——This is a sad Place.

Mrs. Bev. We come to take you from it. To tell you that the World goes well again. That Providence has seen our Sorrows, and sent the Means to heal 'em—Your Uncle dy'd Yesterday.

Bev. My Uncle!—No, do not say so—O! I am sick at Heart!

Mrs. Bev. Indeed!——I meant to bring you Comfort.

Bev. Tell me he lives then——If you wou'd give me Comfort, tell me he lives.

Mrs. Bev. And if I did——I have no Power to raise the Dead—He dy'd Yesterday.

Bev. And I am Heir to him?

Jar. To his whole Estate, Sir—But bear it patiently—pray bear it patiently.

Bev. Well, well—(*Pausing*) Why, Fame says I am rich then?

Mrs. Bev. And truly so—Why do you look so wildly?

Bev. Do I? The News was unexpected. But has he left me all?

Jar. All, all, Sir—He cou'd not leave it from you.

Bev. I'm sorry for it.

Cha. Sorry! Why sorry?

Bev. Your Uncle's dead, *Charlotte.*

Char. Peace be with his Soul then—Is it so terrible that an old Man should die?

Bev. He shou'd have been immortal.

Mrs. Bev. Heaven knows I wish'd not for his Death. 'Twas the Will of Providence that he shou'd die—Why are you disturb'd so?

Bev. Has Death no Terrors in it?

Mrs. Bev. Not an old Man's Death. Yet if it troubles you, I wish him living.

Bev. And I, with all my Heart.

Char. Why, what's the Matter?

Bev. Nothing—How heard you of his Death?

Mrs. Bev. His Steward came Express. Wou'd I had never known it!

Bev. Or had heard it one Day sooner——For I have a Tale to tell, shall turn you into Stone; or if the Power of Speech remain, you shall kneel down and curse me.

Mrs. Bev. Alas! What Tale is this? And why are we to curse you?—I'll bless you for ever.

Bev. No; I have deserv'd no Blessings. The World holds not such another Wretch. All this large Fortune, this second Bounty of Heaven, that might have heal'd our Sorrows, and satisfy'd our utmost Hopes, in a curs'd Hour I sold last Night.

Char. Sold! How sold!

Mrs. Bev. Impossible!—It cannot be!

Bev. That Devil *Stukely*, with all Hell to aid him, tempted me to the Deed. To pay false Debts of Honour, and to redeem past Errors, I sold the Reversion—Sold it for a scanty Sum, and lost it among Villains.

Char. Why, farewell all then.

Bev. Liberty and Life—Come, kneel and curse me.

Mrs. Bev. Then hear me Heaven! (*Kneels*) Look down with Mercy on his Sorrows! Give Softness to his Looks, and Quiet to his Heart! Take from his Memory the Sense of what is past, and cure him of Despair! On Me! on Me! if Misery must be the Lot of either, multiply Misfortunes! I'll bear 'em patiently, so He is happy! These Hands shall toil for his Support! These Eyes be lifted up for hourly Blessings on him! And every Duty of a fond and faithful Wife be doubly done to cheer and comfort him!——So hear me! So reward me!   (*Rises.*

Bev. I wou'd kneel too, but that offended Heaven wou'd turn my Prayers into Curses. What have I to ask for? I who have shook Hands with Hope? Is it for Length of Days that I shou'd kneel? No; My Time is limited. Or is it for this World's Blessings upon You and Yours? To pour out my

Heart in Wishes for a ruin'd Wife, a Child and Sister? O! no! For I have done a Deed to make Life horrible t'you.——

Mrs. Bev. Why horrible? Is Poverty so horrible?—— The real Wants of Life are few. A little Industry will supply 'em all—And Chearfulness will follow——It is the Privilege of honest Industry, and we'll enjoy it fully.

Bev. Never, never——O, I have told you but in Part. The irrevocable Deed is done.

Mrs. Bev. What Deed?——And why do you look so at me?

Bev. A Deed that dooms my Soul to Vengeance—— That seals Your Misery here, and Mine hereafter.

Mrs. Bev. No, no; You have a Heart too good for't—— Alas! he raves, *Charlotte*——His Looks too terrify me— Speak Comfort to him—He can have done no Deed of Wickedness.

Char. And yet I fear the worst——What is it, Brother?

Bev. A Deed of Horror.

Jar. Ask him no Questions, Madam—This last Misfortune has hurt his Brain. A little Time will give him Patience.

Enter Stukely

Bev. Why is this Villain here?

Stu. To give you Liberty and Safety. There, Madam's his Discharge. (*Giving a Paper to Mrs.* Beverley) Let him fly this Moment. The Arrest last Night was meant in Friendship; but came too late.

Char. What mean you, Sir?

Stu. The Arrest was too late, I say; I wou'd have kept his Hands from Blood, but was too late.

Mrs. Bev. His Hands from Blood!—Whose Blood?—O, Wretch! Wretch!

Stu. From *Lewson's* Blood.

Char. No, Villain! Yet what of *Lewson*? Speak quickly.

Stu. You are ignorant then! I thought I heard the Murderer at Confession.

Char. What Murderer?—And who is murder'd? Not *Lewson*?—Say he lives, and I'll kneel and worship you.

Stu. In Pity, so I wou'd; but that the Tongues of all cry

Murder. I came in Pity, not in Malice; to save the Brother, not kill the Sister. Your *Lewson*'s dead.

Char. O horrible!—Why who has kill'd him? And yet it cannot be. What Crime had He committed that he shou'd die? Villain! he lives! he lives! and shall revenge these Pangs.

Mrs. Bev. Patience, sweet *Charlotte*!

Char. O, 'tis too much for Patience!

Mrs. Bev. He comes in Pity, he says. O! execrable Villain! The Friend is kill'd then, and this the Murderer?

Bev. Silence, I charge you—Proceed, Sir.

Stu. No. Justice may stop the Tale—and here's an Evidence.

Enter Bates

Bates. The News, I see has reach'd you. But take Comfort, Madam. (*To* Char.) There's one Without enquiring for you —Go to him and lose no Time.

Char. O Misery! Misery!   (*Exit.*

Mrs. Bev. Follow her, *Jarvis.* If it be true that *Lewson*'s dead, her Grief may kill her.

Bates. *Jarvis* must stay here, Madam. I have some Questions for him.

Stu. Rather let him fly. His Evidence may crush his Master.

Bev. Why ay; this looks like Management.

Bates. He found you quarrelling with *Lewson* in the Street last Night.   (*To* Bev.

Mrs. Bev. No; I am sure he did not.

Jar. Or if I did—

Mrs. Bev. 'Tis false, old Man—They had no Quarrel; there was no Cause for Quarrel.

Bev. Let him proceed, I say—O! I am sick! sick!——Reach me a Chair.   (*He sits down.*

Mrs. Bev. You droop, and tremble, Love—Your Eyes are fixt too—Yet You are innocent. If *Lewson*'s dead, You kill'd him not.

Enter Dawson

Stu. Who sent for *Dawson*?

Bates. 'Twas I—We have a Witness too, you little think of—Without there!

Stu. What Witness?

Bates. A right one. Look at him.

Enter Lewson *and* Charlotte

Stu. Lewson! O Villains! Villains! (*To* Bates *and* Dawson.

Mrs. *Bev.* Risen from the Dead! Why, this is unexpected Happiness!

Char. Or is't his Ghost? (*To* Stukely) That Sight wou'd please you, Sir.

Jar. What Riddle's this?

Bev. Be quick and tell it—My Minutes are but few.

Mrs. *Bev.* Alas! why so? You shall live long and happily.

Lew. While Shame and Punishment shall rack that Viper. (*Pointing to* Stukely) The Tale is short—I was too busy in his Secrets, and therefore doom'd to die. *Bates*, to prevent the Murder, undertook it—I kept aloof to give it Credit—

Char. And gave Me Pangs unutterable.

Lew. I felt 'em all, and wou'd have told you—But Vengeance wanted ripening. The Villain's Scheme was but half executed. The Arrest by *Dawson* follow'd the suppos'd Murder—And now, depending on his once wicked Associates, he comes to fix the Guilt on *Beverley*.

Mrs. *Bev.* O! execrable Wretch!

Bates. Dawson and I are Witnesses of this.

Lew. And of a thousand Frauds. His Fortune ruin'd by Sharpers and false Dice; and *Stukely* sole Contriver and Possessor of all.

Daw. Had he but stopt on this Side Murder, we had been Villains still.

Mrs. *Bev.* Thus Heaven turns Evil into Good; and by permitting Sin, warns Men to Virtue.

Lew. Yet punishes the Instrument. So shall our Laws; tho' not with Death. But Death were Mercy. Shame,

Beggary, and Imprisonment, unpity'd Misery, the Stings of
Conscience, and the Curses of Mankind shall make Life
hateful to him——till at last, his own Hand end him——
How does my Friend? (*To* Bev.

Bev. Why, well. Who's he that asks me?

Mrs. Bev. 'Tis *Lewson*, Love——Why do you look so
at him?

Bev. They told me he was murder'd. (*Wildly.*

Mrs. Bev. Ay; but he lives to save us.

Bev. Lend me your Hand—The Room turns round.

Mrs. Bev. O Heaven!

Lew. This Villain here, disturbs him. Remove him from
his Sight——And for your Lives, see that you guard him.
(Stukely *is taken off by* Dawson *and* Bates.) How is it, Sir?

Bev. 'Tis here—and here. (*Pointing to his Head and
Heart.*) And now it tears me!

Mrs. Bev. You feel convuls'd too—What is't disturbs you?

Lew. This sudden Turn of Joy perhaps—He wants Rest
too—Last Night was dreadful to him. His Brain is giddy.

Char. Ay, never to be cur'd—Why, Brother!—O! I fear!
I fear!

Mrs. Bev. Preserve him, Heaven!—My Love! my Life!
look at me!—How his Eyes flame!

Bev. A Furnace rages in this Heart—I have been too hasty.

Mrs. Bev. Indeed!—O me! O me!—Help, *Jarvis*! Fly,
fly for Help! Your Master dies else—Weep not, but fly, (*Ex.*
Jar.) What is this hasty Deed?—Yet do not answer me—My
Fears have guess'd it.

Bev. Call back the Messenger—'Tis not in Medicine's
Power to help me.

Mrs. Bev. Is it then so?

Bev. Down, restless Flames!—(*Laying his Hand on his
Heart*) down to your native Hell—There you shall rack me
—O! for a Pause from Pain!

Mrs. Bev. Help *Charlotte*! Support him, Sir! (*To* Lewson)
This is a killing Sight!

Bev. That Pang was well—It has numb'd my Senses.—
Where's my Wife?—Can you forgive me, Love?

Mrs. *Bev.* Alas! for what?

Bev. (*Starting again*) And there's another Pang—Now all is quiet—Will you forgive me?

Mrs. *Bev.* I will—Tell me for what?

Bev. For meanly dying.

Mrs. *Bev.* No—do not say it.

Bev. As truly as my Soul must answer it—Had *Jarvis* staid this Morning, all had been well. But press'd by Shame—pent in a Prison—tormented with my Pangs for You—driven to Despair and Madness—I took the Advantage of his Absence, corrupted the poor Wretch he left to guard me, and——swallow'd Poison.

Mrs. *Bev.* O! fatal Deed!

Char. Dreadful and cruel!

Bev. Ay, most accurs'd—And now I go to my Account. This Rest from Pain brings Death; yet 'tis Heaven's Kindness to me. I wish'd for Ease, a Moment's Ease, that cool Repentance and Contrition might soften Vengeance—Bend me, and let me kneel. (*They lift him from his Chair and support him on his Knees*) I'll pray for You too. Thou Power that mad'st me, hear me! If for a Life of Frailty, and this too hasty Deed of Death, thy Justice dooms me, here I acquit the Sentence. But if, enthron'd in Mercy where thou sit'st, thy Pity has beheld me, send me a Gleam of Hope; that in these last and bitter Moments my Soul may taste of Comfort! And for these Mourners here, O! let their Lives be peaceful, and their Deaths happy!—Now raise me. (*They lift him to the Chair.*)

Mrs. *Bev.* Restore him, Heaven! Stretch forth thy Arm omnipotent, and snatch him from the Grave!—O save him! save him!

Bev. Alas! that Prayer is fruitless. Already Death has seiz'd me—Yet Heaven is gracious—I ask'd for Hope, as the bright Presage of Forgiveness, and like a Light, blazing thro' Darkness, it came and chear'd me—'Twas all I liv'd for, and now I die.

Mrs. *Bev.* Not yet!—Not yet!—Stay but a little and I'll die too.

Bev. No; live, I charge you.—We have a little One. Tho'

I have left him, You will not leave him.—To *Lewson*'s Kindness I bequeath him—Is not this *Charlotte*? We have liv'd in Love, tho' I have wrong'd you—Can you forgive me, *Charlotte*?

Char. Forgive you!—O my poor Brother!

Bev. Lend me your Hand, Love—so—raise me—No—'twill not be—My Life is finish'd—O! for a few short Moments! to tell you how my Heart bleeds for you—That even now, thus dying as I am, dubious and fearful of Hereafter, my bosom Pang is for Your Miseries. Support her Heaven!——And now I go——O, Mercy! Mercy!   (*Dies.*

Lew. Then all is over——How is it, Madam?——My poor *Charlotte* too!

Enter Jarvis

Jar. How does my Master, Madam? Here's Help at Hand——Am I too late then?   (*Seeing* Beverley.

Char. Tears! Tears! Why fall you not?——O wretched Sister!——Speak to her, *Lewson*—Her Grief is speechless.

Lew. Remove her from this Sight——Go to her, *Jarvis*——Lead and support her. Sorrow like Hers forbids Complaint——Words are for lighter Griefs——Some ministring Angel bring her Peace!   (*Jar. and Char. lead her off.*
And Thou, poor breathless Corps, may thy departed Soul have found the Rest it pray'd for! Save but one Error, and this last fatal Deed, thy Life was lovely. Let frailer Minds take Warning; and from Example learn, that Want of Prudence is Want of Virtue.

> *Follies, if uncontroul'd, of every Kind,*
> *Grow into Passions, and subdue the Mind ;*
> *With Sense and Reason hold superior Strife,*
> *And conquer Honour, Nature, Fame and Life.*

FINIS

DOUGLAS:

A

TRAGEDY.

As it is ACTED at the

THEATRE-ROYAL

IN

COVENT-GARDEN.

Non ego sum vates, sed prisci conscius ævi.

EDINBURGH:

Printed for G. HAMILTON & J. BALFOUR, W. GRAY & W. PETER.

M,DCC,LVII.

The Original Edition

[Price One Shilling Sixpence.]

PROLOGUE

Spoken by Mr. SPARKS

IN antient times, when Britain's *trade was arms,*
And the lov'd music of her youth, alarms;
A god–like race sustain'd fair England's *fame:*
Who has not heard of gallant PIERCY's *name?*
Ay, and of DOUGLAS? *Such illustrious foes*
In rival Rome *and* Carthage *never rose!*
From age to age bright shone the British *fire,*
And every hero was a hero's sire.
When powerful fate decreed one warrior's doom,
Up sprung the Phœnix from his parent's tomb.
But whilst these generous rivals fought and fell,
Those generous rivals lov'd each other well:
Tho' many a bloody field was lost and won,
Nothing in hate, in honour all was done.
When PIERCY *wrong'd defy'd his prince or peers,*
Fast came the DOUGLAS, *with his* Scottish *spears;*
And, when proud DOUGLAS *made his King his foe,*
For DOUGLAS, PIERCY *bent his* English *bow.*
Expell'd their native homes by adverse fate,
They knock'd alternate at each other's gate:
Then blaz'd the castle, at the midnight hour,
For him whose arms had shook its firmest tow'r.

This night a DOUGLAS *your protection claims;*
A wife! a mother! Pity's softest names:
The story of her woes indulgent hear,
And grant your suppliant all she begs, a tear.
In confidence she begs; and hopes to find
Each English *breast, like noble* PIERCY's, *kind.*

DRAMATIS PERSONÆ

As represented at LONDON

Lord RANDOLPH,	Mr. RIDOUT
GLENALVON,	Mr. SMITH
NORVAL, DOUGLAS,	Mr. BARRY
STRANGER,	Mr. SPARKS
SERVANTS.	

WOMEN

MATILDA, Lady RANDOLPH,	Mrs. WOFFINGTON
ANNA,	Mrs. VINCENT

PROLOGUE

Spoken at EDINBURGH

IN days of classic fame, when Persia's Lord
Oppos'd his millions to the Grecian sword,
Flourish'd the state of Athens, small her store,
Rugged her soil, and rocky was her shore,
Like Caledonia's: yet she gain'd a name
That stands unrivall'd in the rolls of fame.

  Such proud pre-eminence not valour gave,
(For who than Sparta's dauntless sons more brave?)
But learning, and the love of every art,
That Virgin Pallas and the Muse impart.

  Above the rest the Tragic Muse admir'd
Each Attic breast, with noblest passions fir'd.
In peace their poets with their heroes shar'd
Glory, the hero's, and the bard's reward.
The Tragic Muse each glorious record kept,
And, o'er the kings she conquer'd, Athens wept.

  Here let me cease, impatient for the scene,
To you I need not praise the Tragic Queen:
Oft has this audience soft compassion shown
To woes of heroes, heroes not their own.
This night our scenes no common tear demand,
He comes, the hero of your native land!
DOUGLAS, a name thro' all the world renown'd,
A name that rouses like the trumpet's sound!
Oft have your fathers, prodigal of life,
A DOUGLAS follow'd thro' the bloody strife;
Hosts have been known at that dread name to yield,
And, DOUGLAS dead, his name hath won the field.

  Listen attentive to the various tale,
Mark if the author's kindred feelings fail;
Sway'd by alternate hopes, alternate fears,
He waits the test of your congenial tears.
If they shall flow, back to the Muse he flies,
And bids your heroes in succession rise:
Collects the wand'ring warriors as they roam,
DOUGLAS assures them of a welcome-home.

DRAMATIS PERSONÆ

As represented at EDINBURGH

Lord RANDOLPH,	Mr. YOUNGER
GLENALVON,	Mr. LOVE
NORVAL, DOUGLAS,	Mr. DIGGS
STRANGER,	Mr. HAYMAN
SERVANTS, &c.	

WOMEN

MATILDA, Lady RANDOLPH,	Mrs. WARD
ANNA,	Mrs. HOPKINS

DOUGLAS:

A

TRAGEDY

ACT I

The court of a castle surrounded with woods

Enter Lady RANDOLPH

Ye woods and wilds, whose melancholy gloom
Accords with my soul's sadness, and draws forth
The voice of sorrow from my bursting heart,
Farewel a while: I will not leave you long;
For in your shades I deem some spirit dwells,
Who from the chiding stream, or groaning oak,
Still hears, and answers to MATILDA's moan.
O DOUGLAS! DOUGLAS! if departed ghosts
Are e'er permitted to review this world,
Within the circle of that wood thou art,
And with the passion of immortals hear'st
My lamentation: hear'st thy wretched wife
Weep for her husband slain, her infant lost.
My brother's timeless death I seem to mourn;
Who perish'd with thee on this fatal day.
To thee I lift my voice; to thee address
The plaint which mortal ear has never heard.
O disregard me not; tho' I am call'd
Another's now, my heart is wholly thine.
Incapable of change, affection lies
Buried, my DOUGLAS, in the bloody grave.
But RANDOLPH comes, whom fate has made my Lord,
To chide my anguish, and defraud the dead.

Enter Lord RANDOLPH

Again these weeds of woe! say, do'st thou well
To feed a passion which consumes thy life?
The living claim some duty; vainly thou
Bestow'st thy cares upon the silent dead.

Lady RANDOLPH

Silent, alas! is he for whom I mourn:
Childless, without memorial of his name,
He only now in my remembrance lives.
This fatal day stirs my time-settled sorrow,
Troubles afresh the fountain of my heart.

Lord RANDOLPH

When was it pure of sadness! These black weeds
Express the wonted colour of thy mind,
For ever dark and dismal. Seven long years
Are pass'd, since we were join'd by sacred ties:
Clouds all the while have hung upon thy brow,
Nor broke, nor parted by one gleam of joy.
Time, that wears out the trace of deepest anguish,
As the sea smooths the prints made in the sand,
Has past o'er thee in vain.

Lady RANDOLPH
               If time to come
Should prove as ineffectual, yet, my Lord,
Thou canst not blame me. When our Scottish youth
Vy'd with each other for my luckless love,
Oft I besought them, I implor'd them all
Not to assail me with my father's aid,
Nor blend their better destiny with mine.
For melancholy had congeal'd my blood,
And froze affection in my chilly breast.
At last my Sire, rous'd with the base attempt
To force me from him, which thou rend'red'st vain,
To his own daughter bow'd his hoary head,
Besought me to commiserate his age,

And vow'd he should not, could not die in peace,
Unless he saw me wedded, and secur'd
From violence and outrage. Then, my Lord!
In my extreme distress I call'd on thee,
Thee I bespake, profess'd my strong desire
To lead a single, solitary life,
And begg'd thy Nobleness, not to demand
Her for a wife whose heart was dead to love.
How thou persisted'st after this, thou know'st,
And must confess that I am not unjust,
Nor more to thee than to myself injurious.

Lord RANDOLPH

That I confess; yet ever must regret
The grief I cannot cure. Would thou wert not
Compos'd of grief and tenderness alone,
But had'st a spark of other passions in thee,
Pride, anger, vanity, the strong desire
Of admiration, dear to woman kind;
These might contend with, and allay thy grief,
As meeting tides and currents smooth our firth.

Lady RANDOLPH

To such a cause the human mind oft owes
Its transient calm, a calm I envy not.

Lord RANDOLPH

Sure thou art not the daughter of Sir MALCOLM:
Strong was his rage, eternal his resentment:
For when thy brother fell, he smil'd to hear
That DOUGLAS' son in the same field was slain.

Lady RANDOLPH

Oh! rake not up the ashes of my fathers:
Implacable resentment was their crime,
And grievous has the expiation been.
Contending with the DOUGLAS, gallant lives
Of either house were lost; my ancestors

Compell'd, at last, to leave their ancient seat
On Tiviot's pleasant banks; and now, of them
No heir is left. Had they not been so stern,
I had not been the last of all my race.

Lord RANDOLPH

Thy grief wrests to its purposes my words.
I never ask'd of thee that ardent love,
Which in the breasts of fancy's children burns.
Decent affection and complacent kindness
Were all I wish'd for; but I wish'd in vain.
Hence with the less regret my eyes behold
The storm of war that gathers o'er this land:
If I should perish by the Danish sword,
MATILDA would not shed one tear the more.

Lady RANDOLPH

Thou do'st not think so: woeful as I am
I love thy merit, and esteem thy virtues.
But whither go'st thou now?

Lord RANDOLPH

                              Straight to the camp,
Where every warrior on the tip-toe stands
Of expectation, and impatient asks
Each who arrives, if he is come to tell
The Danes are landed.

Lady RANDOLPH

                    O, may adverse winds,
Far from the coast of Scotland, drive their fleet!
And every soldier of both hosts return
In peace and safety to his pleasant home!

Lord RANDOLPH

Thou speak'st a woman's, hear a warrior's wish:
Right from their native land, the stormy north,
May the wind blow, till every keel is fix'd
Immoveable in Caledonia's strand!

Then shall our foes repent their bold invasion,
And roving armies shun the fatal shore.

Lady RANDOLPH

War I detest: but war with foreign foes,
Whose manners, language, and whose looks are strange,
Is not so horrid, nor to me so hateful,
As that which with our neighbours oft we wage.
A river here, there an ideal line,
By fancy drawn, divides the sister kingdoms.
On each side dwells a people similar,
As twins are to each other; valiant both;
Both for their valour famous thro' the world.
Yet will they not unite their kindred arms,
And, if they must have war, wage distant war,
But with each other fight in cruel conflict.
Gallant in strife, and noble in their ire,
The battle is their pastime. They go forth
Gay in the morning, as to summer sport;
When ev'ning comes, the glory of the morn,
The youthful warrior is a clod of clay.
Thus fall the prime of either hapless land;
And such the fruit of Scotch and English wars.

Lord RANDOLPH

I'll hear no more: this melody would make
A soldier drop his sword, and doff his arms,
Sit down and weep the conquests he has made;
Yea, (like a monk), sing rest and peace in heav'n
To souls of warriors in his battles slain.
Lady, farewell: I leave thee not alone;
Yonder comes one whose love makes duty light. *Exit.*

Enter ANNA

ANNA

Forgive the rashness of your ANNA's love:
Urg'd by affection, I have thus presum'd

To interrupt your solitary thoughts;
And warn you of the hours that you neglect,
And lose in sadness.

Lady RANDOLPH

So to lose my hours
Is all the use I wish to make of time.

ANNA

To blame thee, Lady, suits not with my state:
But sure I am, since death first prey'd on man,
Never did sister thus a brother mourn.
What had your sorrows been if you had lost,
In early youth, the husband of your heart?

Lady RANDOLPH

Oh!

ANNA

Have I distress'd you with officious love,
And ill-tim'd mention of your brother's fate?
Forgive me, Lady: humble tho' I am,
The mind I bear partakes not of my fortune:
So fervently I love you, that to dry
These piteous tears, I'd throw my life away.

Lady RANDOLPH

What power directed thy unconscious tongue
To speak as thou hast done? to name——

ANNA

I know not:
But since my words have made my mistress tremble,
I will speak so no more; but silent mix
My tears with hers.

Lady RANDOLPH

No, thou shalt not be silent.
I'll trust thy faithful love, and thou shalt be

Henceforth th'instructed partner of my woes.
But what avails it? Can thy feeble pity
Roll back the flood of never-ebbing time?
Compel the earth and ocean to give up
Their dead alive?

ANNA

What means my noble mistress?

Lady RANDOLPH

Didst thou not ask what had my sorrows been——
If I in early youth had lost a husband?——
In the cold bosom of the earth is lodg'd,
Mangl'd with wounds, the husband of my youth;
And in some cavern of the ocean lies
My child and his.——————

ANNA

O! Lady, most rever'd!
The tale wrapt up in your amazing words
Deign to unfold.

Lady RANDOLPH

Alas! an antient feud,
Hereditary evil, was the source
Of my misfortunes. Ruling fate decreed,
That my brave brother should in battle save
The life of DOUGLAS' son, our house's foe:
The youthful warriors vow'd eternal friendship.
To see the vaunted sister of his friend
Impatient, DOUGLAS to Balarmo came,
Under a borrow'd name.——My heart he gain'd;
Nor did I long refuse the hand he begg'd:
My brother's presence authoris'd our marriage.
Three weeks, three little weeks, with wings of down,
Had o'er us flown, when my lov'd Lord was call'd
To fight his father's battles; and with him,
In spite of all my tears, did MALCOLM go.

Scarce were they gone, when my stern Sire was told
That the false stranger was Lord DOUGLAS' son.
Frantic with rage, the Baron drew his sword,
And question'd me. Alone, forsaken, faint,
Kneeling beneath his sword, fault'ring I took
An oath equivocal, that I ne'er would
Wed one of DOUGLAS' name. Sincerity,
Thou first of virtues, let no mortal leave
Thy onward path! altho' the earth should gape,
And from the gulph of hell destruction cry
To take dissimulation's winding way.

ANNA

Alas! how few of woman's fearful kind
Durst own a truth so hardy!

Lady RANDOLPH

                    The first truth
Is easiest to avow. This moral learn,
This precious moral, from my tragic tale.——
In a few days the dreadful tidings came
That DOUGLAS and my brother both were slain.
My Lord! my life! my husband!—mighty God!
What had I done to merit such affliction?

ANNA

My dearest Lady! many a tale of tears
I've listen'd to; but never did I hear
A tale so sad as this.

Lady RANDOLPH

                    In the first days
Of my distracting grief, I found myself——
As women wish to be who love their Lords.
But who durst tell my father? The good priest
Who join'd our hands, my brother's antient tutor,
With his lov'd MALCOLM, in the battle fell:
They two alone were privy to the marriage.

On silence and concealment I resolv'd,
Till time should make my father's fortune mine.
That very night on which my son was born,
My nurse, the only confident I had,
Set out with him to reach her sister's house:
But nurse, nor infant, have I ever seen
Or heard of, ANNA, since that fatal hour.
My murder'd child!——had thy fond mother fear'd
The loss of thee, she had loud fame defy'd,
Despis'd her father's rage, her father's grief,
And wander'd with thee thro' the scorning world.

ANNA

Not seen nor heard of! then perhaps he lives.

Lady RANDOLPH

No. It was dark December: wind and rain
Had beat all night. Across the Carron lay
The destin'd road; and in its swelling flood
My faithful servant perish'd with my child.
O hapless son! of a most hapless sire!——
But they are both at rest; and I alone
Dwell in this world of woe, condemn'd to walk,
Like a guilt-troubl'd ghost, my painful rounds:
Nor has despiteful fate permitted me
The comfort of a solitary sorrow.
Tho' dead to love, I was compell'd to wed
RANDOLPH, who snatch'd me from a villain's arms;
And RANDOLPH now possesses the domains,
That by Sir MALCOLM's death on me devolv'd;
Domains, that should to DOUGLAS' son have giv'n
A Baron's title, and a Baron's power.
Such were my soothing thoughts, while I bewail'd
The slaughter'd father of a son unborn.
And when that son came, like a ray from heav'n,
Which shines and disappears; alas! my child!
How long did thy fond mother grasp the hope
Of having thee, she knew not how, restor'd.

Year after year hath worn her hope away;
But left still undiminish'd her desire.

ANNA

The hand, that spins th'uneven thread of life,
May smooth the length that's yet to come of yours.

Lady RANDOLPH

Not in this world: I have consider'd well
Its various evils, and on whom they fall.
Alas! how oft does goodness wound itself,
And sweet affection prove the spring of woe!
O! had I died when my lov'd husband fell!
Had some good angel op'd to me the book
Of providence, and let me read my life,
My heart had broke when I beheld the sum
Of ills, which one by one I have endur'd.

ANNA

That God, whose ministers good angels are,
Hath shut the book in mercy to mankind.
But we must leave this theme: GLENALVON comes:
I saw him bend on you his thoughtful eyes,
And hitherwards he slowly stalks his way.

Lady RANDOLPH

I will avoid him. An ungracious person
Is doubly irksome in an hour like this.

ANNA

Why speaks my Lady thus of RANDOLPH's heir?

Lady RANDOLPH

Because he's not the heir of RANDOLPH's virtues.
Subtle and shrewd, he offers to mankind
An artificial image of himself:
And he with ease can vary to the taste
Of different men, its features. Self-deny'd,

And master of his appetites he seems:
But his fierce nature, like a fox chain'd up,
Watches to seize unseen the wish'd-for prey.
Never were vice and virtue pois'd so ill,
As in GLENALVON's unrelenting mind.
Yet is he brave and politic in war,
And stands aloft in these unruly times.
Why I describe him thus I'll tell hereafter:
Stay and detain him till I reach the castle.

                              [*Exit* Lady RANDOLPH.

ANNA

O happiness! where art thou to be found?
I see thou dwellest not with birth and beauty,
Tho' grac'd with grandeur, and in wealth array'd:
Nor dost thou, it would seem, with virtue dwell;
Else had this gentle Lady miss'd thee not.

Enter GLENALVON

GLENALVON

What dost thou muse on, meditating maid?
Like some entranc'd and visionary seer
On earth thou stand'st, thy thoughts ascend to heaven.

ANNA

Wou'd that I were, e'en as thou say'st, a seer,
To have my doubts by heav'nly vision clear'd!

GLENALVON

What dost thou doubt of? what hast thou to do
With subjects intricate? Thy youth, thy beauty,
Cannot be question'd: think of these good gifts;
And then thy contemplations will be pleasing.

ANNA

Let women view yon monument of woe,
Then boast of beauty: who so fair as she?

But I must follow: this revolving day
Awakes the memory of her antient woes.   [*Exit* ANNA.

GLENALVON *solus*

So!——Lady RANDOLPH shuns me; by and by
I'll woo her as the lion wooes his brides.
The deed's a-doing now, that makes me lord
Of these rich valleys, and a chief of power.
The season is most apt; my sounding steps
Will not be heard amidst the din of arms.
RANDOLPH has liv'd too long: his better fate
Had the ascendant once, and kept me down:
When I had seiz'd the dame, by chance he came,
Rescu'd, and had the Lady for his labour;
I 'scap'd unknown: a slender consolation!
Heaven is my witness that I do not love
To sow in peril, and let others reap
The jocund harvest. Yet I am not safe:
By love, or something like it, stung, inflam'd,
Madly I blabb'd my passion to his wife,
And she has threaten'd to acquaint him of it.
The way of woman's will I do not know:
But well I know the Baron's wrath is deadly.
I will not live in fear: the man I dread
Is as a Dane to me; ay, and the man
Who stands betwixt me and my chief desire.
No bar but he; she has no kinsman near;
No brother in his sister's quarrel bold;
And for the righteous cause, a stranger's cause,
I know no chief that will defy GLENALVON.

End of the FIRST ACT

ACT II

A Court, &c.

Enter Servants and a Stranger at one door, and Lady
RANDOLPH *and* ANNA *at another*

Lady RANDOLPH

What means this clamour? Stranger! speak secure;
Hast thou been wrong'd? have these rude men presum'd
To vex the weary traveller on his way?

First SERVANT

By us no stranger ever suffer'd wrong:
This man with outcry wild has call'd us forth;
So sore afraid he cannot speak his fears.

Enter Lord RANDOLPH *and young man, with their swords
drawn and bloody*

Lady RANDOLPH

Not vain the Stranger's fears! how fares my Lord?

Lord RANDOLPH

That it fares well, thanks to this gallant youth,
Whose valour sav'd me from a wretched death!
As down the winding dale I walk'd alone,
At the cross way four armed men attack'd me:
Rovers, I judge, from the licentious camp,
Who would have quickly laid Lord RANDOLPH low,
Had not this brave and generous Stranger come,
Like my good angel in the hour of fate,
And, mocking danger, made my foes his own.
They turn'd upon him: but his active arm
Struck to the ground, from whence they rose no more,
The fiercest two; the others fled amain,
And left him master of the bloody field.
Speak, Lady RANDOLPH: upon Beauty's tongue

Dwell accents pleasing to the brave and bold.
Speak, noble Dame, and thank him for thy Lord.

Lady RANDOLPH

My Lord, I cannot speak what now I feel.
My heart o'erflows with gratitude to heav'n,
And to this noble youth, who all unknown
To you and yours, deliberated not,
Nor paus'd at peril, but humanely brave
Fought on your side, against such fearful odds.
Have you yet learn'd of him whom we should thank?
Whom call the saviour of Lord RANDOLPH's life?

Lord RANDOLPH

I ask'd that question, and he answer'd not:
But I must know who my deliverer is.   (*to the Stranger.*)

STRANGER

A low born man, of parentage obscure,
Who nought can boast but his desire to be
A soldier, and to gain a name in arms.

Lord RANDOLPH

Whoe'er thou art, thy spirit is ennobl'd
By the great King of Kings! thou art ordain'd
And stamp'd a hero by the sovereign hand
Of Nature! blush not, flower of modesty
As well as valour, to declare thy birth.

STRANGER

My name is NORVAL: on the Grampian hills
My father feeds his flocks; a frugal swain,
Whose constant cares were to increase his store,
And keep his only son, myself, at home.
For I had heard of battles, and I long'd
To follow to the field some warlike Lord:
And heaven soon granted what my Sire deny'd.
This moon which rose last night, round as my shield,

Had not yet fill'd her horns, when, by her light,
A band of fierce Barbarians, from the hills,
Rush'd like a torrent down upon the vale,
Sweeping our flocks and herds. The shepherds fled
For safety, and for succour. I alone,
With bended bow, and quiver full of arrows,
Hover'd about the enemy, and mark'd
The road he took, then hasted to my friends;
Whom, with a troop of fifty chosen men,
I met advancing. The pursuit I led,
Till we o'ertook the spoil-encumber'd foe.
We fought and conquer'd. E're a sword was drawn,
An arrow from my bow had pierc'd their chief,
Who wore that day the arms which now I wear.
Returning home in triumph, I disdain'd
The shepherd's slothful life: and having heard
That our good King had summon'd his bold Peers
To lead their warriors to the Carron side,
I left my father's house, and took with me
A chosen servant to conduct my steps;——
Yon trembling coward who forsook his master.
Journeying with this intent, I past these towers,
And, heaven-directed, came this day to do
The happy deed that gilds my humble name.

Lord RANDOLPH

He is as wise as brave. Was ever tale
With such a gallant modesty rehears'd?
My brave deliverer! thou shalt enter now
A nobler list, and in a monarch's sight
Contend with princes for the prize of fame.
I will present thee to our Scottish King,
Whose valiant spirit ever valour lov'd.
Ha! my MATILDA! wherefore starts that tear?

Lady RANDOLPH

I cannot say: for various affections,
And strangely mingled, in my bosom swell;

Yet each of them may well command a tear.
I joy that thou art safe, and I admire
Him and his fortunes who hath wrought thy safety;
Yea, as my mind predicts, with thine his own.
Obscure and friendless, he the army fought,
Bent upon peril, in the range of death
Resolv'd to hunt for fame, and with his sword
To gain distinction which his birth deny'd.
In this attempt unknown he might have perish'd,
And gain'd, with all his valour, but oblivion.
Now grac'd by thee, his virtue serves no more
Beneath despair. The soldier now of hope
He stands conspicuous; fame and great renown
Are brought within the compass of his sword.
On this my mind reflected, whilst you spoke,
And bless'd the wonder-working Lord of heaven.

Lord RANDOLPH

Pious and grateful ever are thy thoughts!
My deeds shall follow where thou point'st the way.
Next to myself, and equal to GLENALVON,
In honour and command shall NORVAL be.

NORVAL

I know not how to thank you. Rude I am
In speech and manners: never till this hour
Stood I in such a presence: yet, my Lord,
There's something in my breast which makes me bold
To say, that NORVAL ne'er will shame thy favour.

Lady RANDOLPH

I will be sworn thou wilt not. Thou shalt be
My knight; and ever, as thou didst to-day,
With happy valour guard the life of RANDOLPH.

Lord RANDOLPH

Well hast thou spoke. Let me forbid reply.   [*To* NORVAL.
We are thy debtors still; thy high desert

O'ertops our gratitude. I must proceed,
As was at first intended, to the camp.
Some of my train I see are speeding hither,
Impatient doubtless of their Lord's delay.
Go with me, NORVAL, and thine eyes shall see
The chosen warriors of thy native land,
Who languish for the fight, and beat the air
With brandish'd swords.

NORVAL

Let us begone, my Lord.

Lord RANDOLPH

[*To* Lady RANDOLPH.

About the time that the declining fun
Shall his broad orbit o'er yon hills suspend,
Expect us to return. This night once more
Within these walls I rest; my tent I pitch
To-morrow in the field. Prepare the feast.
Free is his heart who for his country fights:
He in the eve of battle may resign
Himself to social pleasure; sweetest then,
When danger to a soldier's soul endears
The human joy that never may return.

[*Exeunt* RANDOLPH *and* NORVAL.

Lady RANDOLPH *and* ANNA

Lady RANDOLPH

His parting words have struck a fatal truth.
O DOUGLAS! DOUGLAS! tender was the time
When we two parted, ne'er to meet again!
How many years of anguish and despair
Has heav'n annex'd to those swift passing hours
Of love and fondness! Then my bosom's flame
Oft, as blown back by the rude breath of fear,
Return'd, and with redoubled ardour blaz'd.

ANNA

May gracious heav'n pour the sweet balm of peace

Into the wounds that fester in your breast!
For earthly consolation cannot cure them.

Lady RANDOLPH

One only cure can heav'n itself bestow;—
A grave—that bed in which the weary rest.
Wretch that I am! Alas! why am I so?
At every happy parent I repine!
How blest the mother of yon gallant NORVAL!
She for a living husband bore her pains,
And heard him bless her when a man was born:
She nurs'd her smiling infant on her breast;
Tended the child, and rear'd the pleasing boy:
She, with affection's triumph, saw the youth
In grace and comeliness surpass his peers:
Whilst I to a dead husband bore a son,
And to the roaring waters gave my child.

ANNA

Alas! alas! why will you thus resume
Your grief afresh? I thought that gallant youth
Would for a while have won you from your woe.
On him intent you gazed, with a look
Much more delighted, than your pensive eye
Has deign'd on other objects to bestow.

Lady RANDOLPH

Delighted, say'st thou? Oh! even there mine eye
Found fuel for my life-consuming sorrow.
I thought, that had the son of DOUGLAS liv'd,
He might have been like this young gallant stranger,
And pair'd with him in features and in shape;
In all endowments, as in years, I deem,
My boy with blooming NORVAL might have number'd.
Whilst thus I mus'd, a spark from fancy fell
On my sad heart, and kindled up a fondness
For this young stranger, wand'ring from his home,
And like an orphan cast upon my care.

I will protect thee, (said I to myself)
With all my power, and grace with all my favour.

Anna

Sure heav'n will bless so generous a resolve.
You must, my noble Dame, exert your power:
You must awake: devices will be fram'd,
And arrows pointed at the breast of Norval.

Lady Randolph

Glenalvon's false and crafty head will work
Against a rival in his kinsman's love,
If I deter him not: I only can.
Bold as he is, Glenalvon will beware
How he pulls down the fabric that I raise.
I'll be the artist of young Norval's fortune.
'Tis pleasing to admire! most apt was I
To this affection in my better days;
Tho' now I seem to you shrunk up, retir'd
Within the narrow compass of my woe.
Have you not sometimes seen an early flower
Open its bud, and spread its silken leaves,
To catch sweet airs, and odours to bestow;
Then, by the keen blast nipt, pull in its leaves,
And, tho' still living, die to scent and beauty!
Emblem of me: affliction, like a storm,
Hath kill'd the forward blossom of my heart.

Enter Glenalvon

Glenalvon

Where is my dearest kinsman, noble Randolph?

Lady Randolph

Have you not heard, Glenalvon, of the base——

Glenalvon

I have: and that the villains may not 'scape,
With a strong band I have begirt the wood.

If they lurk there, alive they shall be taken,
And torture force from them th' important secret,
Whether some foe of RANDOLPH hir'd their swords,
Or if——

Lady RANDOLPH

That care becomes a kinsman's love.
I have a counsel for GLENALVON's ear.   [*Exit* ANNA.

GLENALVON

To him your counsels always are commands.

Lady RANDOLPH

I have not found so; thou art known to me.

GLENALVON

Known!

Lady RANDOLPH

And most certain is my cause of knowledge.

GLENALVON

What do you know? By the most blessed cross,
You much amaze me. No created being,
Yourself except, durst thus accost GLENALVON.

Lady RANDOLPH

Is guilt so bold! and dost thou make a merit
Of thy pretended meekness! This to me,
Who, with a gentleness which duty blames,
Have hitherto conceal'd what, if divulg'd,
Would make thee nothing; or, what's worse than that,
An outcast beggar, and unpitied too!
For mortals shudder at a crime like thine.

GLENALVON

Thy virtue awes me. First of womankind!
Permit me yet to say, that the fond man,
Whom love transports beyond strict virtue's bounds,
If he is brought by love to misery,

In fortune ruin'd, as in mind forlorn,
Unpitied cannot be. Pity's the alms
Which on such beggars freely is bestow'd:
For mortals know that love is still their lord,
And o'er their vain resolves advances still:
As fire, when kindled by our shepherds, moves
Thro' the dry heath before the fanning wind.

Lady RANDOLPH

Reserve these accents for some other ear.
To love's apology I listen not.
Mark thou my words; for it is meet thou should'st.
His brave deliverer RANDOLPH here retains.
Perhaps his presence may not please thee well.
But, at thy peril, practise ought against him:
Let not thy jealousy attempt to shake
And loosen the good root he has in RANDOLPH;
Whose favourites I know thou hast supplanted.
Thou look'st at me, as if thou fain would'st pry
Into my heart. 'Tis open as my speech.
I give this early caution, and put on
The curb, before thy temper breaks away.
The friendless Stranger my protection claims:
His friend I am, and be not thou his foe.   [*Exit.*

Manet GLENALVON

Child that I was, to start at my own shadow,
And be the shallow fool of coward conscience!
I am not what I have been; what I should be.
The darts of destiny have almost pierc'd
My marble heart. Had I one grain of faith
In holy legends, and religious tales,
I should conclude there was an arm above,
That fought against me, and malignant turn'd,
To catch myself, the subtle snare I set.
Why, rape and murder are not simple means!
Th' imperfect rape to RANDOLPH gave a spouse;
And the intended murder introduc'd

A favourite to hide the sun from me;
And worst of all, a rival. Burning hell!
This were thy centre, if I thought she lov'd him!
'Tis certain she contemns me; nay, commands me,
And waves the flag of her displeasure o'er me,
In his behalf. And shall I thus be brav'd?
Curb'd, as she calls it, by dame chastity?
Infernal fiends, if any fiends there are
More fierce than hate, ambition, and revenge,
Rise up and fill my bosom with your fires,
And policy remorseless! Chance may spoil
A single aim; but perseverance must
Prosper at last. For chance and fate are words:
Persistive wisdom is the fate of man.
Darkly a project peers upon my mind,
Like the red moon when rising in the east,
Cross'd and divided by strange-colour'd clouds.
I'll seek the slave who came with NORVAL hither,
And for his cowardice was spurned from him.
I've known a follower's rankled bosom breed
Venom most fatal to his heedless Lord.   [*Exit.*

End of the SECOND ACT

ACT III

A Court, &c. as before

Enter ANNA

ANNA

Thy vassals, Grief! great Nature's order break,
And change the noon-tide to the midnight hour.
Whilst Lady RANDOLPH sleeps, I will walk forth,
And taste the air that breathes on yonder bank.
Sweet may her slumbers be! Ye ministers

Of gracious heaven who love the human race,
Angels and seraphs who delight in goodness!
Forsake your skies, and to her couch descend!
There from her fancy chace those dismal forms
That haunt her waking; her sad spirit charm
With images celestial, such as please
The bless'd above upon their golden beds.

Enter SERVANT

SERVANT

One of the vile assassins is secur'd.
We found the villain lurking in the wood:
With dreadful imprecations he denies
All knowledge of the crime. But this is not
His first essay: these jewels were conceal'd
In the most secret places of his garment;
Belike the spoils of some that he has murder'd.

ANNA

Let me look on them. Ha! here is a heart,
The chosen crest of DOUGLAS' valiant name!
These are no vulgar jewels. Guard the wretch. [*Exit* ANNA.

Enter Servants with a Prisoner

PRISONER

I know no more than does the child unborn
Of what you charge me with.

First SERVANT

                        You say so, Sir!
But torture soon shall make you speak the truth.
Behold the Lady of Lord RANDOLPH comes:
Prepare yourself to meet her just revenge.

Enter Lady RANDOLPH *and* ANNA

ANNA

Summon your utmost fortitude, before

You speak with him. Your dignity, your fame,
Are now at stake. Think of the fatal secret,
Which in a moment from your lips may fly.

Lady RANDOLPH

Thou shalt behold me, with a desperate heart,
Hear how my infant perish'd. See, he kneels.

[The Prisoner kneels.]

PRISONER

Heav'n bless that countenance, so sweet and mild!
A judge like thee makes innocence more bold.
O save me, Lady! from these cruel men,
Who have attack'd and seiz'd me; who accuse
Me of intended murder. As I hope
For mercy at the judgment seat of God,
The tender lamb, that never nipt the grass,
Is not more innocent than I of murder.

Lady RANDOLPH

Of this man's guilt what proof can ye produce?

First SERVANT

We found him lurking in the hollow Glynn.
When view'd and call'd upon, amaz'd, he fled.
We overtook him, and inquir'd from whence
And what he was: he said, he came from far,
And was upon his journey to the camp.
Not satisfy'd with this, we search'd his cloaths,
And found these jewels; whose rich value plead
Most powerfully against him. Hard he seems
And old in villainy. Permit us try
His stubbornness against the torture's force.

PRISONER

O gentle Lady! by your Lord's dear life!
Which these weak hands, I swear, did ne'er assail;
And by your children's welfare, spare my age!

Let not the iron tear my antient joints,
And my grey hairs bring to the grave with pain.

Lady RANDOLPH

Account for these: thine own they cannot be:
For these, I say: be stedfast to the truth;
Detected falshood is most certain death.

[ANNA *removes the Servants and returns.*]

PRISONER

Alas! I'm sore beset! let never man,
For sake of lucre, sin against his soul!
Eternal justice is in this most just!
I, guiltless now, must former guilt reveal.

Lady RANDOLPH

O! ANNA hear!——once more I charge thee speak
The truth direct: for these to me foretel
And certify a part of thy narration;
With which if the remainder tallies not,
An instant and a dreadful death abides thee.

PRISONER

Then, thus adjur'd, I'll speak to you as just
As if you were the minister of heaven,
Sent down to search the secret sins of men.
  SOME eighteen years ago, I rented land
Of brave Sir MALCOLM, then BALARMO's Lord;
But falling to decay, his servants seiz'd
All that I had, and then turn'd me and mine,
(Four helpless infants and their weeping mother)
Out to the mercy of the winter winds.
A little hovel by the river's side
Receiv'd us: there hard labour, and the skill
In fishing, which was formerly my sport,
Supported life. Whilst thus we poorly liv'd,
One stormy night, as I remember well,
The wind and rain beat hard upon our roof:

Red came the river down, and loud and oft
The angry spirit of the water shriek'd.
At the dead hour of night was heard the cry
Of one in jeopardy. I rose, and ran
To where the circling eddy of a pool,
Beneath the ford, us'd oft to bring within
My reach whatever floating thing the stream
Had caught. The voice was ceas'd; the person lost:
But looking sad and earnest on the waters,
By the moon's light I saw, whirl'd round and round,
A basket: soon I drew it to the bank,
And nestled curious there an infant lay.

Lady RANDOLPH

Was he alive?

PRISONER

He was.

Lady RANDOLPH

Inhuman that thou art!
How could'st thou kill what waves and tempests spar'd?

PRISONER

I am not so inhuman.

Lady RANDOLPH

Didst thou not?

ANNA

My noble Mistress, you are mov'd too much:
This man has not the aspect of stern murder;
Let him go on, and you, I hope, will hear
Good tidings of your kinsman's long lost child.

PRISONER

The needy man, who has known better days,
One whom distress has spited at the world,
Is he whom tempting fiends would pitch upon

To do such deeds, as makes the prosperous men
Lift up their hands and wonder who could do them.
And such a man was I; a man declin'd,
Who saw no end of black adversity:
Yet for the wealth of kingdoms, I would not
Have touch'd that infant with a hand of harm.

Lady RANDOLPH

Ha! dost thou say so? Then perhaps he lives!

PRISONER

Not many days ago he was alive.

Lady RANDOLPH

O! God of heav'n! Did he then die so lately?

PRISONER

I did not say he died; I hope he lives.
Not many days ago these eyes beheld
Him, flourishing in youth, and health, and beauty.

Lady RANDOLPH

Where is he now?

PRISONER

Alas! I know not where.

Lady RANDOLPH

Oh fate! I fear thee still. Thou riddler, speak
Direct and clear; else I will search thy soul.

ANNA

Permit me, ever honour'd! Keen impatience,
Tho' hard to be restrain'd, defeats itself.——
Pursue thy story with a faithful tongue,
To the last hour that thou didst keep the child.

PRISONER

Fear not my faith, tho' I must speak my shame.
Within the cradle, where the infant lay,

Was stow'd a mighty store of gold and jewels:
Tempted by which we did resolve to hide,
From all the world, this wonderful event,
And like a peasant breed the noble child.
That none might mark the change of our estate,
We left the country, travell'd to the North,
Bought flocks and herds, and gradually brought forth
Our secret wealth. But God's all-seeing eye
Beheld our avarice, and smote us sore.
For one by one all our own children died,
And he, the Stranger, sole remain'd the heir
Of what indeed was his. Fain then would I,
Who with a father's fondness lov'd the boy,
Have trusted him, now in the dawn of youth,
With his own secret: but my anxious wife,
Foreboding evil, never would consent.
Mean while the stripling grew in years and beauty;
And, as we oft observ'd, he bore himself,
Not as the offspring of our cottage blood;
For nature will break out: mild with the mild,
But with the froward he was fierce as fire,
And night and day he talk'd of war and arms.
I set myself against his warlike bent;
But all in vain: for when a desperate band
Of robbers from the savage mountains came——

Lady RANDOLPH

Eternal Providence! What is thy name?

PRISONER

My name is NORVAL; and my name he bears.

Lady RANDOLPH

'Tis he; 'tis he himself! It is my son!
O sovereign mercy! 'Twas my child I saw!
No wonder, ANNA, that my bosom burn'd.

ANNA

Just are your transports: ne'er was woman's heart

Prov'd with such fierce extremes. High fated Dame!
But yet remember that you are beheld
By servile eyes; your gestures may be seen
Impassion'd strange; perhaps your words o'erheard.

Lady RANDOLPH

Well dost thou counsel, ANNA: heaven bestow
On me that wisdom which my state requires!

ANNA

The moments of deliberation pass,
And soon you must resolve. This useful man
Must be dismiss'd in safety, 'ere my Lord
Shall with his brave deliverer return.

PRISONER

If I, amidst astonishment and fear,
·Have of your words and gestures rightly judg'd,
Thou art the daughter of my antient master;
The child I rescu'd from the flood is thine.

Lady RANDOLPH

With thee dissimulation now were vain.
I am indeed the daughter of Sir MALCOLM;
The child thou rescu'dst from the flood is mine.

PRISONER

Bless'd be the hour that made me a poor man!
My poverty hath sav'd my master's house!

Lady RANDOLPH

Thy words surprize me: sure thou dost not feign:
The tear stands in thine eye: such love from thee
Sir MALCOLM's house deserv'd not; if aright
Thou told'st the story of thy own distress.

PRISONER

Sir MALCOLM of our Barons was the flower;
The fastest friend, the best, the kindest master:

But ah! he knew not of my sad estate.
After that battle, where his gallant son,
Your own brave brother, fell, the good old Lord
Grew desperate and reckless of the world;
And never, as he erst was wont, went forth
To overlook the conduct of his servants.
By them I was thrust out, and them I blame:
May heav'n so judge me as I judg'd my master!
And God so love me as I love his race!

Lady RANDOLPH

His race shall yet reward thee. On thy faith
Depends the fate of thy lov'd master's house.
Rememb'rest thou a little lonely hut,
That like a holy hermitage appears
Among the clifts of Carron?

PRISONER

           I remember
The cottage of the clifts.

Lady RANDOLPH

           'Tis that I mean:
There dwells a man of venerable age,
Who in my father's service spent his youth:
Tell him I sent thee, and with him remain,
Till I shall call upon thee to declare,
Before the King and Nobles, what thou now
To me hast told. No more but this, and thou
Shalt live in honour all thy future days:
Thy son so long shall call thee father still,
And all the land shall bless the man, who sav'd
The son of DOUGLAS, and Sir MALCOLM's heir.
Remember well my words: if thou should'st meet
Him whom thou call'st thy son, still call him so;
And mention nothing of his nobler father.

PRISONER

Fear not that I shall mar so fair an harvest,

By putting in my sickle 'ere 'tis ripe.
Why did I leave my home and antient dame?
To find the youth to tell him all I knew,
And make him wear these jewels in his arms;
Which might, I thought, be challeng'd, and so bring
To light the secret of his noble birth.

> [Lady RANDOLPH *goes towards the Servants.*

Lady RANDOLPH

This man is not th'assassin you suspected,
Tho' chance combin'd some likelihoods against him.
He is the faithful bearer of the jewels
To their right owner, whom in haste he seeks.
'Tis meet that you should put him on his way,
Since your mistaken zeal hath dragg'd him hither.

> [*Exeunt Stranger and Servants.*

Lady RANDOLPH *and* ANNA

Lady RANDOLPH

My faithful ANNA! dost thou share my joy?
I know thou dost. Unparallel'd event!
Reaching from heav'n to earth, Jehovah's arm
Snatch'd from the waves, and brings to me my son!
Judge of the widow, and the orphan's father!
Accept a widow's and a mother's thanks
For such a gift! What does my ANNA think
Of the young eaglet of a valiant nest?
How soon he gaz'd on bright and burning arms,
Spurn'd the low dunghill where his fate had thrown him,
And tower'd up to the region of his sire!

ANNA

How fondly did your eyes devour the boy!
Mysterious nature, with the unseen cord
Of powerful instinct, drew you to your own.

Lady RANDOLPH

The ready story of his birth believ'd

Supprest my fancy quite; nor did he owe
To any likeness my so sudden favour:
But now I long to see his face again,
Examine every feature, and find out
The lineaments of DOUGLAS, or my own.
But most of all I long to let him know
Who his true parents are, to clasp his neck,
And tell him all the story of his father.

ANNA

With wary caution you must bear yourself
In public, lest your tenderness break forth,
And in observers stir conjectures strange.
For, if a cherub in the shape of woman
Should walk this world, yet defamation would,
Like a vile cur, bark at the angel's train——
To-day the Baron started at your tears.

Lady RANDOLPH

He did so, ANNA! well thy Mistress knows,
If the least circumstance, mote of offence,
Should touch the Baron's eye, his sight would be
With jealousy disorder'd, But the more
It does behove me instant to declare
The birth of DOUGLAS, and assert his rights.
This night I purpose with my son to meet,
Reveal the secret, and consult with him:
For wise he is, or my fond judgment errs.
As he does now, so look'd his noble father,
Array'd in nature's ease: his mien, his speech,
Were sweetly simple, and full oft deceiv'd
Those trivial mortals who seem always wise.
But, when the matter match'd his mighty mind,
Up rose the Hero: on his piercing eye
Sat Observation: on each glance of thought
Decision follow'd, as the thunder-bolt
Pursues the flash.

ANNA

That demon haunts you still:
Behold GLENALVON.

Lady RANDOLPH

Now I shun him not.
This day I brav'd him in behalf of NORVAL;
Perhaps too far: at least my nicer fears
For DOUGLAS thus interpret.

Enter GLENALVON

GLENALVON

Noble Dame!
The hov'ring Dane at last his men hath landed:
No band of pirates; but a mighty host,
That come to settle where their valour conquers;
To win a country, or to lose themselves.

Lady RANDOLPH

But whence comes this intelligence, GLENALVON?

GLENALVON

A nimble courier sent from yonder camp,
To hasten up the chieftains of the north,
Inform'd me, as he past, that the fierce Dane
Had on the eastern coast of Lothian landed,
Near to that place where the sea-rock immense,
Amazing Bass, looks o'er a fertile land.

Lady RANDOLPH

Then must this western army march to join
The warlike troops that guard Edina's tow'rs.

GLENALVON

Beyond all question. If impairing time
Has not effac'd the image of a place,
Once perfect in my breast, there is a wild
Which lies to westward of that mighty rock,

And seems by nature formed for the camp
Of water-wafted armies, whose chief strength
Lies in firm foot, unflank'd with warlike horse:
If martial skill directs the Danish lords,
There inaccessible their army lies
To our swift scow'ring horse, the bloody field
Must man to man, and foot to foot, be fought.

Lady RANDOLPH

How many mothers shall bewail their sons!
How many widows weep their husbands slain!
Ye dames of Denmark! ev'n for you I feel,
Who sadly sitting on the sea-beat shore,
Long look for lords that never shall return.

GLENALVON

Oft has th'unconquer'd Caledonian sword
Widow'd the north. The children of the slain
Come, as I hope, to meet their fathers' fate.
The monster war, with her infernal brood,
Loud yelling fury, and life-ending pain,
Are objects suited to GLENALVON's soul.
Scorn is more grievous than the pains of death:
Reproach more piercing than the pointed sword.

Lady RANDOLPH

I scorn thee not, but when I ought to scorn;
Nor e'er reproach, but when insulted virtue
Against audacious vice asserts herself.
I own thy worth, GLENALVON; none more apt
Than I to praise thine eminence in arms,
And be the echo of thy martial fame.
No longer vainly feed a guilty passion.
Go and pursue a lawful mistress, glory.
Upon the Danish crests redeem thy fault,
And let thy valour be the shield of RANDOLPH.

GLENALVON

One instant stay, and hear an alter'd man.

When beauty pleads for virtue, vice abash'd
Flies its own colours, and goes o'er to virtue.
I am your convert; time will shew how truly:
Yet one immediate proof I mean to give.
That youth, for whom your ardent zeal to-day,
Somewhat too haughtily, defy'd your slave,
Amidst the shock of armies I'll defend,
And turn death from him, with a guardian arm.
Sedate by use, my bosom maddens not
At the tumultuous uproar of the field.

Lady RANDOLPH

Act thus, GLENALVON, and I am thy friend:
But that's thy least reward. Believe me, Sir,
The truly generous is the truly wise;
And he who loves not others, lives unblest.

[*Exit* Lady RANDOLPH.

GLENALVON *solus*

Amen! and virtue is its own reward!——
I think that I have hit the very tone
In which she loves to speak. Honey'd assent,
How pleasing art thou to the taste of man,
And woman also! flattery direct
Rarely disgusts. They little know mankind
Who doubt its operation: 'tis my key,
And opes the wicket of the human heart.
How far I have succeeded now I know not.
Yet I incline to think her stormy virtue
Is lull'd a while: 'tis her alone I fear:
Whilst she and RANDOLPH live, and live in faith
And amity, uncertain is my tenure.
Fate o'er my head suspends disgrace and death,
By that weak hair, a peevish female's will.
I am not idle: but the ebbs and flows
Of fortune's tide cannot be calculated.
That slave of NORVAL's I have found most apt:
I shew'd him gold, and he has pawn'd his soul

To say and swear whatever I suggest.
NORVAL, I'm told, has that alluring look,
'Twixt man and woman, which I have observ'd
To charm the nicer and fantastic dames,
Who are, like Lady RANDOLPH, full of virtue.
In raising RANDOLPH's jealousy I may
But point him to the truth. He seldom errs
Who thinks the worst he can of womankind.

The End of the THIRD ACT

ACT IV

Flourish of Trumpets

Enter Lord RANDOLPH *attended*

Lord RANDOLPH

Summon an hundred horse, by break of day,
To wait our pleasure at the castle gate.

Enter Lady RANDOLPH

Lady RANDOLPH

Alas! my Lord! I've heard unwelcome news;
The Danes are landed.

Lord RANDOLPH

          Ay, no inroad this
Of the Northumbrian bent to take a spoil:
No sportive war, no tournament essay,
Of some young knight resolv'd to break a spear,
And stain with hostile blood his maiden arms.
The Danes are landed: we must beat them back,
Or live the slaves of Denmark.

Lady RANDOLPH

          Dreadful times!

Lord RANDOLPH

The fenceless villages are all forsaken;
The trembling mothers and their children lodg'd
In wall-girt towers and castles; whilst the men
Retire indignant. Yet, like broken waves,
They but retire more awful to return.

Lady RANDOLPH

Immense, as fame reports, the Danish host——

Lord RANDOLPH

Were it as numerous as loud fame reports,
An army knit like ours wou'd pierce it thro':
Brothers, that shrink not from each other's side,
And fond companions, fill our warlike files:
For his dear offspring, and the wife he loves,
The husband, and the fearless father arm.
In vulgar breasts heroic ardor burns,
And the poor peasant mates his daring lord.

Lady RANDOLPH

Men's minds are temper'd, like their swords, for war;
Lovers of danger, on destruction's brink
They joy to rear erect their daring forms.
Hence, early graves; hence, the lone widow's life;
And the sad mother's grief-embitter'd age.
Where is our gallant guest?

Lord RANDOLPH

                              Down in the vale
I left him, managing a fiery steed,
Whose stubbornness had foil'd the strength and skill
Of every rider. But behold he comes,
In earnest conversation with GLENALVON.

Enter NORVAL *and* GLENALVON

GLENALVON! with the lark arise; go forth,
And lead my troops that ly in yonder vale:
Private I travel to the royal camp:

NORVAL, thou goest with me. But say, young man!
Where didst thou learn so to discourse of war,
And in such terms as I o'erheard to-day?
War is no village science, nor its phrase
A language taught amongst the shepherd swains.

NORVAL

Small is the skill my Lord delights to praise
In him he favours.——Hear from whence it came.
Beneath a mountain's brow, the most remote
And inaccessible by shepherds trod,
In a deep cave, dug by no mortal hand,
A hermit liv'd; a melancholy man,
Who was the wonder of our wand'ring swains.
Austere and lonely, cruel to himself,
Did they report him; the cold earth his bed,
Water his drink, his food the shepherd's alms.
I went to see him, and my heart was touch'd
With rev'rence and with pity. Mild he spake,
And, entring on discourse, such stories told
As made me oft revisit his sad cell.
For he had been a soldier in his youth;
And fought in famous battles, when the Peers
Of Europe, by the bold GODFREDO led,
Against th'usurping Infidel display'd
The cross of Christ, and won the Holy Land.
Pleas'd with my admiration, and the fire
His speech struck from me, the old man wou'd shake
His years away, and act his young encounters:
Then, having shew'd his wounds, he'd sit him down,
And all the live-long day discourse of war.
To help my fancy, in the smooth green turf
He cut the figures of the marshall'd hosts;
Describ'd the motions, and explain'd the use
Of the deep column, and the lengthen'd line,
The square, the crescent, and the phalanx firm.
For all that Saracen or Christian knew
Of war's vast art, was to this hermit known.

Lord RANDOLPH

Why did this soldier in a desart hide
Those qualities that should have grac'd a camp?

NORVAL

That too at last I learn'd. Unhappy man!
Returning homewards by Messina's port,
Loaded with wealth and honours bravely won,
A rude and boist'rous captain of the sea
Fasten'd a quarrel on him. Fierce they fought:
The stranger fell, and with his dying breath
Declar'd his name and lineage! Mighty God!
The soldier cried, my brother! Oh! my brother!

Lady RANDOLPH

His brother!

NORVAL

Yes; of the same parents born;
His only brother. They exchang'd forgiveness:
And happy, in my mind, was he that died:
For many deaths has the survivor suffer'd.
In the wild desart on a rock he sits,
Or on some nameless stream's untrodden banks,
And ruminates all day his dreadful fate.
At times, alas! not in his perfect mind,
Holds dialogues with his lov'd brother's ghost;
And oft each night forsakes his sullen couch,
To make sad orisons for him he slew.

Lady RANDOLPH

To what mysterious woes are mortals born!
In this dire tragedy were there no more
Unhappy persons? did the parents live?

NORVAL

No; they were dead: kind heav'n had clos'd their eyes
Before their son had shed his brother's blood.

Lord RANDOLPH

Hard is his fate; for he was not to blame!
There is a destiny in this strange world,
Which oft decrees an undeserved doom:
Let schoolmen tell us why.—From whence these sounds?

[*Trumpets at a distance.*]

Enter an OFFICER

OFFICER

My Lord, the trumpets of the troops of Lorn:
The valiant leader hails the noble RANDOLPH.

Lord RANDOLPH

Mine antient guest! does he the warriors lead?
Has Denmark rous'd the brave old Knight to arms?

OFFICER

No; worn with warfare, he resigns the sword.
His eldest hope, the valiant JOHN of Lorn,
Now leads his kindred bands.

Lord RANDOLPH

GLENALVON, go.
With hospitality's most strong request
Intreat the chief.   [*Exit* GLENALVON.]

OFFICER

My Lord, requests are vain.
He urges on, impatient of delay,
Stung with the tidings of the foe's approach.

Lord RANDOLPH

May victory sit on the warrior's plume!
Bravest of men! his flocks and herds are safe;
Remote from war's alarms his pastures lie,
By mountains inaccessible secur'd:
Yet foremost he into the plain descends,
Eager to bleed in battles not his own.

Such were the heroes of the antient world:
Contemners they of indolence and gain;
But still for love of glory, and of arms,
Prone to encounter peril, and to lift
Against each strong antagonist the spear.
I'll go and press the hero to my breast.

        [*Exit* RANDOLPH.

Manent Lady RANDOLPH *and* NORVAL

Lady RANDOLPH

The soldier's loftiness, the pride and pomp
Investing awful war, NORVAL, I see,
Transport thy youthful mind.

NORVAL

      Ah! should they not?
Bless'd be the hour I left my father's house!
I might have been a shepherd all my days,
And stole obscurely to a peasant's grave.
Now, if I live, with mighty chiefs I stand;
And, if I fall, with noble dust I lie.

Lady RANDOLPH

There is a gen'rous spirit in thy breast,
That could have well sustain'd a prouder fortune.
This way with me; under yon spreading beech,
Unseen, unheard, by human eye or ear,
I will amaze thee with a wond'rous tale.

NORVAL

Let there be danger, Lady, with the secret,
That I may hug it to my grateful heart,
And prove my faith. Command my sword, my life:
These are the sole possessions of poor NORVAL.

Lady RANDOLPH

Know'st thou these gems?

NORVAL

             Durst I believe mine eyes
I'd say I knew them, and they were my father's.

Lady RANDOLPH

Thy father's, say'st thou! ah! they were thy father's!

NORVAL

I saw them once, and curiously inquir'd
Of both my parents, whence such splendor came;
But I was check'd, and more could never learn.

Lady RANDOLPH

Then learn of me, thou art not NORVAL's son.

NORVAL

Not NORVAL's son!

Lady RANDOLPH

           Nor of a shepherd sprung.

NORVAL

Lady, who am I then?

Lady RANDOLPH

           Noble thou art;
For noble was thy Sire!

NORVAL

           I will believe—
O! tell me farther! Say who was my father?

Lady RANDOLPH

DOUGLAS!

NORVAL

Lord DOUGLAS, whom to day I saw?

Lady RANDOLPH

His younger brother.

NORVAL

           And in yonder camp?

Lady Randolph

Alas!

Norval

You make me tremble——Sighs and tears!
Lives my brave father?

Lady Randolph

    Ah! too brave indeed!
He fell in battle 'ere thyself was born.

Norval

Ah me unhappy! 'ere I saw the light?
But does my mother live? I may conclude,
From my own fate, her portion has been sorrow.

Lady Randolph

She lives; but wastes her life in constant woe,
Weeping her husband slain, her infant lost.

Norval

You that are skill'd so well in the sad story
Of my unhappy parents, and with tears
Bewail their destiny, now have compassion
Upon the offspring of the friends you lov'd!
O! tell me who, and where my mother is!
Oppress'd by a base world, perhaps she bends
Beneath the weight of other ills than grief;
And desolate, implores of heav'n the aid
Her son should give. It is, it must be so——
Your countenance confesses that she's wretched.
O! tell me her condition! Can the sword——
Who shall resist me in a parent's cause?

Lady Randolph

Thy virtue ends her woe.——My son, my son!
I am thy mother, and the wife of Douglas!

         [Falls upon his neck.

NORVAL

O heav'n and earth, how wondrous is my fate!
Art thou my mother? Ever let me kneel!

Lady RANDOLPH

Image of DOUGLAS! Fruit of fatal love!
All that I owe thy Sire, I pay to thee.

NORVAL

Respect and admiration still possess me,
Checking the love and fondness of a son.
Yet I was filial to my humble parents.
But did my Sire surpass the rest of men,
As thou excellest all of womankind?

Lady RANDOLPH

Arise, my son! In me thou dost behold
The poor remains of beauty once admir'd:
The autumn of my days is come already;
For sorrow made my summer haste away.
Yet in my prime I equal'd not thy father:
His eyes were like the eagle's, yet sometimes
Liker the dove's; and, as he pleas'd, he won
All hearts with softness, or with spirit aw'd.

NORVAL

How did he fall? Sure 'twas a bloody field
When DOUGLAS died. O I have much to ask!

Lady RANDOLPH

Hereafter thou shalt hear the lengthen'd tale
Of all thy father's and thy mother's woes.
At present this: thou art the rightful heir
Of yonder castle, and the wide domains
Which now Lord RANDOLPH, as my husband, holds.
But thou shalt not be wrong'd; I have the power
To right thee still: before the King I'll kneel,
And call Lord DOUGLAS to protect his blood.

NORVAL

The blood of DOUGLAS will protect itself.

Lady RANDOLPH

But we shall need both friends and favour, boy,
To wrest thy lands and lordship from the gripe
Of RANDOLPH and his kinsman. Yet I think
My tale will move each gentle heart to pity,
My life incline the virtuous to believe.

NORVAL

To be the son of DOUGLAS is to me
Inheritance enough. Declare my birth,
And in the field I'll seek for fame and fortune.

Lady RANDOLPH

Thou dost not know what perils and injustice
Await the poor man's valour. O! my son!
The noblest blood in all the land's abash'd,
Having no lacquey but pale poverty.
Too long hast thou been thus attended, DOUGLAS!
Too long hast thou been deem'd a peasant's child.
The wanton heir of some inglorious chief
Perhaps has scorn'd thee in the youthful sports,
Whilst thy indignant spirit swell'd in vain!
Such contumely thou no more shalt bear;
But how I purpose to redress thy wrongs
Must be hereafter told. Prudence directs
That we should part before yon chiefs return.
Retire, and from thy rustic follower's hand
Receive a billet, which thy mother's care,
Anxious to see thee, dictated before
This casual opportunity arose
Of private conference. Its purport mark;
For as I there appoint we meet again.
Leave me, my son! and frame thy manners still
To NORVAL's, not to noble DOUGLAS' state.

NORVAL

I will remember. Where is NORVAL now?
That good old man.

Lady RANDOLPH

                    At hand conceal'd he lies,
An useful witness. But beware, my son,
Of yon GLENALVON; in his guilty breast
Resides a villain's shrewdness, ever prone
To false conjecture. He hath griev'd my heart.

NORVAL

Has he indeed? Then let yon false GLENALVON
Beware of me.   [*Exit* DOUGLAS.

Manet Lady RANDOLPH

                    There burst the smother'd flame!
O! thou all righteous and eternal King!
Who father of the fatherless art call'd,
Protect my son!——Thy inspiration, Lord!
Hath fill'd his bosom with that sacred fire,
Which in the breasts of his forefathers burn'd:
Set him on high like them, that he may shine
The star and glory of his native land!
Then let the minister of death descend,
And bear my willing spirit to its place.
Yonder they come. How do bad women find
Unchanging aspects to conceal their guilt?
When I, by reason, and by justice urg'd,
Full hardly can dissemble with these men
In nature's pious cause.

Enter Lord RANDOLPH *and* GLENALVON

Lord RANDOLPH

                    Yon gallant chief,
Of arms enamour'd, all repose disclaims.

Lady RANDOLPH

Be not, my Lord, by his example sway'd:

Arrange the business of to-morrow now,
And, when you enter, speak of war no more.

                    [*Exit* Lady RANDOLPH.

Manent Lord RANDOLPH *and* GLENALVON

Lord RANDOLPH

'Tis so, by heav'n! her mien, her voice, her eye,
And her impatience to be gone, confirm it.

GLENALVON

He parted from her now: behind the mount,
Amongst the trees, I saw him glide along.

Lord RANDOLPH

For sad, sequester'd virtue she's renown'd!

GLENALVON

Most true, my Lord.

Lord RANDOLPH

                 Yet this distinguish'd Dame
Invites a youth, the acquaintance of a day,
Alone to meet her at the midnight hour.
This assignation, [*shews a letter*] the assassin freed,
Her manifest affection for the youth,
Might breed suspicion in a husband's brain,
Whose gentle consort all for love had wedded;
Much more in mine. MATILDA never lov'd me.
Let no man, after me, a woman wed,
Whose heart he knows he has not; tho' she brings
A mine of gold, a kingdom for her dowry,
For let her seem, like the night's shadowy queen,
Cold and contemplative;—He cannot trust her:
She may, she will, bring shame and sorrow on him;
The worst of sorrows, and the worst of shames!

GLENALVON

Yield not, my Lord, to such afflicting thoughts;
But let the spirit of an husband sleep,

Till your own senses make a sure conclusion.
This billet must to blooming NORVAL go:
At the next turn awaits my trusty spy;
I'll give it him refitted for his master.
In the close thicket take your secret stand;
The moon shines bright, and your own eyes may judge
Of their behaviour.

Lord RANDOLPH

Thou dost counsel well.

GLENALVON

Permit me now to make one slight essay.
Of all the trophies which vain mortals boast,
By wit, by valour, or by wisdom won,
The first and fairest, in a young man's eye,
Is woman's captive heart. Successful love
With glorious fumes intoxicates the mind;
And the proud conqueror in triumph moves
Air-born, exalted above vulgar men.

Lord RANDOLPH

And what avails this maxim?

GLENALVON

Much, my Lord!
Withdraw a little: I'll accost young NORVAL,
And with ironical derisive counsel
Explore his spirit. If he is no more
Than humble NORVAL, by thy favour rais'd,
Brave as he is, he'll shrink astonish'd from me:
But if he be the fav'rite of the fair,
Lov'd by the first of Caledonia's dames,
He'll turn upon me, as the lion turns
Upon the hunter's spear.

Lord RANDOLPH

'Tis shrewdly thought.

GLENALVON

When we grow loud, draw near. But let my Lord
His rising wrath restrain.   [*Exit* RANDOLPH.

Manet GLENALVON

                              'Tis strange, by heav'n!
That she should run full tilt her fond career,
To one so little known. She too that seem'd
Pure as the winter stream, when ice emboss'd
Whitens its course. Even I did think her chaste,
Whose charity exceeds not. Precious sex,
Whose deeds lascivious pass GLENALVON's thoughts!
                                        NORVAL *appears.*

His port I love; he's in a proper mood
To chide the thunder, if at him it roar'd.
Has NORVAL seen the troops?

NORVAL

                              The setting sun,
With yellow radiance lighten'd all the vale,
And as the warriors mov'd, each polish'd helm,
Corslet, or spear, glanc'd back his gilded beams.
The hill they climb'd, and halting at its top,
Of more than mortal size, tow'ring, they seem'd,
An host angelic, clad in burning arms.

GLENALVON

Thou talk'st it well; no leader of our host,
In sounds more lofty, speaks of glorious war.

NORVAL

If I shall e'er acquire a leader's name,
My speech will be less ardent. Novelty
Now prompts my tongue, and youthful admiration
Vents itself freely; since no part is mine
Of praise pertaining to the great in arms.

GLENALVON

You wrong yourself, brave Sir; your martial deeds

Have rank'd you with the great: but mark me NORVAL;
Lord RANDOLPH's favour now exalts your youth
Above his veterans of famous service.
Let me, who know these soldiers, counsel you.
Give them all honour; seem not to command:
Else they will scarcely brook your late sprung power,
Which nor alliance props, nor birth adorns.

NORVAL

Sir, I have been accustom'd all my days
To hear and speak the plain and simple truth:
And tho' I have been told, that there are men
Who borrow friendship's tongue to speak their scorn,
Yet in such language I am little skill'd.
Therefore I thank GLENALVON for his counsel,
Altho' it sounded harshly. Why remind
Me of my birth obscure? Why slur my power
With such contemptuous terms?

GLENALVON

                    I did not mean
To gall your pride, which now I see is great.

NORVAL

My pride!

GLENALVON

          Suppress it as you wish to prosper.
Your pride's excessive. Yet for RANDOLPH's sake
I will not leave you to its rash direction.
If thus you swell, and frown at high-born men,
Will high-born men endure a shepherd's scorn?

NORVAL

A shepherd's scorn!

GLENALVON

               Yes, if you presume
To bend on soldiers these disdainful eyes,
As if you took the measure of their minds,

And said in secret, you're no match for me;
What will become of you?

NORVAL

               If this were told——   [*Aside*.
Hast thou no fears for thy presumptuous self?

GLENALVON

Ha! Dost thou threaten me?

NORVAL

                Didst thou not hear?

GLENALVON

Unwillingly I did; a nobler foe
Had not been question'd thus. But such as thee——

NORVAL

Whom dost thou think me?

GLENALVON
Norval.

NORVAL

                 So I am——
And who is NORVAL in GLENALVON's eyes?

GLENALVON

A peasant's son, a wand'ring beggar-boy;
At best no more, even if he speaks the truth.

NORVAL

False as thou art, dost thou suspect my truth?

GLENALVON

Thy truth! thou'rt all a lie; and false as hell
Is the vain-glorious tale thou told'st to RANDOLPH.

NORVAL

If I were chain'd, unarm'd, and bedrid old,
Perhaps I should revile: But as I am
I have no tongue to rail. The humble NORVAL

Is of a race who strive not but with deeds.
Did I not fear to freeze thy shallow valour,
And make thee sink too soon beneath my sword,
I'd tell thee—what thou art. I know thee well.

GLENALVON

Dost thou not know GLENALVON, born to command
Ten thousand slaves like thee?

NORVAL

               Villain, no more:
Draw and defend thy life. I did design
To have defy'd thee in another cause:
But heaven accelerates its vengeance on thee.
Now for my own and Lady RANDOLPH's wrongs.

Enter Lord RANDOLPH

Lord RANDOLPH

Hold, I command you both. The man that stirs
Makes me his foe.

NORVAL

           Another voice than thine
That threat had vainly sounded, noble RANDOLPH.

GLENALVON

Hear him, my Lord; he's wondrous condescending!
Mark the humility of shepherd NORVAL!

NORVAL

Now you may scoff in safety.   [*Sheaths his sword.*

Lord RANDOLPH

              Speak not thus,
Taunting each other; but unfold to me
The cause of quarrel, then I judge betwixt you.

NORVAL

Nay, my good Lord, tho' I revere you much,
My cause I plead not, nor demand your judgment.

I blush to speak; I will not, cannot speak
Th' opprobrious words that I from him have borne.
To the liege-lord of my dear native land
I owe a subject's homage; but even him
And his high arbitration I'd reject.
Within my bosom reigns another lord;
Honour, sole judge and umpire of itself.
If my free speech offend you, noble RANDOLPH,
Revoke your favours, and let NORVAL go
Hence as he came, alone, but not dishonour'd.

Lord RANDOLPH

Thus far I'll mediate with impartial voice:
The antient foe of Caledonia's land
Now waves his banners o'er her frighted fields.
Suspend your purpose, till your country's arms
Repel the bold invader; then decide
The private quarrel.

GLENALVON

I agree to this.

NORVAL

And I.

Enter SERVANT

SERVANT

The banquet waits.

Lord RANDOLPH

We come.

[*Exit* RANDOLPH.

GLENALVON

NORVAL,
Let not our variance mar the social hour,
Nor wrong the hospitality of RANDOLPH.
Nor frowning anger, nor yet wrinkl'd hate,

Shall stain my countenance. Smooth thou thy brow;
Nor let our strife disturb the gentle Dame.

NORVAL

Think not so lightly, Sir, of my resentment;
When we contend again, our strife is mortal.

The End of the FOURTH ACT

ACT V

The Wood

Enter DOUGLAS

This is the place, the centre of the grove.
Here stands the oak, the monarch of the wood.
How sweet and solemn is this mid-night scene!
The silver moon, unclouded, holds her way
Thro' skies where I could count each little star.
The fanning west wind scarcely stirs the leaves;
The river, rushing o'er its pebbled bed,
Imposes silence with a stilly sound.
In such a place as this, at such an hour,
If ancestry can be in ought believ'd,
Descending spirits have convers'd with man,
And told the secrets of the world unknown.

Enter Old NORVAL

NORVAL

'Tis he. But what if he should chide me hence?
His just reproach I fear.　　　[DOUGLAS *turns and sees him.*
　　　　　　Forgive, forgive,
Canst thou forgive the man, the selfish man,
Who bred Sir MALCOLM's heir a shepherd's son?

DOUGLAS

Kneel not to me: thou art my father still:
Thy wish'd-for presence now compleats my joy.
Welcome to me, my fortunes thou shalt share,
And ever honour'd with thy DOUGLAS live.

Old NORVAL

And dost thou call me father? O my son!
I think that I could die to make amends
For the great wrong I did thee. 'Twas my crime
Which in the wilderness so long conceal'd
The blossom of thy youth.

DOUGLAS

               Not worse the fruit,
That in the wilderness the blossom blow'd.
Amongst the shepherds, in the humble cote,
I learn'd some lessons, which I'll not forget
When I inhabit yonder lofty towers.
I, who was once a swain, will ever prove
The poor man's friend; and, when my vassals bow,
NORVAL shall smooth the crested pride of DOUGLAS.

NORVAL

Let me but live to see thine exaltation!
Yet grievous are my fears. O leave this place,
And those unfriendly towers.

DOUGLAS

               Why should I leave them?

NORVAL

Lord RANDOLPH and his kinsman seek your life.

DOUGLAS

How know'st thou that?

NORVAL

             I will inform you how.
When evening came, I left the secret place

Appointed for me by your mother's care,
And fondly trod in each accustom'd path
That to the castle leads. Whilst thus I rang'd,
I was alarm'd with unexpected sounds
Of earnest voices. On the persons came;
Unseen I lurk'd, and overheard them name
Each other as they talk'd, Lord RANDOLPH this,
And that GLENALVON: still of you they spoke,
And of the Lady: threat'ning was their speech,
Tho' but imperfectly my ear could hear it.
'Twas strange, they said, a wonderful discov'ry;
And ever and anon they vow'd revenge.

DOUGLAS

Revenge! for what?

NORVAL

     For being what you are;
Sir MALCOLM's heir: how else have you offended?
When they were gone, I hied me to my cottage,
And there sat musing how I best might find
Means to inform you of their wicked purpose.
But I could think of none: at last perplex'd
I issued forth, encompassing the tower
With many a weary step and wishful look.
Now Providence hath brought you to my sight,
Let not your too couragious spirit scorn
The caution which I give.

DOUGLAS

     I scorn it not.
My mother warn'd me of GLENALVON's baseness:
But I will not suspect the noble RANDOLPH.
In our encounter with the vile assassins,
I mark'd his brave demeanor: him I'll trust.

NORVAL

I fear you will too far.

DOUGLAS

Here in this place
I wait my mother's coming: she shall know
What thou hast told: her counsel I will follow:
And cautious ever are a mother's counsels.
You must depart; your presence may prevent
Our interview.

NORVAL

My blessing rest upon thee!
O may heav'n's hand, which sav'd thee from the wave,
And from the sword of foes, be near thee still;
Turning mischance, if ought hangs o'er thy head,
All upon mine!   [*Exit* Old NORVAL.

DOUGLAS

He loves me like a parent;
And must not, shall not lose the son he loves,
Altho' his son has found a nobler father.
Eventful day! how hast thou chang'd my state!
Once on the cold, and winter shaded side
Of a bleak hill, mischance had rooted me,
Never to thrive, child of another soil:
Transplanted now to the gay sunny vale,
Like the green thorn of May my fortune flowers.
Ye glorious stars! high heav'n's resplendent host!
To whom I oft have of my lot complain'd,
Hear and record my soul's unalter'd wish!
Dead or alive, let me but be renown'd!
May heav'n inspire some fierce gigantic Dane,
To give a bold defiance to our host!
Before he speaks it out I will accept;
Like DOUGLAS conquer, or like DOUGLAS die.

Enter Lady RANDOLPH

Lady RANDOLPH

My son! I heard a voice——

DOUGLAS

　　　　　　——The voice was mine.

Lady RANDOLPH

Didst thou complain aloud to nature's ear,
That thus in dusky shades, at mid-night hours,
By stealth the mother and the son should meet?

　　　　　　　　　　　　[*Embracing him.*

DOUGLAS

No; on this happy day, this better birth-day,
My thoughts and words are all of hope and joy.

Lady RANDOLPH

Sad fear and melancholy still divide
The empire of my breast with hope and joy.
Now hear what I advise.

DOUGLAS

　　　　　First, let me tell
What may the tenor of your counsel change.

Lady RANDOLPH

My heart forebodes some evil!

DOUGLAS

　　　　　　　'Tis not good.——
At eve, unseen by RANDOLPH and GLENALVON,
The good old NORVAL in the grove o'erheard
Their conversation: oft they mention'd me
With dreadful threatnings; you they sometimes nam'd.
'Twas strange, they said, a wonderful discov'ry;
And ever and anon they vow'd revenge.

Lady RANDOLPH

Defend us gracious God! we are betray'd:
They have found out the secret of thy birth;
It must be so. That is the great discovery.

Sir MALCOLM's heir is come to claim his own;
And he will be reveng'd. Perhaps even now,
Arm'd and prepar'd for murder, they but wait
A darker and more silent hour, to break
Into the chamber where they think thou sleep'st.
This moment, this, heav'n hath ordain'd to save thee!
Fly to the camp, my son!

DOUGLAS

         And leave you here?
No: to the castle let us go together,
Call up the antient servants of your house,
Who in their youth did eat your father's bread.
Then tell them loudly that I am your son.
If in the breasts of men one spark remains
Of sacred love, fidelity, or pity,
Some in your cause will arm. I ask but few
To drive those spoilers from my father's house.

Lady RANDOLPH

O Nature, Nature! what can check thy force?
Thou genuine offspring of the daring DOUGLAS!
But rush not on destruction: save thyself,
And I am safe. To me they mean no harm.
Thy stay but risks thy precious life in vain.
That winding path conducts thee to the river.
Cross where thou seest a broad and beaten way,
Which running eastward leads thee to the camp.
Instant demand admittance to Lord DOUGLAS.
Shew him these jewels, which his brother wore.
Thy look, thy voice, will make him feel the truth,
Which I by certain proof will soon confirm.

DOUGLAS

I yield me and obey: but yet my heart
Bleeds at this parting. Something bids me stay
And guard a mother's life. Oft have I read
Of wondrous deeds by one bold arm atchiev'd.

Our foes are two: no more: let me go forth,
And see if any shield can guard GLENALVON.

Lady RANDOLPH

If thou regard'st thy mother, or rever'st
Thy father's mem'ry, think of this no more.
One thing I have to say before we part;
Long wert thou lost; and thou art found, my child,
In a most fearful season. War and battle
I have great cause to dread. Too well I see
Which way the current of thy temper sets:
To-day I've found thee. Oh! my long lost hope!
If thou to giddy valour giv'st the rein,
To-morrow I may lose my son for ever.
The love of thee, before thou saw'st the light,
Sustain'd my life when thy brave father fell.
If thou shalt fall, I have nor love nor hope
In this waste world! My son, remember me!

DOUGLAS

What shall I say? how can I give you comfort?
The God of battles of my life dispose
As may be best for you! for whose dear sake
I will not bear myself as I resolv'd.
But yet consider, as no vulgar name
That which I boast sounds amongst martial men.
How will inglorious caution suit my claim?
The post of fate unshrinking I maintain.
My country's foes must witness who I am.
On the invaders heads I'll prove my birth,
'Till friends and foes confess the genuine strain.
If in this strife I fall, blame not your son,
Who if he lives not honour'd, must not live.

Lady RANDOLPH

I will not utter what my bosom feels.
Too well I love that valour which I warn.
Farewel, my son! my counsels are but vain,   [Embracing.
And as high heav'n hath will'd it all must be.   [Separate.

Lady RANDOLPH

Gaze not on me, thou wilt mistake the path;
I'll point it out again.

> [*Just as they are separating, enter from the wood
> Lord* RANDOLPH *and* GLENALVON.]

Lord RANDOLPH

Not in her presence.

Now——

GLENALVON

I'm prepar'd.

Lord RANDOLPH

No: I command thee stay.
I go alone: it never shall be said
That I took odds to combat mortal man.
The noblest vengeance is the most compleat.

> [*Exit* Lord RANDOLPH.

> [GLENALVON *makes some steps to the same side of the
> stage, listens and speaks.*]

GLENALVON

Demons of death come settle on my sword,
And to a double slaughter guide it home!
The lover and the husband both must die.

> [Lord RANDOLPH *behind the scenes.*]

Lord RANDOLPH

Draw, villain! draw.

DOUGLAS

Assail me not, Lord RANDOLPH;
Not as thou lov'st thyself.

> [*Clashing of swords.*]

GLENALVON, *running out*

Now is the time.

Enter Lady RANDOLPH *at the opposite side of the stage, faint and breathless*

Lady RANDOLPH

Lord RANDOLPH, hear me; all shall be thine own:
But spare! Oh spare my son!

Enter DOUGLAS *with a sword in each hand*

My mother's voice!
I can protect thee still.

Lady RANDOLPH

He lives, he lives:
For this, for this to heaven eternal praise!
But sure I saw thee fall.

DOUGLAS

It was GLENALVON.
Just as my arm had master'd RANDOLPH's sword,
The villain came behind me; but I slew him.

Lady RANDOLPH

Behind thee! Ah; thou'rt wounded! O my child,
How pale thou look'st! and shall I lose thee now?

DOUGLAS

Do not despair: I feel a little faintness;
I hope it will not last.   [*Leans upon his sword.*]

Lady RANDOLPH

There is no hope!
And we must part! the hand of death is on thee!
O my beloved child! O DOUGLAS, DOUGLAS!

DOUGLAS

Too soon we part; I have not long been DOUGLAS.
O destiny! hardly thou deal'st with me:
Clouded and hid, a stranger to myself,
In low and poor obscurity I liv'd.

Lady RANDOLPH

Has heav'n preserv'd thee for an end like this?

DOUGLAS

O had I fallen as my brave fathers fell,
Turning with great effort the tide of battle!
Like them I should have smil'd and welcom'd death.
But thus to perish by a villain's hand!
Cut off from nature's and from glory's course,
Which never mortal was so fond to run.

Lady RANDOLPH

Hear justice! hear! stretch thy avenging arm.

[DOUGLAS *falls.*]

DOUGLAS

Unknown I die; no tongue shall speak of me.——
Some noble spirits, judging by themselves,
May yet conjecture what I might have prov'd,
And think life only wanting to my fame:
But who shall comfort thee?

Lady RANDOLPH

Despair! despair!

DOUGLAS

O had it pleas'd high heaven to let me live
A little while!——my eyes that gaze on thee
Grow dim apace! my mother——O! my mother.   [*Dies.*]

Enter Lord RANDOLPH *and* ANNA

Lord RANDOLPH

Thy words, the words of truth, have pierc'd my heart.
I am the stain of knighthood and of arms.
Oh! if my brave deliverer survives
The traitor's sword——

ANNA

Alas! look there, my Lord.

Lord RANDOLPH

The mother and her son! How curst I am!
Was I the cause? No: I was not the cause.
Yon matchless villain did seduce my soul
To frantic jealousy.

ANNA

My Lady lives:
The agony of grief hath but supprest
A while her powers.

Lord RANDOLPH

But my deliverer's dead!
The world did once esteem Lord RANDOLPH well.
Sincere of heart, for spotless honour fam'd:
And, in my early days, glory I gain'd
Beneath the holy banner of the cross.
Now past the noon of life, shame comes upon me;
Reproach, and infamy, and public hate,
Are near at hand: for all mankind will think
That RANDOLPH basely stab'd Sir MALCOLM's heir.

                [Lady RANDOLPH *recovering*.

Lady RANDOLPH

Where am I now? still in this wretched world!
Grief cannot break a heart so hard as mine.
My youth was worn in anguish: but youth's strength,
With hope's assistance, bore the brunt of sorrow;
And train'd me on to be the object now,
On which Omnipotence displays itself,
Making a spectacle, a tale of me,
To awe its vassal, man.

Lord RANDOLPH

O misery!
Amidst thy raging grief I must proclaim
My innocence.

Lady RANDOLPH

Thy innocence!

Lord RANDOLPH

My guilt
Is innocence compar'd with what thou think'st it.

Lady RANDOLPH

Of thee I think not: what have I to do
With thee or any thing? My son! my son!
My beautiful! my brave! how proud was I
Of thee, and of thy valour! My fond heart
O'erflowed this day with transport, when I thought
Of growing old amidst a race of thine,
Who might make up to me their father's childhood,
And bear my brother's and my husband's name:
Now all my hopes are dead! A little while
Was I a wife! a mother not so long!
What am I now?——I know.——But I shall be
That only whilst I please; for such a son
And such a husband make a woman bold.   [*Runs out.*

Lord RANDOLPH

Follow her, ANNA: I myself would follow,
But in this rage she must abhor my presence.   *Exit* ANNA.

Enter Old NORVAL

NORVAL

I hear the voice of woe; heaven guard my child!

Lord RANDOLPH

Already is the idle gaping crowd,
The spiteful vulgar, come to gaze on RANDOLPH.
Begone.

NORVAL

I fear thee not. I will not go.
Here I'll remain. I'm an accomplice, Lord,
With thee in murder. Yes, my sins did help
To crush down to the ground this lovely plant.
O noblest youth that ever yet was born!

Sweetest and best, gentlest and bravest spirit,
That ever bless'd the world! Wretch that I am,
Who saw that noble spirit swell and rise
Above the narrow limits that confin'd it,
Yet never was by all thy virtues won
To do thee justice, and reveal the secret,
Which timely known, had rais'd thee far above
The villain's snare! Oh! I am punish'd now!
These are the hairs that should have strew'd the ground,
And not the locks of DOUGLAS.

    [*Tears his hair, and throws himself upon the body of*
        DOUGLAS.

Lord RANDOLPH

I know thee now: thy boldness I forgive;
My crest is fallen. For thee I will appoint
A place of rest, if grief will let thee rest.
I will reward, altho' I cannot punish.
Curst, curst GLENALVON, he escap'd too well,
Tho' slain and baffled by the hand he hated.
Foaming with rage and fury to the last,
Cursing his conqueror, the felon dy'd.

Enter ANNA

ANNA

My Lord, my Lord!

Lord RANDOLPH

    Speak: I can hear of horror.

ANNA

Horror indeed!

Lord RANDOLPH

    MATILDA?

ANNA

    Is no more;
She ran, she flew like light'ning up the hill,

Nor halted till the precipice she gain'd,
Beneath whose low'ring top the river falls
Ingulph'd in rifted rocks: thither she came,
As fearless as the eagle lights upon it,
And headlong down——

Lord RANDOLPH

                    'Twas I! alas! 'twas I
That fill'd her breast with fury; drove her down
The precipice of death! Wretch that I am!

ANNA

O had you seen her last despairing look!
Upon the brink she stood, and cast her eyes
Down on the deep: then lifting up her head
And her white hands to heaven, seeming to say,
Why am I forc'd to this? she plung'd herself
Into the empty air.

Lord RANDOLPH

                    I will not vent,
In vain complaints, the passion of my soul.
Peace in this world I never can enjoy.
These wounds the gratitude of RANDOLPH gave.
They speak aloud, and with the voice of fate
Denounce my doom. I am resolv'd. I'll go
Straight to the battle, where the man that makes
Me turn aside must threaten worse than death.
Thou, faithful to thy mistress, take this ring,
Full warrant of my power. Let every rite
With cost and pomp upon their funerals wait:
For RANDOLPH hopes he never shall return.

FINIS

EPILOGUE

AN Epilogue I ask'd; but not one word
Our bard will write. He vows, 'tis most absurd
With comic wit to contradict the strain
Of tragedy, and make your sorrows vain.
Sadly he says, that pity is the best,
The noblest passion of the human breast:
For when its sacred streams the heart o'erflow,
In gushes pleasure with the tide of woe;
And when its waves retire, like those of Nile,
They leave behind them such a golden soil,
That there the virtues without culture grow,
There the sweet blossoms of affection blow.
These were his words:—void of delusive art
I felt them; for he spoke them from his heart.
Nor will I now attempt, with witty folly,
To chase away celestial melancholy.

THE

IRON CHEST:

A PLAY;

IN THREE ACTS.

WRITTEN BY

GEORGE COLMAN,

THE YOUNGER.

FIRST REPRESENTED AT THE THEATRE ROYAL DRURY-
LANE, ON SATURDAY, 12TH MARCH, 1796.

THE THIRD EDITION.

LONDON:
PRINTED BY T. WOODFALL,
FOR MESSRS. CADELL AND DAVIES,
IN THE STRAND.

1798.

DRAMATIS PERSONÆ

Sir Edward Mortimer,	*Mr. Kemble*
Fitzharding,	*Mr. Wroughton*
Wilford,	*Mr. Bannister jun.*
Adam Winterton,	*Mr. Dodd*
Rawbold,	*Mr. Barrymore*
Samson,	*Mr. Suett*
Boy,	*Master Welsh*
Cook,	*Mr. Hollingsworth*
Peter,	*Mr. Banks*
Walter,	*Mr. Maddocks*
Simon,	*Mr. Webb*
Gregory,	*Mr. Trueman*
Armstrong,	*Mr. Kelly*
Orson,	*Mr. R. Palmer*
1st Robber,	*Mr. Dignum*
2d Robber,	*Mr. Sedgwick*
3d Robber,	*Mr. Bannister*
Robber's Boy,	*Master Webb*
Helen,	*Miss Farren*
Blanch,	*Mrs. Gibbs*
Dame Rawbold,	*Miss Tidswell*
Barbara,	*Signora Storace*
Judith,	*Miss De Camp*

SCENE, *in the New Forest, in Hampshire, and on its Borders*

THE IRON CHEST;

A PLAY,

IN THREE ACTS

ACT I. SCENE I

The inside of RAWBOLD'S COTTAGE. *Several children, squalid and beggarly, discovered in different parts of the room : some asleep.* DAME RAWBOLD *seated, leaning over the embers of the fire.* BARBARA *seated near her.* SAMSON *standing in the front of the stage. A narrow stair-case in the back scene. A taper burning. The whole scene exhibits poverty and wretchedness.* ·

GLEE

SAMSON

Five times, by the taper's light,
    The hour-glass I have turn'd to night.
First Boy. Where's father ?
Samson.   He's gone out to roam:
        If he have luck,
        He'll bring a buck,
    Upon his lusty shoulders, home.

The different voices

    Home! home!
    He comes not home!
    Hark! from the woodland vale below,
    The distant clock sounds, dull, and slow!
        Bome! bome! bome!

Sam. Five o'clock, and father not yet returned from New Forest! An he come not shortly, the Sun will rise, and roast

the venison on his shoulders.—Sister Barbara!—Well, your
rich men have no bowels for us lowly! they little think,
while they are gorging on the fat haunch of a goodly buck,
what fatigues we poor honest souls undergo in stealing it.—
Why, sister Barbara!

Barb. I am here, brother Sampson.   (*getting up*)

Sam. Here!—marry, out upon you for an idle baggage!
why, you crawl like a snail.

Barb. I prithee, now, do not chide me, Samson!

Sam. 'Tis my humour. I am father's head man in his
poaching. The rubs I take from him, who is above me, I
hand down to you, who are below me. 'Tis the way of office
—where every miserable devil domineers it over the next
more miserable devil that's under him. You may scold sister
Margery, an you will—she's your younger by a twelvemonth.

Barb. Truly, brother, I would not make any one unhappy, for the world. I am content to do what I can to
please, and to mind the house.

Sam. Truly, a weighty matter! Thou art e'en ready to hang
thyself, for want of something to while away time. What hast
thou much more to do than to trim the faggots, nurse thy
mother, boil the pot, patch our jackets, kill the poultry,
cure the hogs, feed the pigs, and comb the children?

Barb. Many might think that no small charge, Samson.

Sam. A mere nothing.—While father and I (bate us but
the mother and children) have the credit of purloining every
single thing that you have the care of. We are up early, and
down late, in the exercise of our industry.

Barb. I wish father, and you, would give up the calling.

Sam. No—there is one keen argument to prevent us.

Bar. What's that, brother?

Sam. Hunger. Wouldst have us be rogues, and let our
family starve? Give up poaching and deer-stealing! Oons!
dost think we have no conscience? Yonder sits mother, poor
soul—old, helpless, and crazy.

Barb. Alas! brother, 'tis heart-aching to look upon her.
This very time three years she got her maim. It was a piteous
tempest!

Sam. Aye—'twas rough weather.

Barb. I never pass the old oak, that was shivered that night, in the storm, but I am ready to weep. It remembers me of the time when all our poor family went to ruin.

Sam. Pish—no matter: The cottage was blown down—the barn fired—father undone—Well, landlords are flinty hearted —no help! what then? We live, don't we? (*sullenly*)

Barb. Troth, brother, very sadly. Father has grown desperate; all is fallen to decay. We live by pilfering on the Forest—and our poor mother distracted, and unable to look to the house. The rafter, which fell in the storm, struck so heavy upon her brain, I fear me 'twill never again be settled.

Moth. Children! Barbara! where's my eldest daughter? She is my darling.

Barb. I am here, mother.

Sam. Peace, fool! you know she's doating.

Moth. Look to the cattle, Barbara! We must to market to morrow. My husband's a rich man. We thrive! we thrive! Ha, ha, ha!—oh!

Barb. Oh brother! I cannot bear to see her thus— though, alas! we have long been used to it. The little ones too—scarce cloath'd—hungry—almost starving!—Indeed, we are a very wretched family.

Sam. Hark! Methought I heard a tread.—Hist! be wary. We must not open in haste, for fear of surprises.

(*A knock at the Cottage door.*)

DUET

Samson. Who knocks at this dead hour?

Rawbold (*without*).   A friend.

Samson. How should we know,
          A friend from foe?
      A signal you must give.

Rawbold (*without.*)   Attend.

(RAWBOLD *gives three knocks, which* SAMSON *counts, singing at intervals.*)

Samson. ——One, two, three!

         'Tis he.

        Give me the word we fixt to night.

           'Tis Roebuck (*in a whisper to Barbara*)

Rawbold (*without.*) Roebuck.

Samson.   That is right,

     Enter now by candle-light.

Rawbold. Open now by candle light.

    SAMSON *opens the door, and* RAWBOLD *enters*

Raw. Bar the door. So, softly.

Sam. What success, father?

Raw. Good: my limbs ache for't.

Moth. O brave husband! Welcome from the court. Thou shalt be made a knight; and I a lady. Ha! ha!

Raw. Rest, rest, poor soul!—How you stand! (*to* SAMSON) The chair, you gander!

Sam. (*to* Barbara) Why how you stand! the chair, you gander!   (*They bring* RAWBOLD *a chair: he sits.*)

Raw. Here—take my gun—'tis unscrewed. The keepers are abroad. I had scarce time to get it in my pocket.

   (*He pulls the gun from a pocket under his coat, in three pieces, which* SAMSON *screws together, while they are talking.*)

Fie! 'tis sharp work! Barbara, you jade, come hither.

Sam. Barbara, you jade, come hither.

Raw. Who bid thee chide her, lout! Kiss thy old father, wench. Kiss me, I say.—So—why dost tremble? I am rough as a tempest. Evil fortune has blown my lowring nature into turbulence; but thou art a blossom that dost bend thy head so sweetly under my gusts of passion, 'tis pity they should e'er harm thee.

Barb. Indeed, father, I am glad to see you safe returned.

Raw. I believe thee. Take the keys. Go to the locker, in the loft, and bring me a glass to recruit me.

                        (BARBARA *goes out.*

Sam. Well, father, and so——

Raw. Peace.—I ha' shot a buck.

Sam. O rare! Of all the sure aims, on the borders of the New Forest, here, give me old Gilbert Rawbold; though I, who am his son, say it, that should not say it.—Where have you stow'd him, father?

Raw. Under the furze, behind the hovel. Come night again, we will draw him in, boy. I have been watch'd.

Sam. Watch'd! O, the pestilence! our trade will be spoiled if the Groom Keepers be after us. The law will persecute us, father.

Raw. Do'st know Mortimer?

Sam. What, Sir Edward Mortimer? Aye, sure. He is head Keeper of the forest. 'Tis he who has shut himself up in melancholy. Sees no rich, and does so much good to the poor.

Raw. He has done me naught but evil. A gun cannot be carried on the border, here, but he has scent on't, at a league's distance. He is a thorn to me. His scouts this night were after me—all on the watch. I'll be revenged—I'll—So, the brandy.—*Enter* BARBARA, *with the Liquor.*

Raw. (*after drinking*) 'Tis right, i' faith!

Sam. That 'tis I'll be sworn; for I smuggled it myself. We do not live so near the coast for nothing.

Raw. Sir Edward Mortimer, look to it!

Barb. Sir Edward Mortimer! O, dear father, what of him?

Raw. Aye, now thou art all agog! Thou would'st hear somewhat of that smooth-tongued fellow, his secretary—his clerk, Wilford; whom thou so often meet'st in the forest. I have news on't. Look how you walk thither again. What, thou wouldst betray me to him, I warrant;—conspire against your father.

Sam. Aye! conspire against your father—and your tender loving brother, you viper, you!

Barb. Beshrew me, father, I meant no harm: and, indeed, indeed, Wilford is as handsome a—I mean as good a youth as ever breathed. If I thought he meant ill by you, I should hate him.

Raw. When didst see him last?—Speak!

Barb. You terrify me so, father, I am scarce able to

speak. Yesternoon, by the copse: 'Twas but to read with him
the book of sonnets, he gave me.

Sam. That's the way your sly, grave rogues, work into
the hearts of the females. I never knew any good come of
a girl's reading sonnets, with a learned clerk, under a
copse.

Raw. Let me hear no more of your meetings. I am content to think you would not plot my undoing.

Barb. I?—O father!

Raw. But he may plot yours. Mark me—Fortune has
thrust me forth to prowl, like the wolf;—but the wolf is
anxious for its young. I am an outcast whom hunger has
hardened. I violate the law; but feeling is not dead within
me: and, callous villain as I am accounted, I would tear that
greater villain piecemeal, who would violate my child, and
rob an old man of the little remains of comfort wretchedness
has left him.

(*A knocking at the door. A voice without.* Hilliho! ho!)

Raw. How now!

Sam. There! an they be not after us already. I'll—We
have talk'd, too, 'till 'tis broad day light.

Wilford (*without*). Open, good master Rawbold; I would
speak to you suddenly.

Barb. O heaven! 'tis the voice of Wilford himself.

Raw. Wilford! I'm glad on't—Now he shall—I'm glad
on't. Open the door: Quickly, I say—He shall smart for it.

Sam. Are you mad, father? 'Tis we shall smart for it.
Let in the keeper's head man! The hind quarter of a buck
has hung these fourteen days, in the pantry.

Raw. Open, I say.

Sam. O Lord! I defy any secretary's nose not to smell
stolen venison the moment 'tis thrust into our hovel.

SAMSON *opens the door. Enter* WILFORD

Wilf. Save you, good people! You are Gilbert Rawbold,
as I take it.

Raw. I am. Your message here, young man, bodes me no

good: but I *am* Gilbert Rawbold—and here's my daughter. Do'st know her?

Wilf. Ah, Barbara, good wench! how fares it with you?

Raw. Look on her well—then consult your own conscience. 'Tis difficult, haply, for a secretary to find one. You are a villain.

Wilf. You lie.—Hold, I crave pardon. You are her father. She is innocent, and you are unhappy: I respect virtue and misfortune too much to shock the one or insult the other.

Raw. Sdeath! why meet my daughter in the forest?

Wilf. Because I love her.

Raw. And would ruin her.

Wilf. That's a strange way of shewing one's love, methinks. I have a simple notion, Gilbert, that the thought of having taken a base advantage of a poor girl's affection might go nigh to break a man's sleep, and give him unquiet dreams: now, I love my night's rest, and shall do nothing to disturb it.

Raw. Would'st not poison her mind?

Wilf. 'Tis not my method, friend, of dosing a patient. Look ye, Gilbert; Her mind is a fair flower, stuck in the rude soil, here, of surrounding ignorance, and smiling in the chill of poverty:—I would feign cheer it with the little sun-shine I possess of comfort and information. My parents were poor like her's. Should occasion serve, I might, haply, were all parties agreed, make her my wife. To offer ought else would affect her, you, and myself; and I have no talent at making three people uneasy at the same time.

Raw. Your hand. On your own account, we are friends.

Barb. O dear father!

Raw. Be silent. Now to your errand. 'Tis from Mortimer.

Wilf. I come from Sir Edward.

Raw. I know his malice. He would oppress me with his power. He would starve me, and my family. Search my house.

Sam. No, father no. You forget the hind quarter in the pantry.   (*aside*)

Raw. Let him do his worst: but let him beware. A tyrant; a villain!

Wilf. Harkye—he is my master. I owe him my gratitude;—every thing:—and had you been any but my Barbara's father, and spoken so much against him, my indignation had work'd into my knuckles, and cram'd the words down your rusty throat.

Sam. I do begin to perceive how this will end. Father will knock down the secretary, as flat as a buck.

Raw. Why am I singled out? Is there no mark for the vengeance of office to shoot its shaft at but me? This morning, as he dog'd me in the forest————

Wilf. Hush, Rawbold. Keep your counsel. Should you make it publick he must notice it.

Raw. Did he not notice it?

Wilf. No matter—but he has sent me thus early, Gilbert, with this relief to your distresses, which he has heard of. Here are twenty marks, for you, and your family.

Raw. From Sir Edward Mortimer?

Wilf. 'Tis his way;—but he would not have it mentioned. He is one of those judges who, in their office, will never warp the law to save offenders: but his private charity bids him assist the needy, before their necessities drive them to crimes which his publick duty must punish.

Raw. Did Mortimer do this? did he? heaven bless him! Oh, young man, if you knew half the misery—my wife—my children—Shame on't! I have stood many a tug, but the drops, now, fall in spite of me. I am not ungrateful; but I cannot stand it. We will talk of Barbara when I have more man about me. (*Exit up the stair-case.*

Wilf. Farewell. I must home to the lodge quickly. Ere this, I warrant, I am looked for.

Barb. Farewell.

QUINTETTO

Wilford

The Sun has tipt the hills with red;
The lout now flourishes his flail;
The punchy Parson waddles from his bed,
Heavy, and heated, with his last night's ale.
Adieu! adieu! I must be going;
The dapper village cock is crowing.
    Adieu, my little Barbara!

Barbara

Adieu!—and should you think upon
The lowly cottage, when you're gone,
Where two old Oaks, with ivy deckt,
Their branches o'er the roof project,
I pray, good sir, just recollect
    That there lives little Barbara.

Samson

And Samson too, good sir, in smoke and smother;
Barbara's very tender—loving brother.

First Boy, to Samson

Brother, look! the Sun, aloof,
Peeps through the crannies of the roof.
Give us food, good brother, pray!
For we eat nothing yesterday.

Children.	Give us food, good brother, pray!
Samson.	Oh, fire and faggot! what a squalling!
Barbara.	Do not chide 'em.—
Samson.	Damn their bawling!

Hungry stomachs there's no balking:
I wish I could stop their mouths with talking:
But very good meat is, cent per cent,
Dearer than very good argument.

Wilford.	Adieu, adieu! I must be going;
	The dapper village cock is crowing.
	Adieu, my little Barbara! }
Barbara.	Oh, think on little Barbara! }

Children. Give us food!
Samson.   Curse their squalling!
Wilford and Barbara. Adieu! adieu!
Samson. Damn their bawling!

Samson, Wilford, and Barbara

Adieu my little Barbara! ⎫
Oh, think on little Barbara! ⎬
You'll think on little Barbara. ⎭

SCENE II. *An old fashion'd Hall, in* Sir EDWARD
MORTIMER's *Lodge*

*Several Servants cross the Stage, with Flaggons,
Tankards, Cold meat, &c. &c.*

Enter ADAM WINTERTON

Wint. Softly, varlets, softly! See you crack none of the
stone flaggons. Nay, 'tis plain your own breakfasts be toward, by your skuttling thus.—A goodly morning! Why,
you giddy-pated knave, (*to one of the servants.*) is it so you
carry a dish of pottery? No heed of our good master Sir
Edward Mortimer's ware? Fie, Peter Pickbone, fie!

Serv. I am in haste, master Steward, to break my fast.

Wint. To break thy fast!—to break thy neck, it should
seem. Ha! ha! good i'faith!—Go thy ways knave! (*Exit
servant.*) 'Tis thus the rogues ever have me. I would
feign be angry with them, but, straight, a merry jest passeth
across me, and my choler is over. To break thy neck it
should seem! ha, ha! 'twas well conceited, by St. Thomas!
——My table-book, for the business of the day. Ah, my
memory holds not as it did. It needs the spur. (*Looking over
his book.*) Nine and forty years have I been house-steward,
and butler. Let me see.—Six winters ago, come Christmas
eve, died my old master, Sir Marmaduke.—Ah! he was
a heavy loss. I look'd to drop before him. He was hale
and tough:—but, thank heaven, I ha' seen him out, my

dear old master!—Let me see—my tables; (*Looking over them and singing.*

When birds do carrol on the bush,
With a heigh no nonny——heigho!

Enter COOK

Cook. Master Steward! Good master Winterton!

Wint. Who calls merry old Adam Winterton? Ha, Jacob Cook! Well bethought—the dinner. Nay, I bear a brain: thinking men will combine. I never see Jacob Cook but it reminds me of ordering dinner. We must have——what say my tables?——we must have, Jacob——Nay, by St. Thomas, I perceive 'twas Christmas eve *seven* years died my good old master, Sir Marmaduke.

Cook. I pray you despatch me, good master steward. I would bestir in time.

Wint. Then I would counsel thee to rise earlier, Jacob; for truth to say thou art a sluggard. Ha! good i'faith!—Let me see;—Dinner—oh! Hast thou prepared the fare I order'd yester-night?

Cook. All kill'd, and ready: but will not Sir Edward Mortimer pall on his diet? 'Tis the very same bill of fare we serv'd yesterday.

Wint. Hey—let me see—I have settled the dinners, throughout the week, in my tables. Now, by our lady, I have mistaken, and read Thursday twice over!—Ha! ha! ha!—A pestilence upon me! Well, Sir Edward, (heaven bless him!) must bear with me. He must e'en dine today on what he dined on yesterday!—'tis too late to be changed. Get thee gone, knave, get thee gone!

Cook. (*Going out*)—Age has so overdone this old Dry-bones, he'll shortly tumble from the spit.— 'Thursday twice over!'—This comes of being able to read. An old buzzard!
(*Exit.*

Wint. These fatigues of office somewhat wear a man. I have had a long lease on't. I ha' seen out Queen Mary, Queen Elizabeth, and King James. 'Tis e'en almost time that I should retire, to begin to enjoy myself. Eh! by St. Thomas! hither trips the fair mistress Blanch. Of all the waiting gentlewomen I ever looked on, during the two last reigns, none stir'd my fancy like this little rose-bud.

Enter BLANCH

Blanch. A good day, good Adam Winterton.

Wint. What wag! what tulip! I never see thee but I am a score of years the younger.

Blanch. Nay, then, let us not meet often, or you will soon be in your second child-hood.

Wint. What, you come from your mistress, the Lady Helen, in the forest here; and would speak with Sir Edward Mortimer, I warrant?

Blanch. I would. Is his melancholy worship stirring yet?

Wint. Fie, you mad-cap! He is my master, and your Lady's Friend.

Blanch. Yes, truly, it seems, her only one, poor Lady: he protects her now she is left an orphan.

Wint. A blessing on his heart! I would it were merrier. Well, she is much beholden to Sir Edward for his consolation: and he never affords her his advice but his bounty is sure to follow it.

Blanch. Just so a crow will nourish its nestling: he croaks first, and then gives her food.

Wint. Ha, ha! good i'faith!—but wicked. Thy company will corrupt, and lead me astray. Should they happen to marry, (and I have my fancies on't) I'll dance a galliard with thee, in the hall, on the round Oak table. Sbud! when I was a youth, I would ha' caper'd with St. Vitus, and beat him.

Blanch. You are as likely to dance, now, as they to marry. What has hindered them, if the parties be agreed?— yet I have, now, been with my mistress these two years since Sir Edward first came hither, and placed her in the cottage, hard by his lodge.

Wint. Tush! family reasons.—Thou knowest nothing: thou art scarce catch'd. Two years back, when we came from

Kent, and Sir Edward first entered on his office, here, of Head Keeper, thou wert a Colt, running wild about New Forest. I hired you myself, to attend on madam Helen.

Blanch. Nay I shall never forget it. But you were as frolicksome, then, as I, methinks. Dost remember the box on the ear I gave thee, Adam?

Wint. Peace, peace, you pie! an you prate thus I'll stop your mouth. I will, by St. Thomas!

Blanch. An I be inclined to the contrary, I do not think you are able to stop it.

Wint. Out, you baggage! thou hast more tricks than a kitten. Well, go thy ways. Sir Edward is at his study, and there thou wilt find him. Ah, mistress Blanch! had you but seen me in the early part of Queen Elizabeth's reign!

Blanch. How old art thou now, Adam?

Wint. Four score, come Martlemas: and, by our Lady, I can run with a lapwing.

Blanch. Canst thou?—Well said!—Thou art a merry old man, and shalt have a kiss of me, on one condition.

Wint. Shall I! odsbud, name it, and 'tis mine.

Blanch. Then, catch me. (*Runs off.*)

Wint. Pestilence on't! there was a time when my legs had serv'd:—but, to speak truth, I never thrust them, now, into my scarlet hose that they do not remember me of two sticks of red sealing-wax. I was a clean limb'd stripling, when I first stood behind Sir Marmaduke's arm chair, in the old Oak eating-room.

SONG. *Adam Winterton*

Sir Marmaduke was a hearty Knight;
        Good man! Old man!
He's painted standing bolt upright,
        With his hose roll'd over his knee;—
His Perriwig's as white as chalk;
        And on his fist he holds a Hawk;
            And he looks like the head
            Of an ancient family.

II

His dining room was long and wide;
      Good man! Old man!
His Spaniels lay by the fire-side!—
    And in other parts, d'ye see,
Cross-bows, tobacco-pipes, old hats,
A saddle, his wife, and a litter of cats;
      And he look'd like the head
    Of an ancient family.

III

He never turn'd the poor from his gate;
      Good man! Old man!
But always ready to break the pate
    Of his Country's enemy.
What Knight could do a better thing,
Than serve the poor, and fight for his King.
      And so may every head
    Of an ancient family.

Enter WILFORD

Wilf. Every new act of Sir Edward's charity sets me a thinking; and the more I think the more I am puzzled. 'Tis strange that a man should be so ill at ease, who is continually doing good. At times, the wild glare of his eye is frightful; and, last night, when I was writing for him, in the library, I could not help fancying I was shut up with the devil. I would stake my life there's a secret; and I could almost give my life to unravel it. I must to him, for my morning's employment. (*Crossing the stage.*)

Wint. Ah! boy! Wilford! secretary! whither away, lad?

Wilf. Mr. Winterton!—Aye, marry, this good old man has the clue, could I but coax him to give it to me.—A good morning to you, Sir!

Wint. Yea, and the like to thee, boy. Come, thou shalt have a cup of Canary, from my corner cup-board, yonder.

Wilf. Not a drop.

Wint. Troth, I bear thee a good will for thy honest, old, dead father's sake.

Wilf. I do thankfully perceive it, Sir. Your placing me in Sir Edward's family, some nine months ago, when my poor father died, and left me friendless, will never out of my memory.

Wint. Tut, boy, no merit of mine in assisting the friendless. 'Tis our duty, child. I could never abide to see honest industry chop fallen. I love to have folks merry about me, to my heart.

Wilf. I would you could instill some mirth into our good master Sir Edward. You are an old domestick—the only one he brought with him, two years back, from Kent,—and might venture to give his spirits a jog. He seems devour'd with spleen, and melancholy.

Wint. You are a prying boy.—Go to.—I have told thee, a score of times, I would not have thee curious about our worthy master's humour. By my troth, I am angry with thee. What, a boy like you?——a——Thou hast put me in choler. Continue this, and I'll undo thee;—I'll un——sbud! I'll unprotect thee.—Ha, good i'faith! Nay, marry, my rage holds not long:—flash and out again. Unprotect thee!—ha! 'twas exceeding good, by Saint Thomas!

Wilf. I should cease to pry, sir, would you but once, (as I think you have more than once seem'd inclined) gratify my much-raised curiosity.

Wint. Well said, i' faith! I do not doubt thee. I warrant thou wouldst cease to inquire, when I had told thee all thou wouldst know.—What, green-horn, didst think to trap the old man?—Go thy ways, boy! I have a head.—Old Adam Winterton can sift a subtle speech to the bottom.

Wilf. Ah, good sir, you need not tell me that. Young as I am, I can admire that experience, in another, which I want myself.

Wint. There is something marvellous engaging in this young man! You have a world of promise, boy. Sixty years ago, in Queen Elizabeth's time, I was just such another. I remember Marian Potpan, the farmer's daughter, of Stocks Green, was then enamour'd of me. Well, beware how you offend Sir Edward.

Wilf. I would not, willingly, for the world. He has been the kindest master to me. He has inform'd my mind, relieved my distresses, cloath'd me, shelter'd me:—but, whilst my fortunes ripen in the warmth of his goodness, the frozen gloom of his countenance chills me.

Wint. Well, well, take heed how you prate on't. Out on these babbling boys! There is no keeping a secret with younkers in a family.

Wilf. (*very eagerly.*) What, then there *is* a secret!——'Tis as I guessed after all.

Wint. Why, how now, hot head?——Mercy on me! an this tinder-box boy do not make me shake with apprehension. Is it thus you take my frequent council?

Wilf. Dear sir, 'tis your council which most I covet. Give me but that; admit me to your confidence; steer me with your advice, which I ever held excellent, and, with such a pilot, I may sail prosperously through a current which, otherwise, might wreck me.

Wint. 'Tis melting to see how unfledged youth will shelter itself, like a chicken, under the wing of such a tough old cock as myself! Well, well, I'll think on't, boy.

Wilf. The old answer.—Yet, he softens apace: could I but clench him now—Faith, sir, 'tis a raw morning; and I care not if I taste the canary your kindness offer'd.

Wint. Aha! lad! say'st thou so? Just my modest humour when I was young. I ever refused my glass at first, but I came to it ere I had quitted my company. Here's the key of the corner cup-board, yonder. See you do not crack the bottle, you heedless goose, you!

(WILFORD *takes out the bottle and glasses.*)

Ha! fill it up. Od! it sparkles curiously. Here's to————I prithee, tell me now, Wilford; didst ever in thy life see a waiting-gentlewoman with a more inviting eye than the little Mrs. Blanch?

Wilf. Here's Mrs. Blanch—(*drinks.*)

Wint. Ah, wag! well, go thy ways! Well, when I was of thy age————odsbud! no matter; 'tis past, now;—but here's the little Mrs. Blanch. (*drinks.*)

Wilf. 'Tis thought, here, Sir Edward means to marry her lady, Madam Helen.

Wint. Nay, I know not. She has long been enamour'd of him, poor lady, when he was the gay, the gallant Sir Edward, in Kent. Ah, well! two years make a wond'rous change!

Wilf. Yes, 'tis a good tough love, now a days, that will hold out a couple of twelvemonths.

Wint. Away, I mean not so, you giddy pate! He is all honour; and as steady in his course as the sun: yet I wonder, sometimes, he can bear to look upon her.

Wilf. Eh? why so? Did not he bring her, under his protection, to the Forest; since, 'tis said, she lost her relations?

Wint. Hush, boy! on your life do not name her uncle—I would say her relations.

Wilf. Her uncle! wherefore? Where's the harm in having an uncle, dead or alive?

Wint. Peace, peace! In that uncle lyes the secret.

Wilf. Indeed! how, good Adam Winterton? I prithee, how?

Wint. Ah! 'twas a heavy day! Poor Sir Edward is now a broken spirit—but if ever a good spirit walk'd the earth, in trunk hose, he is one.

Wilf. Let us drink Sir Edward's health.

Wint. That I would, tho' 'twere a mile to the bottom—(*drinks*) Ha, 'tis cheering, i'faith! Well, in troth, I have regard for thee, boy, for thy father's sake.

Wilf. Oh, good sir! and this uncle, you say—

Wint. Of Madam Helen—ah! there lyes the mischief.

Wilf. What mischief can be in him? why, he is dead.

Wint. Come nearer—see you prate not now, on your life. Our good master, Sir Edward, was arraign'd on his account, in open court.

Wilf. Arraign'd! how mean you?

Wint. Alas, boy! tried.—Tried for———nearer yet—his murder.

Wilf. Mu—mur—Murder! (*drops the glass.*)

Wint. Why, what! why, Wilford! out, alas! the boy's passion will betray all! what, Wilford, I say!

Wilf. You have curdled my blood!

Wint. What, varlet, thou darest not think ill of our worthy master?

Wilf. I—I am his secretary. Often alone with him at dead midnight, in his library. The candles in the sockets—and a man glaring upon me who has committed mur—ugh!

Wint. Committed! Thou art a base, lying knave, to say it: and while I wear a rapier, I'll———tush! Heaven help me! I forget I am fourscore. Well, well—hear me, pettish boy, hear me. Why, look now, thou dost not attend.

Wilf. I—I mark; I mark.

Wint. I tell thee, then, our good Sir Edward was beloved in Kent, where he had returned a year before, from his travels. Madam Helen's uncle was hated by all the neighbourhood, rich and poor. A mere brute, dost mark me.

Wilf. Like enough: but when brutes walk upon two legs, the law of the land, thank Heaven! will not suffer us to butcher them.

Wint. Go to, you fire-brand! Our good master labour'd all he could, for many a month, to sooth his turbulence; but in vain. He pick'd a quarrel with Sir Edward, in the publick county assembly; nay, the strong ruffian struck him down, and trampled on him. Think on that, Wilford! on our good master Sir Edward, whose great soul was nigh to burst with the indignity.

Wilf. Well, but the end on't?

Wint. Why, our young master took horse, for his own house, determined, as it appear'd, to send a challenge to this white-liver'd giant, in the morning.

Wilf. I see. He kill'd him in a duel. That's another kind of butchery, which the law allows not; true humanity shudders at; and false honour justifies.

Wint. See, now, how you fly off! Sir Edward's revenge, boy, was baffled. For his antagonist was found dead in the street, that night; killed, by some unknown assassins, on his return from the assembly.

Wilf. Indeed! *unknown* assassins!

Wint. Nay, 'tis plain, our good Sir Edward had no hand

in the wicked act: for he was tried, as I told you, at the next
assize. Mercy on me! 'twas a crouded court; and how gentle
and simple threw up their caps, at his acquittal! Heaven be
thank'd! he was cleared, beyond a shadow of doubt.

Wilf. He was; I breathe again. 'Twas a happy thing.
'Twas the only way left of cleansing him from a foul suspicion.

Wint. Out alas! lad, 'tis his principal grief. He is full of
nice feeling, and high-flown honour: and the thought of being
tried, for such a crime, has given him his heart's wound. Poor
gentleman! he has shun'd the world ever since. He was
once the life of all company——but now!

Mort. (*without*) Winterton!

Wint. Hark! some one calls. Out on thee! thou has sunk
my spirits into my heels. Who calls merry old Adam
Winterton?

Mort. (*without*) Adam Winterton! come hither to me.

Wint. Nay, by our lady, 'tis Sir Edward himself!—Pestilence on't! if I seem sad now, 'twill be noted. I come, good
Sir Edward.

'When birds—(not a word on thy life)—
   do carroll on the bush,'
'With a hey no nonny'——Mercy on me!   (*Exit.*

Wilf. My throat's parch'd, and my blood freezes! A
quart of brandy couldn't moisten the one, nor thaw the other.
This accounts, then, for all. Poor, unhappy gentleman! This
unravels all, from the first day of my service—when a deep
groan made me run into the library, and I found him locking
up his papers, in the iron chest, as pale as ashes.—Eh?—
What can be in that chest?—Perhaps some proof of——no, I
shudder at the suggestion.—'Tis not possible one so good
can be guilty of——I know not what to think—nor what to
resolve. But curiosity is roused, and, come what may, I'll
have an eye upon him.   (*Exit.*

SCENE III. *A Library*

Sir EDWARD MORTIMER discover'd at a Writing Table
ADAM WINTERTON attending:

Mort. 'Tis his first trespass, so we'll quit him, Adam:—
But caution him how he offend again.
As Keeper of the Forest, I should fine him.

Wint. Nay that your worship should. He'll prove ere
     long,
—Mark but my words—a sturdy poacher. Well,
'Tis you know best.

Mort. Well, well, no matter, Adam;—
He has a wife, and child.

Wint. Ah! bless your honour!

Mort. They kill'd his dog?

Wint. Aye, marry, sir:—a lurcher.
Black Martin Wincot the Groom Keeper shot him;
A perilous good aim.—I warrant me,
The rogue has lived this year upon that lurcher.

Mort. Poor wretch!—Oh! well bethought; Send Walter
     to me—
I would employ him: he must ride for me,
On business of much import.

Wint. Lackaday!
That it should chance so! I have sent him forth,
To Winchester, to buy me flannel hose;
For winter's coming on. Good lack! that things
Should fall so crosly!

Mort. Nay, nay, do not fret—
'Tis better that my business cool, good Adam,
Than thy old limbs.

Wint. Ah! you've a kindly heart!

Mort. Is Wilford waiting?

Wint. Wilford! mercy on me!
I tremble now to hear his name. He is—
Here in the hall, sir.

Mort. Send him in, I prithee.

Wint. I shall, sir. Heaven bless you! Heaven bless you!
(Exit.

Mort. Good morning, good old heart! This honest soul
Would feign look cheery in my house's gloom;
And, like a gay and sturdy ever-green,
Smiles, in the midst of blast, and desolation,
Where all around him withers.—Well, well—wither!
Perish this frail and fickle frame!—this clay,
That, in it's dross-like compound, doth contain
The mind's pure ore, and essence.—Oh! that mind!
That mind of man! that god-like spring of action!
That source, whence Learning, Virtue, Honour, flow!—
Which lifts us to the stars; which carries us
O'er the swol'n waters of the angry deep,
As swallows skim the air.—That Fame's sole fountain!
That doth transmit a fair, and spotless name,
When the vile trunk is rotten:—Give me that!
Oh! give me but to live, in after-age,
Remember'd and unsullied!—Heaven and earth!
Let my pure flame of Honour shine in story,
When I am cold in death—and the slow fire,
That wears my vitals now, will no more move me
Than 'twould a corpse within a monument.
(A knock at the door of the library.)
How now! Who's there? Come in.

Enter WILFORD

Wilford! is't you? You were not wont to knock.
Wilf. I fear'd I might surprise you, sir.
Mort. Surprise me!
Wilf. I mean—disturb you, sir:—yes—at your studies—
Disturb you at your studies.
Mort. Very strange!
You were not used to be so cautious.
Wilf. No—
I never used—but I—hum—I have learnt——
Mort. Learnt!
Wilf. Better manners, sir. I was quite raw,

When, in your bounty, you first shelter'd me:
But, thanks to your great goodness, and the lessons
Of Mr. Winterton, I still improve,
And pick up something daily.

   Mort. Aye, indeed!
Winterton!—No, he dare not—Hark you, sir!

                           (stepping up to him)

   Wilf. Sir!

   Mort. (*retreating from him*). What am I about!—Oh,
      Honour! Honour!
Thy pile should be so uniform, displace
One atom of thee, and the slightest breath
Of a rude peasant makes thy owner tremble
For his whole building. Reach me, from the shelf,
The volume I was busied in, last night.

   Wilf. Last night, sir?

   Mort. Aye;—it treats of Alexander.

   Wilf. Oh, I remember, sir—of Macedon.
I made some extracts, by your order. (*goes to the Book-Case.*)

   Mort. Books
(My only commerce, now,) will sometimes rouse me
Beyond my nature, I have been so warm'd,
So heated by a well-turn'd rhapsody,
That I have seem'd the Hero of the tale,
So glowingly described. Draw me a man
Struggling for Fame, attaining, keeping it,
Dead ages since, and the Historian
Decking his memory, in polish'd phrase,
And I can follow him through every turn,
Grow wild in his exploits, myself himself,
Until the thick pulsation of my heart
Wakes me, to ponder on the thing I am.

   Wilf. (*giving him the book*)
To my poor thinking, Sir, this Alexander
Would scarcely rouse a man to follow him.

   Mort. Indeed! why so lad? He is reckon'd brave,
Wise, generous, learn'd, by older heads than thine.

   Wilf. I cannot tell, sir:—I have but a gleaning.—

He conquer'd all the world;—but left unconquer'd
A world of his own passions—and they led him,
(It seems so there) on petty provocation,
Even to murder.

> (MORTIMER *starts*—WILFORD *and he exchange looks—*
> *both confused*)

I have touch'd the string—
'Twas unawares—I cannot help it.   (*aside*)

Mort. (*attempting to recover himself.*) Wilford——Wilford,
I——you mistake the character——I, mark you—he—death
and eternal tortures!

> (*dashes the book on the floor, and seizes* WILFORD)

Slave! I will crush thee! pulverise thy frame!
That no vile particle of prying nature
May——Ha, ha, ha!—I will not harm thee, boy—
O, agony!   (*Exit.*

Wilf. Is this the high-flown honour, and delicate feeling, old Winterton talk'd of, that cannot bear a glance at
the trial?—Delicate! had I been born under a throttling
planet, I had never survived this collaring. This may be
guilt. If so——well, what have I to do with the knowledge
on't!—what *could* I do? cut off my benefactor, who gives
me bread, who is respected for his virtues, pitied for his misfortunes, loved by his family, bless'd by the poor?—Pooh!
he is innocent. This is his pride and shame. He was
acquitted—Thousands witness'd it—thousands rejoiced at it
—thousands—eh? the key left in the iron chest! Circumstance and mystery tempt me at every turn. Ought I—no
matter. These are no common incitements, and I submit to
the impulse. I heard him stride down the stairs. It opens
with a spring, I see. I tremble in every joint (*goes to the*
chest).

Enter Sir EDWARD MORTIMER

Mort. I had forgot the key and——ha! by hell!

(*Sees* WILFORD; *snatches a pistol from the table, runs up to*
him, and holds it to his head. WILFORD *on his knees, claps*

down the lid of the trunk which he has just open'd. After
an apparent struggle of mind, MORTIMER *throws the pistol*
from him.)

Mort. Begone!——Come back.—Come hither to me.
Mark me—I see thou dost at every turn—
And I have noted thee too. Thou hast found
(I know not how) some clue to my disgrace:
Aye, my disgrace—we must not mince it now—
Publick dishonour!—trod on!—buffeted!
Then tried as the foul demon who had foild
My manly means of vengeance. Anguish gnaws me:
Mountains of shame are piled upon me!—Me,
Who have made Fame my idol. 'Twas enough!
But something must be super-added: You,—
A worm, a viper I have warm'd, must plant,
In venom'd sport, your sting into my wounds,
Too tender e'en for tenderness to touch,
And work me into madness. Thou wouldst question
My very——slave!——my very innocence;
Ne'er doubted yet by judges nor arraigners.
Wretch! you have wrung this from me. Be content,
I am sunk low enough.

Wilf. (*returning the key*) Oh, sir! I ever
Honour'd and loved you. But I merit all.
My passions hurried me I know not whither.
Do with me as you please, my kind, wrong'd master!
Discard me—thrust me forth—nay, kill me!——

Mort. Kill you!

Wilf. I know not what I say.—I know but this,
That I would die to serve you.

Enter a Servant

Serv. Sir, your brother.
Is just alighted at the gate.

Mort. My brother!
He could not time it worse. Wilford, remember!
Come, shew me to him.   (*Exit with servant.*

Wilf. Remember! I shall never while I live forget it: nay, I shall never, while I live, forgive myself. My knees knock together still; and the cold drops stand on my forehead, like rain-water on a pent-house.

Enter BARBARA

Barbara. Wilford!

Wilf. Eh? Barbara! How camest thou here?

Barb. With my father, who waits below, to see Sir Edward.

Wilf. He————He is busied; he cannot see him now. He is with his brother.

Barb. Troth, I am sorry for it. My poor father's heart is bursting with gratitude, and he would fain ease it, by pouring out his thanks to his benefactor. Oh, Wilford, your's is a happy lot to have such a master as Sir Edward!

Wilf. Happy? Oh! yes—I—I am very happy.

Barb. Mercy! has any ill befallen you?

Wilf. No; nothing. 'Tis all my happiness. My happiness is like your father's gratitude, Barbara; and, at times, it goes near to choak me.

Barb. Nay, I'm sure there's more in this. Bless me, you look pale! I cou'dn't bear to see you ill, or uneasy, Wilford.

Wilf. Cou'dn't you, Barbara? Well, well, I shall be better presently. 'Tis nothing of import.

Barb. Trust me, I hope not.

Wilf. Well, question me no more on't now, I beseech you, Barbara.

Barb. Believe me, I would not question you but to console you, Wilford. I would scorn to pry into any one's grief; much more your's, Wilford, to satisfy a busy curiosity. Though, I am told, there are such in the world who would.

Wilf. I————I am afraid there are, Barbara. But come, no more of this. 'Tis a passing cloud on my spirits, and will soon blow over.

Barb. Ah! could I govern your fortunes, foul weather should ne'er harm you.

Wilf. Should not it, sweet! Kiss me. (*Kisses her.*) The lips of a woman are a sovereign cordial for melancholy.

DUET

WILFORD AND BARBARA

Wilf.	Sweet little Barbara, when you are advancing,
	Sweet little Barbara, my cares you remove;
Barb.	Poor little Barbara can feel her heart dancing,
	When little Barbara is met by her love.
Wilf.	When I am grieved, love! oh, what would you say?
Barb.	Tattle to you, love,
	And prattle to you, love,
And laugh your grief and care away.	
Wilf.	Sweet little Barbara, &c.
Barb.	Poor little Barbara, &c.
Wilf.	Yet, dearest Barbara, look all through the nation,
	Care, soon or late, my love, is ev'ry man's lot.
Barb.	Sorrow and melancholy, grief and vexation,
	When we are young and jolly, soon is forgot.
Wilf.	When we grow old, love! then what will you say?
Barb.	Tattle to you, love,
	And prattle to you, love,
And laugh your grief and care away.	
Wilf.	Sweet little Barbara, &c.
Barb.	Poor little Barbara, &c.

END OF THE FIRST ACT

ACT II

SCENE I. *The New Forest*

Enter ARMSTRONG *and* ORSON

Arm. Go to—I tell thee Orson, (as I have told thee more than once) thou art too sanguinary.

Ors. And, I tell you, Captain Armstrong—but always under favour, you being our leader—you are too humane.

Arm. Humanity is scarcely counted a fault: if so, 'tis a fault on the right side.

Ors. Umph! perhaps not with us. We are robbers.

Arm. And why should robbers lack humanity? They who plunder most respect it as a virtue, and make a shew on't, to guild their vices. Lawyers, Physicians, Placemen, all——all plunder and slay, but all pretend to humanity.

Ors. They are Regulars, and plunder by licence.

Arm. Then let us Quacks set the Regulars a better example.

Ors. This humanity, Captain, is a high horse you are ever bestride upon. Some day, mark my word, he'll fling you.

Arm. Cruelty is a more dangerous beast:—When the rider's thrown, his brains are kick'd out, and no one pities him.

Ors. Like enough;—but your tough horseman, who ventures boldly, is never dismounted. When I am engaged in a desperate chace, (as we are, Captain,) I stick at nothing. I hate milk sops.

Arm. And love mutiny. Take heed, Orson; I have before caution'd you not to glance at me.

Ors. I say nothing: but if some escape to inform against us, whom we have rob'd, 'tis none of my fault. Dead men tell no tales.

Arm. Wretch! Speak that again, and you shall tell none.

(*holds a carbine to his head.*)

Ors. Flash away!—I don't fear death.

Arm. More shame for thee; for thou art unfit to meet it.

Ors. I know my trade. I set powder, ball, and rope, at defiance.

Arm. Brute! You mistake headstrong insensibility for courage. Do not mistake my horror of it for cowardice: for I, who shudder at cruelty, will fell your boldness to the earth, when I see you practice it. Submit.

Ors. I do. I know not what 'tis, but I have told you, often, there is something about you awes me. I cannot tell——I could kill twenty to your one.

Arm. There 'tis.——Thou wouldst dart upon weak

unguarded man, like a tyger. A ferocious animal, whether crawling or erect, ever shrinks from fair opposition.

Ors. My courage was never yet doubted, Captain.

Arm. Your nerves, fool. Thou art a mere machine. Could I but give it motion, I would take an oak from the forest, here, clap a flint into it for heart, and make as bold a fellow as thou art. Listen to my orders.

Ors. I obey.

Arm. Get thee to our den. Put on thy disguise—then hie thee to the market town for provision, for our company. Here——Here is part of the spoil we took yester-night: see you bring an honest account of what you lay out (*giving money*)

Ors. My honour!——

Arm. Well, I do not doubt thee, here. Our profession is singular; it's followers do not cheat one another. You will not be back till dusk. See you fall not on any poor straggling peasant, as you return.

Ors. I would feign encounter the solitary man, who is sometimes wandering by night about the forest. He is rich.

Arm. Not for your life. 'Tis Sir Edward Mortimer, the head Keeper. Touch him not; 'tis too near home. Besides, he is no object for plunder. I have watch'd him, at midnight, stealing from his lodge, to wander like one crazed. He is good, too, to the poor; and should walk unmolested by Charity's charter. 'Twere pity that he who administers to necessity, all day, should be rifled by necessity at night. An thou shouldst meet him, I charge thee spare him.

Ors. I must, if it be your order. This sparing doctrine will go nigh, at last, to starve all the thieves. When a man takes to the trade of a wolf, he should not go like a lamb to his business. (*Exit.*

Arm. This fellow is downright villain: Harden'd and relentless. I have felt, in my penury, the world trample on me. It has driven me to take that, desperately, which wanting I should starve. Death! my spirit cannot brook to see a sleek knave walk negligently by his fellow in misery, and suffer him to rot. I will wrench that comfort from him

which he will not bestow.—But nature puts a bar:—Let
him administer to my wants, and pass on:—I have done
with him.

SONG

Armstrong

When the Robber his victim has noted,
 When the Free-booter darts on his prey,
Let Humanity spare the devoted;
 Let Mercy forbid him to slay.

Since my hope is by penury blighted,
 My sword must the traveller daunt;
I will snatch from the rich man, benighted,
 The gold he denies to my want.

But the victim when, once, I have noted,
 At my foot when I look on my prey,
Let Humanity spare the devoted;
 Let Mercy forbid me to slay.

SCENE II. *The Hall in* Sir Edward Mortimer's
      Lodge

Enter Fitzharding

Fitz. Well, business must be minded:—but he stays
A tedious time, methinks.—You, fellow!
      (*To a* Servant *crossing the hall.*
Ser. Sir!
Fitz. Where is Sir Tristful? Where's Don Melancholy?
Serv. Who, sir?
Fitz. My brother, knave, Sir Edward Mortimer.
Serv. He was with you, but now, Sir.
Fitz. Sir, I thank you;—
That's information. Louts, and serving-men,
Can never parley straight. I met a fellow,

Here, on my way across the heath,—a Hind—
And ask'd how far to Lymington: I look'd
The answer would have bolted from his chops,
Bounce, like a pellet from a popgun.—No:—
He stared, and scratch'd his empty head, and cried,
'Where do you come from?'——Who brought in my
        luggage?
    Serv. It was not I, sir.
    Fitz. There!—They never can!
Go to your master; pray him to despatch
His household work:—tell him I hate fat Folios.
Plague! when I cross the country, here, to see him,
He leaves me, ram'd into an elbow chair,
With a huge, heavy book, that makes me nod,
Then tumbles on my toes. Tell him, do'st hear,
Captain Fitzharding's company has tired me.
    Serv. Who's company?——
    Fitz. My own, knave.
    Serv. Sir, I shall.   (*Exit.*
    Fitz. A book to me's a sovereign Narcotick;
A lump of opium; every line a dose.
Edward is all deep reading, and black letter;
He shews it in his very chin. He speaks
Mere Dictionary; and he pores on pages
That give plain men the head-ache. 'Scarce, and curious,'
Are baits his learning nibbles at. His brain
Is cram'd with mouldy volumes, cramp, and useless,
Like a librarian's lumber-room.—Poor fellow!
Grief will do much!—well! some it drives to reading,
And some to drinking:—'twill do much!—this trial——
A fool to fret so for't! his honour's clear.
Tut! I'm a soldier—know what honour is.
Had I been slander'd, and a fair Court martial
Cleansed me from calumny, as white as snow,
I had ne'er moped, and fumed, and winced, and kick'd,
But sat down heart-whole. Plague upon't! this house
Appears the very cave of melancholy.
Nay, hold, I lie:—here comes a petticoat.

Enter BLANCH

Od! a rare wench! This is the best edition
In Edward's whole collection. Here, come hither!
Let me peruse you.
   Blanch. Would you speak to me, Sir?
   Fitz. Aye, child. I'm going now to read you.
   Blanch. Read me!
You'll find me full of errors, sir.
   Fitz. No matter.
Come nearer, child: I cannot see to read
At such a distance.
   Blanch. You had better, Sir,
Put on your spectacles.
   Fitz. Aye, there she has me!
A plague upon old Time! old Scythe and Hour-glass
Has set his mark upon me. Harkye, child:
You do not know me. You and I must have
Better acquaintance.
   Blanch. O, I've heard of you.
You are Sir Edward's kinsman, Sir—his brother.
   Fitz. Aye—his half brother—by the mother's side—
His elder brother.
   Blanch. Yes, Sir, I see that.
   Fitz. This gypsey's tongue is like her eye: I know not
Which is the sharpest. Tell me what's your name.
   Blanch. My name is Blanch, Sir—born, here, in the
     forest.
   Fitz. Sbud! I must be a Keeper in this forest.
Whither art going, sweet one?
   Blanch. Home, Sir.
   Fitz. Home!
Why, is not this thy home?
   Blanch. No, Sir; I live
Some half mile hence—with madam Helen, Sir.
I brought a letter from her, to Sir Edward.
   Fitz. Odso, with Helen!—so—with her!—the object
Of my grave brother's groaning passion. Plague!

I would 'twere in the house. I do not like
Your rheumatick, October assignations,
Under an elm, by moonlight. This will end
In flannels and sciatica. My passion
Is not Arcadian. Tell me, pretty one,
Shall I walk with you, home?

   Blanch. No, Sir, I thank you;
It would fatigue you, sadly.

   Fitz. Fatigue me!
Oons! this wild forest filly, here, would make me
Grandfather to Methusaleh. Look here—
Here is a purse of money.

   Blanch. O, the father!
What, will you give me any?

   Fitz. Gold I find
The universal key; the *passe par tout*.
It will unlock a forest maiden's heart,
As easy as a politician's. Here;
Here are two pieces, rose-bud. Buy a top-knot;
Make thyself happy with them.

   Blanch. That I will.
The poor old woman, northward of the lodge,
Lyes sick in bed. I'll take her this, poor soul,
To comfort her.

   Fitz. Hold!—hey the devil!—hold.
This was not meant to comfort an old woman.

   Blanch. Why, wouldn't you relieve her, Sir?

   Fitz. Um?——yes:—
But—pshaw! pooh, prithee—there's a time for all things.
Why tell me of her now,—of an old fool,—
Of comforting the aged, now?

   Blanch. I thought
That you might have a fellow feeling, Sir.

   Fitz. This little pastoral devil's laughing at me!
Oons! come and kiss me, jade. I am a Soldier,
And Justice of the Peace.

   Blanch. Then, shame upon you!
Your double calling might have taught you better.

I see your drift, now. Take your dirt again,

                         (*throws down the money*.)

Good Captain Justice!—Stoop for it,—and think

How an old Soldier, and a Justice looks,

When he is picking up the bribes he offers,

To injure those he should protect;—the helpless,

The poor, and innocent.   [*Exit.*

    Fitz. I warrant me,

Could I but see my face, now, in a glass,

That I look wond'rous sheepish. I'm ashamed

To pick up the two pieces.—Let them lye.—

I would not wrong the innocent;—good reason;—

There be so few that are so:—she is honest;

I must make reparation. Odso! Wilford!

Enter WILFORD

How fares it, boy?

    Wilf. I thank you, Sir. I hope you have enjoy'd

Your health, these three months past, since last you

        honour'd us

With your good presence, at the lodge.

    Fitz. Indifferent.

Some cramps and shooting pains, boy. I have dropt

Some cash here, but I am afraid to bend

To pick it up again, lest it should give me

An aukward twinge. Stoop for it, honest Wilford.

There's a good lad!

    Wilf. Right willingly, Sir.   (*Picks up the money.*)

    Fitz. So!

The Soldier and the Justice save their blushes.—

Now, carry it, I prithee, at your leisure,

To an old gossip, near the lodge here—northward—

I've heard of her—she's bed-ridden, and sick.

You need not say who sent you.

    Wilf. I conceive.

'Tis private bounty; that's true charity.

    Fitz. Nay, pish!—my charity!———

    Wilf. Nay, I could swear

'Tis not the first time you have offer'd this
In secret.

    Fitz. Um!—why no;—not quite the first.
But tell me, lad, how jogs the world here, eh?
In Rueful Castle?—What, some three months back,
We two were cronies. What, hast thou forgot?
Thou wert my favourite here, man.

    Wilf. Sir, you honour'd me
By saying so.

    Fitz. Tut! honour'd!—tut—a fig!
Thou art grown starch, and sad. This air is catching;
Thou art infected. Harkye, Wilford, harkye!
Thou'rt a sly rogue! What, you could never tell me
Of Helen's waiting maid; the little cherry;—
Of——plague upon her name!—of——

    Wilf. Blanch, Sir?

    Fitz. Blanch:
That's it;—the forest fairy.—You and I
Must have some talk about her.

    Wilf. Have you seen her?

    Fitz. Just now: just gone. Od! I have blunder'd hor-
      ribly!
You must know, lad——come hither.

                  (*They retire to the back of the scene.*)

Enter Sir Edward Mortimer

    Mort. Now for my brother, and—Ha! Wilford with him!
That imp is made my scourge. They whisper too!
O! I had rather court the thunder-bolt,
To melt my bones, and pound me to a mass,
Than suffer this vile canker to corrode me.
Wilford!

    Wilf. Who calls?—eh!—'tis Sir Edward.

    Fitz. Mum!

    Mort. I seem to interrupt you.

    Wilf. (*earnestly.*) No, indeed.
No, on my life, sir:—we were only talking
Of——

Fitz. Hold your tongue. Oons! boy, you must not tell.

Mort. Not!

Fitz. Not! no to be sure:—why, 'tis a secret.

Wilf. You shall know all, sir.—'Twas a trifle—nothing—
In faith, you shall know all.

Fitz. In faith, you lie.
Be satisfied, good Edward:—'tis a toy.—
But, of all men, I would not have thee know on't.
It is a tender subject.

Mort. Aye, indeed!

Fitz. May not I have my secret? Oons! good brother,
What would you say, now, should a meddling knave
Busy his brains with matters, though but trivial,
Which concern you alone?

Mort. I'd have him rot:
Die piecemeal; pine; moulder in misery.
Agent, and sacrifice to Heaven's wrath
When castigating plagues are hurl'd on man,
Stands lean, and lynx-eyed Curiosity,
Watching his neighbour's soul. Sleepless himself
To banish sleep from others. Like a Leech
Sucking the blood-drops from a care-worn heart,
He gorges on't—then renders up his food,
To nourish Calumny, his soul-lung'd mate,
Who carries Rumour's trumpet; and whose breath,
Infecting the wide surface of the world,
Strikes pestilence and blight. O, fie, on't! fie!
Whip me the curious wretch from pole to pole!
Who writhes in fire, and scorches all around him,
A victim making victims!

Fitz. By the mass,
'Twere a sound whipping that, from pole to pole!
From constable to constable might serve.
E'en you yourself were like to prove, but now,
This Leech, that's yoke-fellow, you say, to Scandal,
The bad-breath'd trumpeter.

Mort. Your pardon, brother;
I had forgot. Wilford, I've business for you.

Wait for me—aye—an hour after dinner,
Wait for me in the library.

   Wilf. The library!——

I sicken at the sound. (*aside.*) Wait there for you—
     and—

Captain Fitzharding, Sir?

   Mort. For me, alone.

   Wilf. Alone, Sir!

   Mort. Yes,—begone.

   Wilf. I shall, sir—but,

If I have ever breath'd a syllable
That might displease, you may——

   Mort. Fool! breathe no more.

   Wilf. I'm dumb.

I'd rather step into a Lion's den
Than meet him in the library!—I go, Sir.   [*Exit.*

   Fitz. Brother, you are too harsh with that poor boy.

   Mort. Brother, a man must rule his family
In his own way.

   Fitz. Well, well, well—Don't be touchy.

I speak not to offend: I only speak
On a friend's privilege. The Poor are men,
And have their feelings, brother.

   Mort. So have I!

   Fitz. One of the best that we can shew, believe me,

Is mildness to a servant. Servants, brother,
Are born with fortune's yoke about their necks;
And that is galling in itself enough;
We should not goad them under it. The master
Should rather cheer them in their servitude,
With kindly words—not too familiar neither;
But utter'd with that air which true benevolence
Imparts to dignified nobility.

   Mort. Brother, your hand. You have a gentle nature—

May no mischance e'er ruffle it, my brother!
I've known thee from my infancy, old soldier;
And never did I know—I do not flatter—
A heart more stout, more cased with hardy manhood,

More full of milk within. Trust me, dear friend,
If admiration of thy charity
May argue charity in the admirer,
I am not destitute.

   Fitz. You!—I have seen you
Sometimes o'erflow with it.

   Mort. And what avails it?
Honour has been my theme; good will to man
My study. I have labour'd for a name
As white as mountain snow; dazzling, and speckless:
Shame on't! 'tis blur'd with blots! Fate, like a mildew,
Ruins the virtuous harvest I would reap,
And all my crop is weeds.

   Fitz. Why, how now brother!
This is all spleen. You mope yourself too much,
In this dull forest, here. Twenty blue devils
Are dancing jigs, and hornpipes, in your brains.
Fie, fie! be more a man.

   Mort. Well, I have done.

   Fitz. Come, what's for dinner? Od! I mean to eat
Abundantly.

   Mort. I know not, brother. Honest Winterton
Will tell you all.

   Fitz. What he! old Adam? he!
My merry buck of Paradise?——Odso!
I have not seen him. Well, he shall produce
A flaggon of the best; and, after dinner,
We will be jovial. Come, come, rouse you, man!
I came on purpose, thirty miles from home,
To jog your spirits. Prithee, now, be gay!
And, prithee, too, be kind to my young favourite!
To Wilford there.

   Mort. Well, well; I hope I have been.

   Eliz. No doubt, in actions:—but in words, and looks.—
A rugged look's a damper to a greenhorn.
I watch'd him, now, when you frown'd angerly
And he betray'd——

   Mort. Betray'd!

Fitz. Ten thousand fears.

Mort. Oh!

Fitz. The poor devil couldn't shew more scared
Had you e'en held a pistol to his head.   (MORTIMER *starts*)
Why, hey-day! what's the matter?

Mort. Brother!———
Question me not; my nerves are aspin-like;
The slightest breath will shake 'em. Come, good brother.

Fitz. You'll promise to be gay?

Mort. I'll do my best.

Fitz. Why that's well said! A man can do no more.
Od! I believe my rattling talk has given you
A stir already.

Mort. That it has indeed!

Come, brother!   [*Exeunt.*

SCENE III. *Helen's Cottage*

Enter HELEN *and* SAMSON

Helen. Are you he that wish to enter in my service?

Sam. Yes, so please you, Madam Helen, for want of a better.

Helen. Why, I have seen you in the forest—at Rawbold's cottage. He is your father, as I think.

Sam. Yes, so please you, Madam; for want of a better.

Helen. I fear me you may well say that. Your father, as I have heard, bears an ill name in the forest.

Sam. Alas! madam, he is obliged to bear it—for want of a better. We are all famish'd, madam: and the naked and hungry have seldom many friends to speak well of them.

Helen. If I should hire thee, who will give thee a character?

Sam. My father, madam.

Helen. Why, sirrah, he has none of his own.

Sam. The more fatherly in him, madam, to give his son what he has need of for himself. But a knave is often applied to, to vouch for a good servant's honesty. I will serve you as faithfully as your last footman; who, I have heard, ran away this morning.

Helen. Truly, he did so.

Sam. I was told on't, some half hour ago; and ran, hungrily, hither, to offer myself. So, please you, let not poverty stand in the way of my preferment.

Helen. Should I entertain you, what could you do to make yourself useful?

Sam. Any thing. I can wire hares, snare partridges, shoot a buck, and smuggle brandy, for you, madam.

Helen. Fie on you, knave! 'Twere fitter to turn you over to the Verderors of the forest, for punishment, than to encourage you in such practices.

Sam. I would practice any thing better, that might get me bread. I would scrape trenchers, fill buckets, and carry a message. What can a man do! He can't starve.

Helen. Well, sirrah, to snatch thee from evil, I care not if I make trial of thee.

Sam. No! will you?

Helen. Nineteen in twenty might question my prudence for this:—but, whatever loss I may suffer from thy roguery, the thought of having open'd a path to lead a needy wanderer back to virtue will more than repay me.

Sam. O, bless, you, lady! If I do not prove virtuous never trust in man again. I am overjoy'd!

Helen. Get thee to the kitchen. You will find a livery there will suit you.

Sam. A livery! O, the father! Virtuous and a livery, all in a few seconds! Heaven bless you!

Helen. Well, get you to your work.

Sam. I go, madam. If I break any thing to day, be-seech you let it go for nothing; for joy makes my hand tremble. Should you want me, please to cry Samson, and I am with you in a twinkling. Heaven bless you! Here's fortune!   (*Exit.*

Helen. Blanch stays a tedious time. Heaven send Mortimer's health be not worse! He is sadly altered since we

came to the forest. I dream'd, last night, of the fire he saved
me from; and I saw him, all fresh, in manly bloom, bearing
me through the flames, even as it once happened.

Enter BLANCH

Helen. How now, wench! You have almost tired my
patience.

Blanch. And my own legs, madam. If the old footman
had not made so much use of his, by running away, they
might have spared mine.

Helen. Inform me of Sir Edward Mortimer. Hast seen
him?

Blanch. Yes, I have, madam.

Helen. Say; tell me;
How look'd he? how's his health? is he in spirits?
What said he, Blanch? Will he be here to day?

Blanch. A little breath, madam, and I will answer all,
duly.

Helen. O! fie upon thee, wench!
These interrogatories should be answered
Quicker than breath can utter them.

Blanch. That's impossible, lady.

Helen. Thou would'st not say so hadst thou ever loved.
Love has a fleeter messenger than speech,
To tell love's meaning. His expresses post
Upon the orbs of vision, ere the tongue
Can shape them into words. A lover's look
Is his heart's Mercury. O! the Eye's eloquence,
Twin-born with thought, outstrips the tardy voice,
Far swifter than the nimble lightning's flash
The sluggish thunder-peal that follows it.

Blanch. I am not skill'd in eye-talking, madam. I have
been used to let my discourse ride upon my tongue; and,
I have been told, 'twill trot at a good round pace upon
occasion.

Helen. Then let it gallop, now, beseech you, wench,
And bring me news of Mortimer.

Blanch. Then, madam, I saw Sir Edward in his library:

and deliver'd your letter. He will be here, either in the
evening, or on the morrow: 'tis uncertain which—for
his brother, Captain Fitzharding, is arrived, on a visit
to him.

Helen. Is he?—well, that may somewhat raise his
spirits.
That soldier has a pleasant, harmless mind.
Mirth gilds his age, and sits upon his brow
Like sun in winter. I ne'er saw a man
More cheerful in decline, more laughter-loving,
More gay, and frolicksome.

Blanch. Frolicksome enough, if you knew all—But not
so harmless.   (*aside.*)

Helen. He'll scarce be here to night.

Blanch. Who? Sir Edward? Haply not, madam: but his
letter may chance to specify further particulars.

Helen. His letter! Has he written?—fie upon thee!
Why didst not give it me, at once? Where is it?
Thou art turn'd dreamer, wench!—Come, quickly.

Blanch. You talk'd to me so much of reading eyes,
madam, that I e'en forgot the letter. Here it is.

Helen. Come to me, shortly, in my cabinet:
I'll read it there.—I am almost unfit
To open it. I ne'er receive his letters
But my hand trembles. Well, I know 'tis silly,
And yet I cannot help it. I will ring;
Then come to me, good Blanch—not yet. My Mortimer,
Now for your letter!   (*Exit.*)

Blanch. I would they were wedded once, and all this
trembling would be over. I am told your married lady's
feelings are little roused in reading letters from a husband.

Enter SAMSON—*dress'd in a Livery*

Sam. This sudden turn of fortune might puff some men
up with pride. I have look'd in the glass already:—and if
ever man look'd braver in a glass than I, I know nothing
of finery.

Blanch. Hey day! who have we here?

Sam. Oh, lord! this is the maid.——I mean the waiting woman. I warrant we shall be rare company, in a long winter's evening.

Blanch. Why, who are you?

Sam. I'm your fellow-servant:—the new comer. The last footman cast his skin in the pantry this morning, and I have crept into it.

Blanch. Why, sure, it cannot be!—Now I look upon you again, you are Samson Rawbold—old Rawbold's son, of the forest, here.

Sam. The same. I am not like some upstarts. When I am prosperous, I do not turn my back on my poor relations.

Blanch. What, has my lady hired thee?

Sam. She has taken me, like a pad nag, upon trial.

Blanch. I suspect you will play her a jade's trick, and stumble in your probation. You have been caught tripping, ere now.

Sam. An I do not give content 'tis none of my fault. A man's qualities cannot come out all at once. I wish you would teach me a little how to lay a cloth.

Blanch. You are well qualified for your office, truly, not to know that.

Sam. To say truth, we had little practice that way, at home. We stood not upon forms. We had sometimes no cloth for a dinner——

Blanch. And, sometimes, no dinner for a cloth.

Sam. Just so. We had little order in our family.

Blanch. Well, I will instruct you.

Sam. That's kind. I will be grateful. They tell me I have learnt nothing but wickedness, yet: but I will instruct you in any thing I know, in return.

Blanch. There I have no mind to become your scholar. But be steady in your service, and you may outlive your beggary, and grow into respect.

Sam. Nay, an riches rain upon me, respect will grow of course. I never knew a rich man yet who wanted followers to pull off their caps to him.

SONG

Samson

I

A traveller stopt at a widow's gate;
She kept an Inn, and he wanted to bait;——
    But the landlady slighted her guest:
For when Nature was making an ugly race,
She certainly moulded the traveller's face
    As a sample for all the rest.

II

The chamber-maid's sides they were ready to crack,
When she saw his queer nose, and the hump at his back;—
    A hump isn't handsome, no doubt——
And, though 'tis confess'd that the prejudice goes,
Very strongly, in favour of wearing a nose,
    Yet a nose shouldn't look like a snout.

III

A bag full of gold on the table he laid——
'T had a wond'rous effect on the widow and maid!
    And they quickly grew marvellous civil.
The money immediately alter'd the case;
They were charm'd with his hump, and his snout, and his face,
    Tho' he still might have frighten'd the devil.

IV

He paid like a prince—gave the widow a smack——
Then flop'd on his horse at the door, like a sack;
    While the landlady, touching the chink,
Cried—'Sir, should you travel this country again,
'I heartily hope that the sweetest of men
    'Will stop at the widow's to drink.'

Exeunt.

SCENE IV. *The* LIBRARY

WILFORD *discovered*

Wilf. I would Sir Edward were come! The dread of a fearful encounter is, often, as terrible as the encounter itself. Yet my encounters with him, of late, are no trifles. Some few hours back, in this very room, he held a loaded pistol within an inch of my brains. Well, that was passion—he threw it from him on the instant, and—eh!—He's coming. —No. The old wainscot cracks and frightens me out of my wits, and, I verily believe, the great folio dropt on my head, just now, from the shelf, on purpose to increase my terrors.

(*Enter* SIR EDWARD MORTIMER, *at one door of the Library, which he locks after him.* WILFORD *turns round on hearing him shut it.*)

Wilf. What's that?—'Tis he himself! Mercy on me! he has lock'd the door!—What is going to become of me!

Mort. Wilford!—Is no one in the picture gallery?

Wilf. No——not a soul, Sir——Not a human soul— None within hearing, if I were to bawl Ever so loud.

Mort. Lock yonder door.

Wilf. The door, Sir!

Mort. Do as I bid you.

Wilf. What, Sir? Lock——(MORTIMER *waves with his hand.*)

I shall, Sir. (*going to the door and locking it.*) His face has little anger in it, neither: 'Tis rather mark'd with sorrow, and distress.

Mort. Wilford, approach me.—What am I to say For aiming at your life!—Do you not scorn me, Despise me for it?

Wilf. I! Oh, Sir!——

Mort. You must. For I am singled from the herd of men, A vile, heart-broken wretch!

Wilf. Indeed, indeed, Sir,
You deeply wrong yourself. Your equal's love,
The poor man's prayer, the orphan's tear of grati-
    tude,
All follow you:—and I!—I owe you all!
I am most bound to bless you.

   Mort. Mark me, Wilford.—
I know the value of the orphan's tear,
The poor man's prayer, respect from the respected;
I feel to merit these, and to obtain them,
Is to taste here, below, that thrilling cordial
Which the remunerating Angel draws,
From the eternal fountain of delight,
To pour on blessed souls, that enter heaven.
I feel this:—I!—How must my nature, then,
Revolt at him who seeks to stain his hand,
In human blood?—and yet it seems, this day,
I sought your life.—O! I have suffer'd madness—
None know my tortures—pangs!—but I can end them:
End them as far as appertains to thee.—
I have resolv'd it.—Hell born struggles tear me!
But I have ponder'd on't,—and I must trust thee.

   Wilf. Your confidence shall not be——

   Mort. You must swear.

   Wilf. Swear, Sir!—will nothing but an oath, then——

   Mort. Listen.
May all the ills that wait on frail humanity
Be doubled on your head, if you disclose
My fatal secret! May your body turn
Most lazar-like, and loathsome; and your mind
More loathsome than your body! May those fiends
Who strangle babes, for very wantonness,
Shrink back, and shudder at your monstrous crimes,
And, shrinking, curse you! Palsies strike your youth!
And the sharp terrors of a guilty mind
Poison your aged days; while all your nights,
As on the earth you lay your houseless head,
Out-horror horror! May you quit the world

Abhor'd, self-hated, hopeless for the next,
Your life a burthen, and your death a fear!

Wilf. For mercy's sake, forbear! you terrify me!

Mort. Hope this may fall upon thee;—Swear thou
      hopest it,
By every attribute which heaven, earth, hell,
Can lend, to bind, and strengthen conjuration,
If thou betray'st me.

Wilf. Well I———*(hesitating.)*

Mort. No retreating!

Wilf. (after a pause.)
I swear by all the ties that bind a man,
Divine, or human,—never to divulge!

Mort. Remember you have sought this secret:—Yes,
Extorted it. I have not thrust it on you.
'Tis big with danger to you; and to me,
While I prepare to speak, torment unutterable.
Know, Wilford, that——damnation!

Wilf. Dearest Sir!
Collect yourself. This shakes you horribly.
You had this trembling, it is scarce a week,
At Madam Helen's.

Mort. There it is.—Her uncle—

Wilf. Her uncle!

Mort. Him. She knows it not—None know it—
You are the first ordain'd to hear me say,
I am——his murderer.

Wilf. O, heaven!

Mort. His assassin.

Wilf. What, you that—mur—the murder—I am
      choak'd!

Mort. Honour, thou blood-stain'd God! at whose red
      altar
Sit War and Homicide, O, to what madness
Will insult drive thy votaries! By heaven,
In the world's range there does not breathe a man
Whose brutal nature I more strove to soothe,
With long forbearance, kindness, courtesy,

Than his who fell by me. But he disgraced me,
Stain'd me,—oh, death, and shame! the world look'd on,
And saw this sinewy savage strike me down;
Rain blows upon me, drag me to and fro,
On the base earth, like carrion. Desperation,
In every fibre of my frame, cried vengeance!
I left the room, which he had quitted. Chance,
(Curse on the chance!) while boiling with my wrongs,
Thrust me against him, darkling in the street:—
I stab'd him to the heart:—and my oppressor
Roll'd, lifeless, at my foot.
    Wilf. Oh! mercy on me!
How could this deed be cover'd!
    Mort. Would you think it?
E'en at the moment when I gave the blow,
Butcher'd a fellow creature in the dark,
I had all good men's love. But my disgrace,
And my opponent's death, thus link'd with it,
Demanded notice of the magistracy.
They summon'd me, as friend would summon friend,
To acts of import, and communication.
We met: and 'twas resolved, to stifle rumour,
To put me on my trial. No accuser,
No evidence appear'd, to urge it on.—
'Twas meant to clear my fame.—How clear it, then?
How cover it? you say.—Why, by a Lie:—
Guilt's offspring, and its guard. I taught this breast,
Which Truth once made her throne, to forge a lie;
This tongue to utter it.—Rounded a tale,
Smooth as a Seraph's song from Satan's mouth;
So well compacted, that the o'er throng'd court
Disturb'd cool justice, in her judgment seat,
By shouting 'Innocence!' ere I had finish'd.
The Court enlarged me; and the giddy rabble
Bore me, in triumph, home. Aye!—look upon me.—
I know thy sight aches at me.
    Wilf. Heaven forgive me!
I think I love you still:—but I am young;

I know not what to say:—it may be wrong.—
Indeed I pity you.

   Mort. I disdain all pity.—
I ask no consolation. Idle boy!
Think'st thou that this compulsive confidence
Was given to move thy pity?—Love of Fame
(For still I cling to it) has urged me, thus,
To quash thy curious mischief in it's birth.
Hurt honour, in an evil, cursed hour,
Drove me to murder—lying:—'twould again.
My honesty,—sweet peace of mind,—all, all!
Are barter'd for a name. I *will* maintain it.
Should slander whisper o'er my sepulchre,
And my soul's agency survive in death,
I could embody it with heaven's lightning,
And the hot shaft of my insulted spirit
Should strike the blaster of memory
Dead in the church-yard. Boy, I would not kill thee:
Thy rashness and discernment threaten'd danger:
To check them there was no way left but this:—
Save one—your death:—you shall not be my victim.

   Wilf. My death! What, take my life?—My life! to prop
This empty honour?

   Mort. Empty! Groveling fool!

   Wilf. I am your servant, Sir: child of your bounty;
And know my obligation. I have been
Too curious, haply; 'tis the fault of youth.
I ne'er meant injury: if it would serve you,
I would lay down my life; I'd give it freely:—
Could you, then, have the heart to rob me of it?
You could not;—should not.

   Mort. How!

   Wilf. You dare not.

   Mort. Dare not!

   Wilf. Some hours ago you durst not. Passion moved you;
Reflection interposed, and held your arm.
But, should reflection prompt you to attempt it,
My innocence would give me strength to struggle,

And wrest the murderous weapon from your hand.
How would you look to find a peasant boy
Return the knife you level'd at his heart;
And ask you which in heaven would shew the best,
A rich man's honour, or a poor man's honesty?

  Mort. 'Tis plain I dare not take your life. To spare it,
I have endanger'd mine. But dread my power;—
You know not it's extent. Be warn'd in time:
Trifle not with my feelings. Listen, Sir!
Myriads of engines, which my secret working
Can rouse to action, now encircle you.
I speak not vaguely. You have heard my principle;
Have heard, already, what it can effect:
Be cautious how you thwart it. Shun my brother;
Your ruin hangs upon a thread: Provoke me,
And it shall fall upon you. Dare to make
The slightest movement to awake my fears,
And the gaunt criminal, naked and stake-tied,
Left on the heath to blister in the sun,
'Till lingering death shall end his agony,
Compared to thee, shall seem more enviable
Than Cherubs to the damn'd.

  Wilf. O, misery!
Discard me, sir! I must be hateful to you.
Banish me hence. I will be mute as death;
But let me quit your service.

  Mort. Never.—Fool!
To buy this secret, you have sold yourself.
Your movements, eyes, and, most of all, your breath,
From this time forth, are fetter'd to my will.
You have said, truly: you are hateful to me:—
Yet you shall feel my bounty:—that shall flow,
And swell your fortunes; but my inmost soul
Will yearn with loathing, when—hark! some one knocks!
Open the door.

       [WILFORD *opens the door, and* WINTERTON *comes in.*]
  Mort. How now, Winterton?
Did you knock more than once? Speak—did you listen—

—I mean, good Adam, did you wait?—Aye, wait
Long at the door, here?

   Wint. Bless your honour! no.
You are too good to let the old man wait.

   Mort. What, then, our talk, here—Wilford's here and
mine—
Did not detain you at the door?—Ha!—did it?

   Wint. Not half a second.

   Mort. Oh!—well, what's the matter?

   Wint. Captain Fitzharding, Sir, entreats your company.
I've placed another flaggon on the table.
Your worship knows it.—Number thirty-five:—
The supernaculum.

   Mort. Well, well.—I come.
What, has he been alone?

   Wint. No—I've been with him.
Od! he's a merry man! and does so jest!
He calls me first of men, cause my name's Adam.
Well! 'tis exceeding pleasant, by St. Thomas!

   Mort. Come, Adam; I'll attend the Captain.—Wilford,
What I have just now given you in charge,
Be sure to keep fast lock'd. I shall be angry,—
Be very angry if I find you careless.
Follow me, Adam. (*Exit.* MORTIMER—WINTERTON *following.*

   Wilf. This house is no house for me. Fly I will, I am
resolved:—but whither? His threats strike terror into me;
and, were I to reach the pole, I doubt whether I should elude
his grasp. But to live here a slave—slave to his fears,—
his jealousies! Night's coming on. Darkness be my friend!
for I will forth instantly. The thought of my innocence
will cheer me as I wander thro' the gloom. Oh! when
guilty Ambition writhes upon its couch, why should bare-
foot Integrity repine, though it's sweet sleep be canopied
with a ragged hovel!   (*Exit.*

SCENE V. *The inside of an Abbey, in ruins. Part of it converted into an habitation for Robbers. Various entrances to their apartment, through the broken arches of the building, &c. &c.*

Enter JUDITH, *and a* BOY

Jud. Well, sirrah! have you been upon the scout? Are any of our gang returning?

Boy. No, Judith! not a soul.

Jud. The rogues tarry thus to fret me.

Boy. Why, indeed, Judith, the credit of your cookery is lost among thieves. They never come punctual to their meals.

Jud. No tidings of Orson yet, from the market town?

Boy. I have seen nothing of him.

Jud. Brat! thou dost never bring me good news.

Boy. Judith, you are ever so cross with me!

Jud. That wretch Orson slights my love of late. Hence, you hemp-feed, hence! Get to the broken porch of the abbey, and watch. 'Tis all you are good for.

Boy. You know I am but young yet, Judith, but with good instructions, I may be a robber, in time.

Jud. Away, you imp! you will never reach such preferment. (*A whistle without.*) So! I hear some of our party. (*Whistle again; the boy puts his fingers in his mouth, and whistles in answer.*)

Jud. Why must you keep your noise, sirrah?

Boy. Nay, Judith, 'tis one of the first steps we boys learn in the profession. I shall ne'er come to good, if you check me so. Huzza! here come two!

Enter two ROBBERS, *through the broken part of the Scene*

Jud. So! you have found your road at last. A murrain light upon you! is it thus you keep your hours?

1st Rob. What, hag, ever at this trade! Ever grumbling?

Jud. I have reason. I toil to no credit; I watch with no thanks. I trim up the table for your return, and no one returns in due time to notice my industry. Your meat is scorch'd to cinders. Rogues, would it were poison for you!

2d Rob. How the fury raves! Here, take my carbine; 'twas levell'd, some half hour since, at a traveller's head.

Jud. Hah, hah, hah! Rare! Didst shoot him?

1st Rob. Shoot him? No. This devil in petticoats thinks no more of flaying a man, than killing a cock-chafer. I never knew a woman turn to mischief, that she did not outdo a man, clean.

Jud. Did any of you meet Orson on your way?

1st Rob. Aye, there the hand points. When that fellow is abroad you are more savage than customary; and that is needless.

2d Rob. None of our comrades come yet? They will be finely soak'd.

1st Rob. Aye, the rain pours, like a spout, upon the ruins of the old abbey wall here.

Jud. I'm glad on't. May it drench them, and breed agues! 'twill teach them to keep time.

1st Rob. Peace, thou abominable railer! A man had better dwell in purgatory, than have thee in his habitation— Peace, devil! or I'll make thee repent.

Jud. You! 'tis as much as thy life is worth to move my spleen.

1st Rob. What, you will set Orson, your champion, upon me?

Jud. Coward! he should not disgrace himself with chastising thee.

1st Rob. Death and thunder!——

Jud. Aye, attack a woman, do! it suits your hen-hearted valour. Assault a woman!

1st Rob. Well—passion hurried me. But I have a respect for the soft sex, and am cool again. Come Judith, be friends.—Nay, come, do; and I will give thee a farthingale, I took from a lawyer's widow.

Jud. Where is it?

1st Rob. You shall have it.

Jud. Well—I——Hark!

2d Rob. Soft! I think I hear the foot of a comrade.

MUSICAL DIALOGUE AND CHORUS

ROBBERS and JUDITH

> Listen! No; it is the owl,
> That hoots upon the mould'ring tow'r.
> Hark! the rain beats, the night is foul;
> Our comrades stay beyond their hour.
> Listen!
> All's hush'd around the abbey wall.———
> Soft! Now I hear a robber's call!
> Listen!
> They whistle!—Answer it!—'Tis nigh!
> Again! A comrade comes.—'Tis I!
> And here another; and here another!
> Who comes? A brother. Who comes?
> A brother.
> Now they all come pouring in;
> Our jollity will soon begin.
> Sturdy partners, all appear!
> We're here! and here, and here, and here!
> Thus we stout freebooters prowl,
> Then meet to drain the flowing bowl!

(*At different periods of the Musick, the* ROBBERS *enter, through
various parts of the Ruins, in groups.*

Enter ORSON, *with Luggage on his Back, as if return'd
from Market*

1st Rob. See! hither comes Orson at last. He walks in
like Plenty, with provision on his shoulder.

Jud. O, Orson!—why did'st tarry, Orson? I began to
fear. Thou art cold and damp. Let me wring the wet
from thy cloaths. O! my heart leaps to see thee.

1st Rob. Mark how this she-bear hugs her bruin!

Ors. Stand off! this hamper has been wearisome enough.
I want not thee on my neck.

Jud. Villain! 'tis thus you ever use me. I can revenge:—
I can——do not, dear Orson! do not treat me thus.

Ors. Let a man be ever so sweet temper'd, he will meet
somewhat to sour it. I have been vex'd to madness.

2d Rob. How now, Orson, what has vex'd thee now?

Ors. A prize has slipt through my fingers.

3d Rob. Aye! marry, how?

Ors. I met a straggling knave on foot, and the rogue resisted. He had the face to tell me that he was thrust on the world to seek his fortune; and that the little he had about him was his all. Plague on the provision at my back! I had no time to rifle him:—but I have spoil'd him for fortune seeking, I warrant him.

Rob. How?

Ors. Why I beat him to the ground. Whether he will e'er get up again the next passenger may discover.

Jud. Ha! Ha! O, brave! That's my valiant Orson!

3d Rob. Orson, you are ever disobeying our Captain's order. You are too remorseless, and bloody.

Ors. Take heed, then, how you move my anger, by telling me on't. The affair is mine—I will answer to the consequence.

4th Rob. I hear our Captain's signal. Here he comes. Ha!—he is leading one who seems wounded.

Enter ARMSTRONG, *supporting* WILFORD

Arm. Gently, good fellow! come, keep a good heart!

Wilf. You are very kind. I had breathed my last, but for your care. Whither have you led me?

4th Rob. Where you will be well treated, youngster. You are now among as honourable a knot of men as ever cried 'stand' to a traveller.

Wilf. How: among robbers!

4th Rob. Why, so the law's cant calls us gentlemen, who live at large.

Wilf. So! For what am I reserved!

Arm. Fear nothing. You are safe in this asylum. Judith, lead him in. See some of my linen ready, and look to his wound.

Jud. I do not like the office. You are ever at these tricks. 'Twill ruin us in the end. What have we to do with charity?

Arm. Turbulent wretch! obey me.

Jud. Well, I shall. Come, fellow, since it must be so.

Arm. Anon, I'll visit you myself, lad.

Wilf. Heaven bless you! whate'er becomes of my life—and faith, I am almost weary on't—I am bound to your charity. Gently, I pray you—my wound pains.—Gently!

(*Exit, led out by* JUDITH.)

Arm. I would I knew which of you had done this.

1st Rob. Why, what's the matter, Captain?

Arm. Cruelty is the matter. Had not accident led me to the spot where he lay, yon poor boy had bled to death. I learn'd his story, partly, from him, on the way: and know how basely he has been handled by one of you. Well, time must discover him: for he, who had brutality enough to commit the action, can scarcely have courage enough to confess it.

Ors. Courage, Captain, is a quality, I take it, little wanted by any here. What signify words—I did it.

Arm. I suspected thee, Orson. 'Tis scarce an hour since he, whom thou hast wounded, quitted the service of Sir Edward Mortimer, in the forest here; and inquiry will doubtless be made.

2d Rob. Nay, then we are all discover'd.

Arm. Now, mark what thou hast done. Thou hast endanger'd the safety of our party; thou hast broken my order ('tis not the first time, by many) in attacking a passenger:—and what passenger? One whose unhappy case should have claim'd thy pity. He told you he had displeased his master—left the house of comfort, and with his scanty pittance, was wandering round the world to mend his fortune. Like a butcher, you struck the forlorn boy to the earth, and left him to languish in the forest. Would any of our brave comrades have done this?

All. None! None!

Arm. Comrades, in this case, my voice is single. But if it have any weight, this brute, this Orson, shall be thrust from our community, which he has disgraced. Let it not be said, brothers, while want drives us to plunder, that wantonness prompts us to butchery.

Robbers. O brave Captain! away with him!

Ors. You had better ponder on't, ere you provoke me.

Arm. Rascal! do you mutter threats? You cannot terrifye us. Our calling teems with danger—we are not to be daunted by the treachery of an informer. We defye you. Go. You dare not hurt us. You dare not sacrifice so many brave and gallant fellows, to your revenge, and proclaim yourself scoundrel. Begone.

Ors. Well, if I must, I must. I was always a friend to you all: but if you are bent on turning me out—why—fare you well.

Robbers. Aye, aye—Away, Away!

Ors. Farewell, then.   (*Exit.*

Arm. Come, comrades—Think no more of this. Let us drown the choler we have felt in wine and revelry.

FINALE

Jolly Friars tippled here
Ere these Abbey walls had crumbled;
   Still the ruins boast good cheer,
Though long ago the cloisters tumbled.

     The Monks are gone!——
       Well! well!
     That's all one:——
       Let's ring their knell.
Ding dong! ding dong! to the bald-pated monk!
     He set the example,
     We'll follow his sample,
And all go to bed most religiously drunk.
    Peace to the good fat Friar's soul!
      Who, every day,
      Did wet his clay,
    In the deep capacious bowl.
Huzza! Huzza! we'll drink and we'll sing!
    We'll laugh, and we'll quaff,
    And make the welkin ring!

END OF THE SECOND ACT

ACT III

SCENE I. WINTERTON's *Room, in* Sir EDWARD MORTIMER's *Lodge*

SAMSON *and* BLANCH, *discover'd, at a Table, with Bottles and Glasses*

Blanch. Samson, you must drink no more.

Sam. One more glass, Mistress Blanch, and I shall be better company. 'Twill make me loving.

Blanch. Nay, then, you shall not have a drop.

Sam. I will:—and so shall you too. (*filling the glass*) Who knows but it may make you the same.

Blanch. You are wond'rous familiar, Mr. Lout.

Sam. I would not willingly offend. I will endeavour at more respect. My humble duty to you. (*drinks.*)

Blanch. I would counsel you to be cautious of drinking, Samson. Consider where you are. We are now, remember, in Sir Edward Mortimer's Lodge.

Sam. In the Butler's room;—where drinking has always a privilege. (*fills.*)

Blanch. What, another!

Sam. Do not fear. 'Twill not make me familiar again. My lowly respects to you. (*drinks*) This same old Winterton's wine has a marvellous choice flavour. I wonder whether 'twas smuggled.

Blanch. Should you totter with this, now, in the morning, 'twould go nigh to shake your office to the foundation, before night. My Lady would never pardon you.

Sam. 'Twould be hard to turn me adrift, for getting drunk, on the second day of my service.

Blanch. Truly, I think 'twould be reason sufficient.

Sam. 'Twould not be giving a man a fair trial. How should she know but I intend to be sober for a year after?

Blanch. How should she know, indeed! or any one else, who has heard of your former rogueries.

Sam. Well, the worst fault I had was being a sports-man.

Blanch. A sportsman! out on you, rogue! you were a poacher.

Sam. Aye, so the rich nick-name us poor brothers of the field; and lay us by the heels when we do that for hunger which they practice for amusement. Cannot I move you to take a thimble-full, this cold morning?

Blanch. Not a drop, I.

Sam. Hark! I think I hear old Winterton coming back. By our lady, Mistress Blanch, we have made a desperate hole in the bottle, since he left us.

Blanch. We! why, you slanderous rogue, I have not tasted it.

Sam. No—'tis not he.

Blanch. No matter; he will be back on the instant. Leave this idle guzzling, if you have any shame. Think we are attending madam Helen, in her visit to Sir Edward, on his sudden sickness. Think, too, on the confusion from Wilford's flight. Is it a time for you, sot, to tipple, when the whole house is in distress and melancholy?

Sam. Alas! I have too tender a heart, Mistress Blanch; and have need of somewhat, in the midst of this sorrow, to cheer my spirits.

Blanch. This wine will shortly give your professions of amendment the lie.

Sam. Let it give me the lie: 'Tis an affront I can easily swallow. Come, a bargain—an you will take one glass with me, I will give over.

Blanch. Well, on that condition——

Sam. Agreed—for that will just finish the bottle. (*fills*) I will drink no health, now, but of thy giving.

Blanch. Then listen and edifye.—May a man never insult a woman with his company, when drunkenness has made him a brute.

Sam. With all my heart:—But a woman knows that man may be made a brute, when wine is clean out of the question. Eh! Here comes the old man in real earnest.

Enter ADAM WINTERTON

Wint. Well, I am here again.—What, madcap?—In

truth, I have a world of care. Our good master taken ill, on the sudden. Wilford flown:—A base, ungrateful boy!— One that I was so fond of:—And to prove such a profligate! I began to love the young villain like my own child. I had mark'd down the unfortunate boy, in my last testament: I had——Bless me! my cold is wond'rous troublesome to my eyes, this morning. Ah! 'tis a wicked world:—— But old Winterton keeps a merry heart, still. Do I not, pretty mistress Blanch?

Blanch. I hope you do, Adam.

Wint. Nay, on second thought, I do not keep it; for thou hast stolen it from me, tulip! ha! good i' faith!—

Sam. Ha! ha!—Well i' faith that is a good jest! ha! ha!

Wint. Dost think so, varlet? 'Thou hast stolen it from me, tulip!' Well, it was; it was exceeding pleasant, by St. Thomas! Heigho! I must e'en take a glass to console me. One cup to——eh! mercy on me! why the liquor has flown. Ha! the bottle has leak'd, haply.

Sam. Yes, Sir:—I crack'd that bottle, myself, in your absence.

Wint. Crack'd! Why what a careless goose art thou! these unthrifty knaves!—ah! times are sadly changed, for the worse, since I was a boy.

Blanch. Dost think so, Adam?

Wint. Question any man, of my age, and he will say the same. Domesticks never broke bottles in queen Elizabeth's time. Servants were better then—aye, marry, and the bottles were better bottles. 'Tis a degenerate world! Well; heigho!

Blanch. Why dost sigh thus, Adam?

Wint. In truth, this is as heavy a day for me—

Blanch. I hope not, Adam. Come, come, things are not so bad, I warrant thee. You have long drank smilingly of the cup of life, Adam; and when a good man takes his potion without murmuring, Providence seldom leaves the bitterest drop at the bottom. What is the matter, Adam?

Wint. Alas! nothing but evil. These attacks come on our worthy master as thick as hail, and weaken him daily.

He has been grievous ill, in the night, poor soul! and ne'er slept a wink since I brought him the news.

Blanch. What news, good Adam?

Wint. Why of Wilford's flight.—A reprobate! The shock of his baseness has brought on Sir Edward's old symptoms.

Blanch. What call you his old symptoms?

Wint. The shiverings, and trembling fits, which have troubled him these two years. I begin to think the air of this forest doth nourish agues. I can never move him to drink enough of canary. I think, in my conscience, I had been aguish myself, in these woods, had I not drank plenty of canary.

Sam. Mass, when I am ill, this old boy shall be my apothecary. *(aside.*

Blanch. Well, well, he may mend. Do not fancy the worst, ere worse arrives, Adam.

Wint. Nay, worse has arrived, already.

Blanch. Aye! marry, how?

Wint. Wilford's villany. Sir Edward says, he has proofs of the blackest treachery against him.

Blanch. Indeed!

Wint. It chills my old blood to think on't! I had mark'd out the boy as a boy of promise—A learned boy! He had the backs of all the books in our library by heart; and now a hue and cry is after him. Mercy on me! if the wretched lad be taken, Sir Edward will bring him to the charge. We none know what 'tis yet; but time will shew.

Blanch. You surprise me! Wilford turn dishonest! I could scarce have credited this; and after two years trial, too.

Sam. O, monstrous! to turn rogue after two years trial! Had it happened after two days, indeed, 'twere not to be wonder'd at.

Enter a SERVANT

Serv. Mr. Winterton, there is a young woman of the forest, would speak with you.

Wint. Out on't! These cottagers time their business vilely. Well, bid her come in, Simon.

Serv. And, Mistress Blanch, your lady would see you anon, in the breakfast parlour.   (*Exit.*

Blanch. I come quickly. Be not cast down, now, Adam; keep thy old heart merry still.

Wint. Ha! in truth, I know not well, now, what would mend my spirits.

Blanch. What think you of the kiss I promised?

Wint. Ah, wag! go thy way. Od! thou hast nimble legs. Had I o'ertaken thee yesterday——Ah! well, no matter.

Blanch. Come, I will not leave thee comfortless, in these sad times. Here—Here is my hand, Adam.

Wint. Thou wilt shew me a light pair of heels again, now.

Blanch. No, in faith. Come; 'tis more than I would offer to every one. Take it.

Wint. That I will, most willingly. (*Kisses her hand.*)

Blanch. Do not play the rake now, and boast of my favours; for I am told there is a breed of puppies will build stories, to a simple girl's prejudice, on slighter encouragement than this. Be not you one of those empty coxcombs, and so adieu, Adam.   (*Exit.*

Wint. Nay, I was never given to vaunt. 'Sbud! if I had, many a tale had been told, sixty years back, of young, lusty Adam Winterton.—Eh! why, what dost thou titter at, scapegrace?

Sam. I, sir?—Not I.   (*smothering a laugh.*

Wint. I had forgot this varlet. Pestilence on't! Should this knave prate of my little gallantry, I tremble for the good name of poor Mistress Blanch!

Enter BARBARA

Barb. May I come in, good your worship?

Wint. Aye, marry, that thou may'st, pretty one.—Well, though many things have declined, since I was a boy, female beauty keeps its rank still. I do think there be more pretty women now than there were in Queen Elizabeth's reign.

Sam. Flesh! this is our Barbara.   (*aside.*

Wint. Well, and what wouldst have, sweet one, with old Adam——Eh! by St. Thomas, why thou art she I have seen, ere now, with Wilford.

Barb. Beseech you, tell me where he is, Sir.

Wint. Alas, child, he's gone—flown! Eh? what—why, art not well, child?

Barb. Nothing, Sir——I only——I hoped he would have called at our cottage, ere he quitted the forest. Is there no hope that he may come back, Sir?

Wint. None, truly, except force bring him back. Alas, child! the boy has turn'd out naught; and justice is dogging him at the heels.

Barb. What, Wilford, Sir?—my poor—O, Sir, my heart is bursting! I pray you, pardon me. Had he pass'd our cottage in his flight, I would have ran out, and follow'd him all the world over.

Wint. To see what love will do! Just so did Jane Blackthorn take on for me, when Sir Marmaduke carried me to London, in the hard winter.

Barb. Beseech you, forgive me, Sir! I only came to make inquiry, for I had heard a strange tale. I would not have my sorrows make me troublesome to your worship.

Wint. To me? poor wench! nay, that thou art not. I trust, child, I ne'er turn'd a deaf ear, yet, to the unfortunate. 'Tis man's office to listen to the sorrows of a woman, and do all he can to soothe them. Come, come, dry thy tears, chicken.

Barb. I look'd to have been his wife shortly, Sir. He was as kind a youth——And, I am sure, he wanted not gratitude. I have heard him talk of you, as you were his father, Sir.

Wint. Did he? Ah! poor lad. Well, he had good qualities; but, alas! he is now a reprobate. Poor boy! To think, now, that he should speak kindly of the old man, behind his back!

Barb. Alas, this is the second flight to bring unhappiness to our poor family!

Wint. The second! How do'st mean, wench?

Barb. My brother, Sir, left our cottage suddenly, yesterday morning; and we have no tidings of him since.

Sam. Lo you, now, where he stands, to glad the hearts of his disconsolate relations! Sister Barbara, why dost not know me?

Barb. Eh! No—Sure it can't————Brother Samson?

Sam. Mr. Samson—Head serving-man to the Lady Helen, of the New Forest.

Barb. O, the fortune! can it be? what gain'd thee so good a place, Samson?

Sam. Merit. I had no interest to back me. Mine is a rare case—I was promoted on the score of my virtues.

Wint. Out upon thee! thy knaveries have been the talk of the whole forest; and furnish'd daily food for conversation.

Sam. Truly, then, conversation has fared better upon them than I. But my old character is laid aside, with my old jerkin. I am now exalted.

Wint. An I have any forecast, in destiny, friend, thou bidst fair, one day, to be more exalted.—Ha! good i' faith! Come, you must to the kitchen, knave. I must thither myself, to give order for the day.

Barb. Must I return home, then, your worship, with no tidings?

Wint. Ah! heaven help me! what havock doth wanton Cupid make with us all! Well, tarry about the house, with thy brother; we may hear somewhat, haply, anon. Take care of thy sister, knave; and mark what I have said to thee. —'Thou bidst fair one day to be more exalted.' Ha! well, it was exceeding pleasant, by St. Thomas!   (*Exit*.

Sam. Well, Barbara, and how fares father?

Barb. He has done nought but chide, since you disappear'd, Samson. It has sour'd him with us all.

Sam. Well, I will call, soon, and set all even.

Barb. Will you, brother?

Sam. I will. Bid him not be cast down. I will protect the Rawbold family.

Barb. Truly, brother, we are much in need of protection.

Sam. Do not fear. Lean upon my power. I am head of all the male domesticks, at madam Helen's.

Barb. O, the father! of all! and how many be there, brother?

Sam. Why, truly, not so many as there be at the Lodge, here. But I have a boy under me, to chop wood, and draw water.

Barb. The money we had from Sir Edward's bounty is nearly gone, in payment of the debt our father owed. You know he had shortly been imprison'd, else.

Sam. My stock is somewhat low, too.—But, no matter. Keep a good heart. I am now a rising man. I will make you all comfortable.

Barb. Heaven bless you, Samson!

Sam. In three months, I look for a quarter's wages; and then Dick shall have a shirt. I must now take you roundly to task.

Barb. Me, brother!

Sam. Aye, marry. You would throw yourself away on this Wilford—who, as the story goes, is little better than the devil's own imp.

Barb. O, brother! be not so uncharitable. I know not what is against him, but he has not been heard yet. Consider too—were all our actions, at home, to be sifted, I fear me, we might not escape blameless.

Sam. Aye, but he, it seems, is falling, and we are upon the rise; and that makes all the difference. Mass! how gingerly men will sift the faults of those who are getting up hill in the world; and what a rough shake they give those who are going downward!

Barb. I would not be one of those sifters, brother.

Sam. No,—I warrant, now, thou wouldst marry this vagabond.

Barb. That I would, brother. He has cheer'd me in my distress, and I would sooner die than leave him, now he is unfortunate.

Sam. Hast thou no respect for the family? Thou wilt bring endless disgrace on the name of Rawbold. Shame on

you; to take away from our reputation, when we have so
little!

Barb. I thought, brother, you would have shewn more
pity for your poor sister.

Sam. Tush! Love's a mere vapour.

Barb. Ah, brother!

DUET

SAMSON *and* BARBARA

I

Barbara

From break of the morning, were I with my love,
I'd talk till the evening drew nigh;
 And, when the day did close,
 I'd sing him to repose,
And tune my love a lullaby.

II

Samson

From break of the morning, were I with my love,
O! long ere the evening drew nigh,
 Her talk would make me doze,
 Till the musick of my nose
Would play my love a lullaby.

III

Barbara

Our children around us, I'd look on my love,
Each moment in rapture would fly.

Samson

 But love is apt to pall,
 When the brats begin to squall,
And a wife is screaming lullaby.

From break of the morning. &c.   [*Exeunt.*

N

SCENE II. *A Room in Sir* EDWARD MORTIMER'S *Lodge*

MORTIMER *and* HELEN *discover'd*

Hel. Sooth, you look better now; indeed you do.

Mort. Thou'rt a sweet flatterer!

Hel. Ne'er trust me, then,
If I do flatter. This is wilfulness.—
Thou wilt be sick, because thou wilt be sick.
I'll laugh away this fancy, Mortimer.

Mort. What couldst thou do to laugh away my sickness?

Hel. I'll mimick the physician—wise and dull—
With cane at nose, and nod emphatical,
Portentous in my silence; feel your pulse,
With an owl's face, that shall express as much
As Galen's head, cut out in wood, and gilt,
Stuck over an apothecary's door.

Mort. And what wouldst thou prescribe?

Hel. I would distil
Each flower that lavish happiness produced,
Through the world's paradise, ere Disobedience
Scatter'd the seeds of care; then mingle each,
In one huge cup of comfort for thee, love,
To chace away thy dulness. Thou shouldst wanton
Upon the wings of Time, and mock his flight,
As he sail'd with thee tow'rd Eternity.
I'd have each hour, each minute of thy life,
A golden holiday; and should a cloud
O'ercast thee, be it light as gossamer,
That Helen might disperse it with her breath,
And talk thee into sunshine!

Mort. Sweet, sweet Helen!
Death, soften'd with thy voice, might dull his sting,
And steep his darts in balsam. Oh! my Helen,
These warnings which that grisly monarch sends,
Forerunners of his certain visitation,
Of late are frequent with me. It should seem
I was not meant to live long.

Hel. Mortimer!

My Mortimer! You——Oh! for heaven's sake,

Do not talk thus! You chill me. You are well;

Very well.—You give way—Oh, Mortimer!

Banish these fantasies. Think on poor Helen!

Mort. Think on thee, Helen?

Hel. Aye: but not think thus.

You said, my Mortimer, my voice could soothe,

In the most trying struggle.

Mort. Said I so?

Yet, Helen, when my fancy paints a death-bed,

I ever place thee foremost in the scene,

To make the picture touching. After man

Is summon'd, and has made up his account,

Oh! 'tis a bitter after-reck'ning, when

His pallid lips receive the last, sad kiss,

Fond, female anguish prints! Then, Helen, then,

Then comes man's agony! To leave the object

He shelter'd in his heart, grief-struck, and helpless!

To grasp her hand; to fix his hollow eye

Upon her face, and mark her mute despair,

'Till the last flutter of his aching spirit

Hurries him hence, for ever!

Hel. Oh! for pity——

What have I done, that you——   (*bursts into tears.*

Mort. My Helen!

Hel. I did not mean to weep. Oh, Mortimer,

I could not talk so cruelly to you!

I would not pain you thus, for worlds!

Mort. Nay, come;

I meant not this. I did not mean to say

There's danger now; but 'tis the privilege

Of sickness to be grave, and moralize

On that which sickness brings. I prithee, now,

Be comforted. Believe me, I shall mend.

I feel I shall, already.

Hel. Do you, Mortimer?

Do you, indeed, feel so?

Mort. Indeed I do.

Hel. I knew you would:—I said it. Did I not?
I am so glad! You must be cautious now.—
I'll play the nurse to-day—and then, to-morrow,
You shall not brood at home, as you are wont,
But we will ride together, through the forest,
You must have exercise. Oh! I will make you
Fresh as the summer dew-drop, and as healthy
As ruddy Labour, springing from his bed,
To carol o'er the fallow!

Mort. Dearest prattler!
Men would meet sickness with a smiling welcome,
Were all woo'd back to health thus prettily.

Hel. I see it in your looks, now, you are better.

Mort. Scarce possible, so suddenly!

Hel. O, yes;
There is no little movement of your face
But I can mark, on the instant—'Tis my study.
I have so gazed upon it, that, I think,
I can interpret ev'ry turn it has,
And read your inmost soul.

Mort. What?

Hel. Mercy on me!
You change again.

Mort. 'Twas nothing. Do not fear;
These little shocks are usual.—'Twill not last.

Hel. Would you could shake them off!

Mort. I would I could!

Hel. Resolve it, then; and the bare resolution
Will bring the remedy. Rally your spirits;
I prithee, now, endeavour.—This young man,
This boy—this Wilford—he has been ungrateful;
But do not let his baseness wear you thus.
Ev'n let him go.

Mort. I'll hunt him through the world!

Hel. Why, look you there now! Pray be calm.

Mort. Well, well;
I am too boisterous: 'Tis my unhappiness

To seem most harsh where I would shew most kind.
The world has made me peevish.—This same boy
Has somewhat moved me.

   Hel. He's beneath your care.
Seek him not now, to punish him. Poor wretch!
He carries that away, within his breast,
Which will embitter all his life to come,
And make him curse the knowledge on't.

   Mort. The knowledge!————
Has he then breathed————Carries within his breast!
What does he know?

   Hel. His own ingratitude.

   Mort. O, very true.

   Hel. Then leave him to his conscience.
It is a scorpion, sent by Heaven itself,
To fix on hidden crimes; a slow, still stream,
Of moulten lead, kept dropping on the heart,
To scald, and weigh it down. Believe me, love,
There is no earthly punishment so great,
To scourge an evil act, as man's own conscience,
To tell him he is guilty.

   Mort. 'Tis a hell!
I pray you talk no more on't.—I am weak—
I did not sleep last night.

   Hel. Would you sleep now?

   Mort. No, Helen, no. I tire thy patient sweetness.

   Hel. Tire me! nay, that you do not. You forget
How often I have sat by you, and watch'd,
Fanning the busy summer-flies away,
Lest they should break your slumbers. Who comes here?

Enter WINTERTON

What, Winterton! How do'st thou, old acquaintance?
How do'st thou, Adam?

   Wint. Bless your goodness, well.
Is my good master better?

   Hel. Somewhat, Adam.

Wint. Now, by our lady, I rejoice to hear it!
I have a message————.

   Hel. O, no business now!

   Wint. Nay, so I said. Quoth I, his honour's sick;
Perilous sick! but the rogue press'd, and press'd;
I could refuse no longer. Out upon them!
The varlets know old Winterton's good nature.
'Tis my weak side.

   Hel. Who has thus importuned you?

   Wint. To say the truth, a most ill-favour'd varlet.
But he will speak to none but to his worship.
I think 'tis forest business.

   Mort. O, not now:
Another time—to-morrow—when he will.
I am unfit.—They tease me!

   Wint. Ev'n as you please, your worship. I should think
From what he dropt, he can give some account
Of the poor boy.

   Mort. Of Wilford!

   Wint. Troth, I think so.
The knave is shy; but Adam has a head.

   Mort. Quick; send him hither on the instant! Haste!
Fly, Adam, fly!

   Wint. Well now, it glads my heart
To hear you speak so briskly

   Mort. Well, despatch!

   Wint. I go. Heaven bless you both! Heaven send you
     well,
And merry days may come again.   (*Exit.*

   Hel. I fear, this business may distract you, Mortimer:
I would you would defer it, till to-morrow.

   Mort. Not so, sweet. Do not fear. I prithee, now,
Let me have way in this. Retire awhile.
Anon I'll come to thee.

   Hel. Pray now, be careful.
I dread these agitations. Pray, keep calm.
Now do not tarry long. Adieu, my Mortimer!

   Mort. Farewel, awhile, sweet!

Hel. Since it must be so—

Farewel!   (*Exit* HELEN.

Mort. Dear, simple innocence! thy words of comfort
Pour oil upon my fires. Methought her eye,
When first she spake of conscience, shot a glance
Like her dead uncle on me. Well, for Wilford!
That slave can play the Parthian with my fame,
And wound it while he flies. Bring him before me,
Place me the runagate within my gripe,
And I will plant my honour on its base,
Firmer than adamant, tho' hell and death
Should moat the work with blood! Oh, how will sin
Engender sin! Throw guilt upon the soul,
And, like a rock dash'd on the troubled lake,
'Twill form its circles, round succeeding round,
Each wider than the——

Enter ORSON

How now! What's your business?

Ors. Part with your office in the forest: part
Concerns yourself in private.

Mort. How myself?

Ors. Touching a servant of your house; a lad,
Whose heels, I find, were nimbler than his duty.

Mort. Speak; what of him? Quick—Know you where he is?
Canst bring me to him?

Ors. To the very spot.

Mort. Do it.

Ors. Nay, softly.

Mort. I'll reward you—amply—
Ensure your fortunes.

Ors. First ensure my neck.
'Twill do me little good else. I've no heirs;
And, when I die, 'tis like the law will bury me,
At its own charge.

Mort. Be brief, and to your purpose.

Ors. Then, to the business which concerns your office,
Here, in the forest.

Mort. Nay, of that anon.
First of my servant.

Ors. Well, ev'n as you please.
'Tis no rare thing—Let publick duty wait,
Till private interests are settled. But
My story is a chain. Take all together,
'Twill not unlink.

Mort. Be quick then. While we talk,
This slave escapes me.

Ors. Little fear of that.
He's in no plight to journey far to-day.

Mort. Where is he hid?

Ors. Hard by; with robbers.

Mort. Robbers!——
Well, I'm glad on't. 'Twill suit my purpose best.   (*aside.*
—What, has he turn'd to plunder?

Ors. No; not so.
Plunder has turn'd to him. He was knock'd down,
Last night, here in the forest, flat and sprawling;
And the milk-hearted captain of our gang
Has shelter'd him.

Mort. It seems, then, thou'rt a thief?

Ors. I served in the profession: But, last night,
The scurvy rogues cashier'd me. 'Twas a plot,
To ruin a poor fellow in his calling,
And take away my means of getting bread.
I come, now, in revenge. I'll hang my comrades,
In clusters, on the forest oaks, like acorns.

Mort. Where lyes their haunt?

Ors. Give me your honour, first——

Mort. I pledge it, for your safety.

Ors. Send your officers
To the old abbey ruins; you will find
As bold a gang as e'er infested woods,
And fatten'd upon pillage.

Mort. What, so near me!
In some few minutes, then, he's mine! Ho! Winterton!
Now for his lurking place! Hope dawns again.

Remain you here! I may have work for you.   (*to* ORSON.
O! I will weave a web so intricate,
For this base insect! so entangle him!——
Why, Winterton! Thou jewel, Reputation!
Let me secure thee, bright and spotless, now,
And this weak, care-worn body's dissolution,
Will cheaply pay the purchase! Winterton!   (*Exit.*

Ors. There may be danger in my stay here. I will e'en
slink off, in the confusion I have raised. I value not the
reward. I hang my comrades, and that shall content me.
                                                  (*Exit.*

SCENE III. *A Hall in the Lodge*

Enter FITZHARDING

Fitz. Rare scuttling tow'rd! This lodge is little Babel:
And Spleen and Sickness are the household gods
In this, my brother's, castle of confusion.
The hue and cry is up! I am half tempted
To wish the game too nimble for the dogs,
That hunt him at the heels. Dishonest! Well,
I'll ne'er trust looks again. His face hangs out
A goodly sign; but all within, it seems,
Is dirty rooms, stale eggs, prick'd wine, sour beer,
Rank bacon, musty beef, and tallow candles.
I'll be deceived no more.—I'll mix with none,
In future, but the ugly: honest men,
Who can out-grin a Griffin; or the head
Carved on the prow of the good ship the Gorgon.
I'm for carbuncled, weather-beaten faces,
That frighten little children, and might serve
For knockers to hall-gates.—Now—who are you?

Enter SAMSON

Sam. Head serving-man to madam Helen, Sir.

Fitz. Well, I may talk to thee; for thou dost answer
To the description of the sort of men
I have resolved to live with.

Sam. I am proud, Sir,
To find I have your countenance.

Fitz. Can'st tell me
The news of Wilford?

Sam. He is turn'd a rogue, Sir.
An errant knave, Sir. 'Tis a rare thing, now,
To find an honest servant:—We are scarce.

Fitz. Where lyes the Abbey, where they go to seek him?
Dost know it?

Sam. Marry, do I; in the dark.
I have stood near it, many a time, in winter,
To watch the hares, by moonlight.

Fitz. A cold pastime!

Sam. Aye, Sir; 'twas killing work. I've left it off.

Fitz. Think you they will be back soon?

Sam. On the instant:
It is hard by, Sir.—Hark! I hear their horses.
They are return'd, I warrant.

Fitz. Run you, fellow.——
If Wilford's taken, send him here, to me.

Sam. Why he's a rogue, Sir. Would your worship
    stoop
To parley with a rogue!

Fitz. Friend, I will stoop
To prop a sinking man, that's call'd a rogue,
And count him innocent, 'till he's found guilty.
I learn'd it from our English laws; where Mercy
Models the weights that fill the scales of Justice;
And Charity, when Wisdom gives her sentence,
Stands by to prompt her. 'Till detection comes,
I side with the accused.

Sam. Would I had known
Your worship sooner. You're a friend, indeed!
All undiscover'd rogues are bound to pray for you:
—So, Heaven bless you!

Fitz. Well, well—bustle; stir:——
Do as I bid thee.

Sam. Aye Sir.—I shall lean

Upon your worship in my time of need.—
Heaven reward you!——Here's a friend to make!   (*Exit.*

Fitz. I have a kind of movement, still, for Wilford,
cannot conquer. What can be this charge
Sir Edward brings against him?—Should the boy
Prove guilty!—well; why should I pity guilt?
Philosophers would call me driv'ler.—Let them.
Whip a deserter, and Philosophy
Stands by, and says he merits it. That's true:—
But wherefore should Philosophy take snuff,
When the poor culprit writhes? A plague on Stoicks!
I cannot hoop my heart about with iron,
Like an old beer-butt. I would have the vessel
What some call weak:—I'd have it ooze a little.
Better compassion should be set abroach,
Till it run waste, than let a system-monger
Bung it with Logick; or a trencher cap
Bawl out his ethics on it, 'till his thunder
Turns all the liquor sour.—So! Here he comes!

Enter WILFORD

Wilf. I am inform'd it is your pleasure, Sir,
To speak with me.

Fitz. Aye, Wilford. I am sorry—
Faith, very sorry,—you and I meet thus.
How could you quit my brother thus abruptly?
Was he unkind to you?

Wilf. Most bountiful.
He made me all I am. The poor can number
His virtues thick as stars. I owe him, Sir,
A world of gratitude.

Fitz. 'Tis a new mode
Of payment you have taken. Wherefore fly?

Wilf. I was unfit to serve him, Sir.

Fitz. Unfit!

Wilf. I was unhappy, Sir. I fled a house
Where certain misery awaited me,
While I was doom'd to dwell in't.

Fitz. Misery!
What was this certain misery?

Wilf. Your pardon,—
I never will divulge.

Fitz. Indeed!

Wilf. No, never.
Pray do not press me. All that I can say
Is, that I have a strong, and rooted reason,
Which has resolved me. 'Twere impossible
I should be tranquil here. I feel it, Sir,
A duty to myself to quit this roof.

Fitz. Harkye, young man. This smacks of mystery;
And now looks foully. Truth, and Innocence,
Walk round the world in native nakedness;
But Guilt is cloak'd.

Wilf. Whate'er the prejudice
My conduct conjures up, I must submit.

Fitz. 'Twere better now you conjured up your friends:
For I must tell you——No there is no need.
You learn'd it, doubtless, on the way, and know
The danger you now stand in.

Wilf. Danger, Sir!
What? How? I have learn'd nothing, Sir; my guides
Drag'd me in silence hither.

Fitz. Then 'tis fit
I put you on your guard. It grieves me, Wilford,
To say there is a heavy charge against you,
Which, as I gather, may affect your life.

Wilf. Mine!—O, good Heaven!

Fitz. Pray be calm:—for, soon,
Here, in the face of all his family,
My brother will accuse you.

Wilf. He!—What, He!
He accuse *me*! O monstrous! O, look down
You who can read men's hearts!——A charge against me!
Ha, ha! I'm innocent! I'm innocent!

(*much agitated.*)

Fitz. Collect your firmness. You will need it all.

Wilf. I shall, indeed! I pray you tell me, Sir,
What is the charge?

Fitz. I do not know it's purport.
I would not hear on't: for on my voice rests
The issue of this business;—and a judge
Should come unbiass'd to his office. Wilford,
Were twenty brothers waiting my award,
You should have even, and impartial justice.

Wilf. O, you are just! I would all men were so!

Fitz. I hope most men are so. Rally your thoughts.
When you are call'd upon, if Truth will serve you,
Sketch out your story with her chaste, bold pencil:
If Truth should fail you, Wilford, even take
The fairest colours human art can mix,
To give a glow to plausibility.
'Tis self-defence; and 'tis allow'd, when man
Must battle it, with all the world against him.
——Heaven bless you, boy!—that is, I mean—pshaw!
    plague!
—Farewell! and may you prosper!   (*Exit.*

Wilf. Then, all my youthful hopes are blighted in the
bud! The breath of my powerful persecutor will wither
them. Let me recall my actions.—My breast is unclog'd with
crime. This charge is to be open;—in the eye of the world;
of the laws.—Then, why should I fear? I am native of a
happy soil where justice guards equally the life of its poorest
and richest inhabitant. Let him inflict his menaces upon me
in secret. Let him torture my mind and body; he shall not,
cannot, touch my good name.

Enter BARBARA

Barb. O, Wilford! (*falls on his neck.*)

Wilf. Barbara! at such a time, too!

Barb. To be brought back, thus, Wilford! and to go
away without seeing me; without thinking of me!

Wilf. It was not so.—I was hastening to your cottage,
Barbara, when a ruffian, in the forest, encounter'd and
wounded me.

Barb. Wounded you!

Wilf. Be not alarm'd. 'Tis not, as I thought yester-night, of moment. One of his party took me to the Abbey ruins, and gave me timely succour.

Barb. And, was it so! was it indeed so, Wilford?

Wilf. Aye, Barbara. When I was drag'd hither, the whole troop escaped, or they had vouch'd for the truth on't.

Barb. I would they had not escaped. For all here say that you had fled to join them.

Wilf. What! join with robbers! what next shall I be charged with!

Barb. Bethink you, Wilford—the time is short: I know your heart is good; but——

Wilf. But what? Can you suspect it, too, Barbara!

Barb. O! mine is so link'd with it, that I would follow you through beggary, through prisons, Wilford.

Wilf. Prisons! The sound, now, makes me shudder!

Barb. If in a hasty moment you have done ought to wrong Sir Edward, throw yourself on his mercy;—sue for pardon.

Wilf. For pardon!—I shall go mad! Pardon! I am innocent.—Heaven knows I am innocent.

Barb. Heaven be thank'd—The family is all summon'd. O, Wilford! my spirits sink within me.

Wilf. (*aside*) I am, now, but a sorry comforter.—Come, Barbara; be tranquil. You see I am so. Don't——don't you, Barbara? (*agitated*)

Enter a SERVANT

Serv. You must attend in the next room.

Wilf. What, Walter, is it you? Pray tell me if—

Serv. Do not question me. I hold no discourse with any of your stamp.

Wilf. Your tone is strangely changed on the sudden. What have I done?

Serv. You are going to be tried. That's enough for me.

Wilf. I might rather claim your pity on that score, Walter.

Serv. What, pity a man that's going to be tried? O, monstrous!

Wilf. Well, fare you well. I will not upbraid you, Walter. You have many in the world to countenance you. Blacken well your neighbour, and nine in ten are in haste to cry shame upon him, ere he has time, or opportunity, to wipe off the accusation. I follow you.

Serv. Do so.   (*Exit.*

Barb. O, Wilford!

Wilf. Be of good cheer. I go arm'd in honesty, Barbara. I can bear every thing. Every thing, save making you the partner of my misfortunes. That, Barbara———I am sure you love me———that would give me a pang which would ———Farewell!   (*Exit.*

Barb. Alas! I tremble for his safety! should they tear him from me!———

SONG

BARBARA

Down by the river there grows a green willow;
   Sing all for my true love! my true love, O!
I'll weep out the night there, the bank for my pillow;
   And all for my true love, my true love, O!
When bleak blows the wind, and tempests are beating,
I'll count all the clouds, as I mark them retreating,
For true lovers' joys, well a-day! are as fleeting.
     Sing, O for my true love, &c.

Maids come, in pity, when I am departed!
   Sing all for my true love, &c.
When dead, on the bank, I am found broken-hearted,
   And all for my true love, &c.
Make me a grave, all while the wind's blowing,
Close to the stream, where my tears once were flowing,
And over my corse keep the green willow growing.
     'Tis all for my true love, &c.

(*Exit.*

SCENE IV. *An Apartment in the Lodge*

FITZHARDING, WILFORD, *and various domesticks,*
discover'd.—To them enter ADAM WINTERTON

Fitz. Is not Sir Edward coming, Adam?
Wint. Aye, Sir.—
But he is grievous ill.—Since Wilford came,
He had another fit.—But he'll be here.
Ah, boy! that I should live to see this day!
I have a merry heart no longer, now.
Wilf. Good man! you have been ever kind to me.
Wint. Heav'n send you may prove honest! Heaven send it!
—Here comes Sir Edward. Would that I had died
Two reigns ago!

Enter Sir EDWARD MORTIMER

Fitz. Now, brother.—You look pale,
And faint with sickness.
Wint. Here's a chair, your worship.
Mort. No matter.—To our business, brother. Wilford,
You may well guess the struggle I endure
To place you here the mark of accusation.
I gave you ample warning: Caution'd you,
When many might have scourged: and, even now,
While I stand here to crush you,—aye, to crush you,—
My heart bleeds drops of pity for your youth,
Whose rashness plucks the red destruction down,
And pulls the bolt upon you.
Wilf. You know best
The movements of your heart, sir. Man is blind,
And cannot read them: but there is a Judge,
To whose all-seeing eye our inmost thoughts
Lye open. Think to him you, now, appeal.—
Omniscience keeps Heaven's register;
And, soon or late, when Time unfolds the book,
Our trembling souls must answer to the record,
And meet their due reward, or punishment.

Fitz. Now, to the point, I pray you.

Mort. Thus it is, then.
I do suspect—By heaven, the story lingers
Like poison on my tongue—but he will force it—

Fitz. What is it you suspect?

Mort. ——That he has rob'd me.

Wilf. Rob'd! I! O, horrible!

Fitz. Not yet—not yet.
Pray tell me brother—I will be impartial;—
But I am somewhat moved.—Pray tell me, brother,
How ground you this suspicion?

Mort. Briefly, thus.——
You may have noticed, in my library,
A chest (WILFORD *starts*)—You see he changes at the word.

Wilf. And well I may!   (*aside.*

Mort. Where I have told you, brother,
The writings which concern our family,
With jewels, cash, and other articles,
Of no mean value, were deposited.

Fitz. You oftentimes have said so.

Mort. Yesterday,
Chance call'd me, suddenly, away; I left
The key in't—but as suddenly return'd;
And found this Wilford, this young man, whose state,
Whose orphan state, met pity in my house,
'Till pity grew to friendship,—him I found,
Fix'd o'er the chest, upon his knees, intent,
As, now, I think, on plunder; tinging theft
Still blacker with ingratitude; and rifling
The easy fool who shelter'd him. Confusion
Shook his young joints, as he let fall the lid,
And gave me back the key.

Fitz. Did you not search
Your papers on the instant?

Mort. No:—for, first,
(Habit so long had fix'd my confidence)
I deem'd it boyish curiosity;—
But told him this would meet my further question:

And, at that moment, came a servant in,
To say you were arrived. He must have mark'd
Our mix'd emotion.

   Fitz. Is that servant here?

   Serv. 'Twas I, Sir.

   Mort. Was it you? Well, saw you ought
To challenge your attention?

   Serv. Sir, I did.

Wilford was pale, and trembling; and our master
Gave him a look as if 'twould pierce him through;
And cried, 'Remember.'—Then he trembled more,
And we both quitted him.

   Mort. When first we met,
You found me somewhat ruffled.

   Fitz. 'Tis most true.

   Mort. But somewhat more when, afterwards, I saw
Wilford conversing with you—like a snake,
Sun'd by your looks, and basking in your favour.
I bade him quit the room, with indignation,
And wait my coming in the library.

   Fitz. I witness'd that, with wonder.

   Mort. O, good brother!
You little thought, while you so gently school'd me,
In the full flow of your benevolence,
For my harsh bearing tow'rd him, on what ground
That harshness rested. I had made my search,
In the brief interval of absence from you,
And found my property had vanish'd.

   Fitz. Well——
You met him in the library?

   Mort. O never
Can he forget that solemn interview.

   Wilf. Aye, speak to that:—it was a solemn interview.

   Mort. Observe, he does acknowledge that we met.
Guilt was my theme:—he cannot now deny it.

   Wilf. It was a theme of—No.   (*checking himsel*

   Mort. He pleaded innocence:
While every word he spake belied his features,

nd mock'd his protestation. I restrain'd
he chastisement he fear'd; nor wou'd I blazon
he wrong I could not fix; and subject, thus,
y general inquiry, all the guiltless
o foul suspicion. That suspicion lay
ost heavily on him; but the big cloud
f anger he had gather'd burst not on him,
a vengeance, to o'erwhelm him: chill it drop'd,
ut kindly, as the dew, in admonition;
ike tears of fathers o'er a wayward child,
hen love enforces them to ruggedness.

Fitz. What said you to him?

Mort. 'Regulate your life,
n future, better. I, now, spare your youth;
ut dare not to proceed. All I exact,
Tis a soft penance)—that you tarry here;
My eye your guard, my house your gentle prison,
My bounty be your chains. Attempt not flight;
light ripens all my doubt to certainty,
nd justice to the world unlocks my tongue.'—
e fled, and I arraign him.

Fitz. Trust me, brother,
his charge is staggering. Yet accidents
ometimes combine to cast a shade of doubt
pon the innocent. May it be so here!
ere is his trunk: 'twas brought here at my order.
is fit that it be search'd.

Mort. O, that were needless.
e were a shallow villain that would trust
is freight of plunder to so frail a bottom.
chool-boys, who strip the orchard of its fruit,
onceal their thievery better.

Fitz. Yet 'tis found,
uch negligence is often link'd with guilt.
Take note—I say not yet that he is guilty;
ut I scarce heard of crafty villain, yet,
ho did not make some blot in his foul game,
hat lookers-on have thought him blind, and mad,

It was so palpable.—'Tis rarely otherwise:
Heaven's hand is in it, brother: Providence
Marks guilt, as 'twere, with a fatuity.——
Adam, do you inspect it.   (*to* WINTERTON.

   Wilf. Here's the key—
E'en take it, freely.—You'll find little there
I value; save a locket, which my mother
Gave me upon her death-bed; and she added
Her blessing to't. Perhaps, her spirit now
Is grieving for my injuries.

   Wint. (*after opening the trunk*). O, mercy!

   Fitz. How now? What's there?

   Wint. As I'm a wretched man,
The very watch my good old master wore!
And, here, my lady's jewels!

   Wilf. I am innocent.
Just Heaven, hear me!

   Fitz. I must hear you, now.
What can you say?—Oh! Wilford.

   Wilf. Give me breath.
Let me collect myself. First this. (*falls on his knees*)
              May sleep
Ne'er close my burning eyes; may conscience gnaw me;
May engines wrench my entrails from their seat,
And whirl them to the winds before my face,
If I know aught of this!

   Fitz. Make it appear so.—But look there; look there!
                       (*pointing to the trunk*)

   Wilf. Heap circumstance upon me; multiply
Charge upon charge; pile seeming fact on fact;
Still I maintain my innocence. Look at me;
Are these the throes of guilt? Are these convulsions
Of a poor, helpless, friendless, wretched boy,
The struggles of a villain?—One thing more:
I here aver it—to his face aver it—
He knows—Yes, he—Yes, my accuser knows,
I merit not his charge.
           (*a general expression of indignation*

Wint. O! fie on't, fie!

Fitz. Wilford, take heed! A base attempt to blacken
An injured master, will but plunge you deeper.

Wilf. I know what I am doing. I repeat it:
Will die repeating it. Sir Edward Mortimer
Is conscious of my innocence.

Mort. Proceed——
Look at these proofs, and talk.—Unhappy boy,
Thy tongue can do me little mischief, now.

Wilf. Do you not know——

Mort. What?

Wilf. ——'Tis no matter, sir.
But I could swear——

Mort. Nay, Wilford, pause a while.
Reflect that oaths are sacred. Weigh the force
Of these asseverations. Mark it well.
*I swear, by all the ties that bind a man,
Divine or human!* Think on that, and shudder.

Wilf. The very words I utter'd! I am tongue-tied. (*aside.*)

Fitz. Wilford, if there be aught that you can urge,
To clear yourself, advance it.

Wilf. O, I could!
I could say much, but must not.—No, I will not.
Do as you please.—I have no friend—no witness,
Save my accuser. Did he not—pray ask him—
Did he not vaunt his wiles could ruin me?
Did he not menace, in his pride of power,
To blast my name, and crush my innocence?

Fitz. What do you answer, Sir?

Mort. I answer—No.—
More were superfluous, when a criminal
Opposes empty volubility
To circumstantial charge. A stedfast brow
Repels not fact, nor can invalidate
These dumb, but damning witnesses, before him.

(pointing to the trunk.)

Wilf. By the just Pow'er that rules us, I am ignorant
How they came there!—but 'tis my firm belief,

You placed them there, to sink me.

   Fitz. O, too much!
You steel men's hearts against you! Death and shame!
It rouses honest choler. Call the officers.—
He shall meet punishment.   (SERVANTS *going.*)

   Mort. Hold! pray you, hold.
Justice has, thus far, struggled with my pity,
To do an act of duty to the world.
I would unmask a hypocrite; lay bare
The front of guilt, that men may see, and shun it:
'Tis done—and I will, now, proceed no further.
I would not hurt the serpent, but to make
The serpent hurtless. He has lost his sting.
Let him depart, and freely.

   Fitz. Look ye, brother.
This shall not be.—Had he proved innocent,
My friendship had been doubled; you well know
I have been partial to him—but this act
Is so begrimed with black, ungrateful malice,
That I insist on justice. Fly, knaves! run,
And let him be secured. [*Exeunt* SERVANTS.] You tarry here.
                          (*to* WILFORD.)

   Mort. I will not have it thus.

   Fitz. You must—You shall—
'Tis weak else. Oons! I trust I have as much
Of good, straight-forward pity, as may serve;
But, to turn dove—to sit still, and be peck'd at,
It is too tame. His insolence tops all!
Does not this rouse you, too?—Look on these jewels.———
Look at this picture.—'Twas our mother's: Stay,
Let me inspect this nearer. What are here?
Parchments————   (*inspecting the trunk.*)

   Mort. O, look no further—They are deeds,
Which, in his haste, no doubt, he crowded there,
Not knowing what—to look o'er at his leisure—
Family deeds—They all were in my chest.

   Wilf. O, 'tis deep laid!—These, too, to give a colour!
                           (*aside.*)

 Fitz. What have we here? I have your leave, good
  brother,
As arbiter in this. Here is a paper
Of curious enfolding—slipt, as 'twere
By chance, within another. This may be
Of note upon his trial.——What's this drops?
A knife, it seems!

 Mort. What!   (*starting.*)

 Fitz. Marks of blood upon it.

 Mort. Touch it not. Throw it back!—bury it—sink it!
Oh, carelessness and haste! Give me that paper.
Darkness and hell!—Give back the paper.

[MORTIMER *attempts to snatch it*; WILFORD *runs between*
 the two brothers, falls on his knees, and prevents him,
 holding FITZHARDING.]

 Wilf. (*rapidly*) No.
I see—I see!—Preserve it. You are judge!—
My innocence, my life, rests on it!

 Mort. Devils,
Foil me at my own game!—Fate!—Ha, ha, ha!
Sport, Lucifer!——He struck me——

[MORTIMER *is fainting, and falling*; WILFORD *runs and*
 catches him.]

 Wilf. I'll support him.——
Read! read! read!

 Fitz. What is this?—My mind misgives me!
It is my brother's hand!—*To die before me!*
What can this mean?——[*reads.*]
Narrative of my murder of——Oh, great Heav'n!
'If by some chance my guilt should be disclosed,
'May this contribute to redeem the wreck
'Of my lost honour!'—I am horror-struck!

 Wilf. Plain, plain!——Stay! he revives.

 Mort. What has been——soft!
I have been wand'ring with the damn'd, sure.—Brother!—
And—aye—'tis Wilford. Oh! thought flashes on me

Like Lightning. I am brain-scorch'd. Give me leave.
I will speak—Soon I will——a little yet——
Come hither, boy.—Wrong'd boy! O Wilford, Wilford!
　　　　　(*bursts into tears, and falls on* WILFORD'*s neck*

Wilf. Be firm, Sir; pray be firm! my heart bleeds f
　　　you—
Warms for you! Oh! all your former charity
To your poor boy, is in my mind.—Still, still,
I see my benefactor.

Mort. Well, I will—
I will be firm. One struggle, and 'tis over.
I have most foully wrong'd you! Ere I die—
And I feel death-struck—let me haste to make
Atonement.—Brother, note. The jewels,
Yes, and that paper—Heaven and accident
Ordain'd it so!—were placed—Curse on my flesh,
To tremble thus!—were placed there by my hand.

Fitz. O, mercy on me!

Mort. More. I fear'd this boy;
He knew my secret; and I blacken'd him,
That, should he e'er divulge the fatal story,
His word might meet no credit. Infamy
Will brand my mem'ry for't: Posterity,
Whose breath I made my god, will keep my shame
Green in her damning record. Oh! I had—
I had a heart o'erflowing with good thoughts
For all mankind! One fatal, fatal turn,
Has poison'd all! Where is my honour, now?
To die!—To have my ashes trampled on,
By the proud foot of scorn! Polluted! Hell—
Who dares to mock my guilt? Is't you—or you?
—Wrack me that grinning fiend! Damnation!
Who spits upon my grave? I'll stab again—
I'll——Oh!　　　　　　　　　　　　　　(*falls*

Fitz. This rives my heart in twain. Why, brother
　　brother!
His looks are ghastly.

Enter SERVANT

Serv. Sir, the officers.

Fitz. Away, knave! Send them hence—the boy is innocent.

Serv. What, Wilford?

Fitz. Aye. Tell it your fellows. Hence!—
ou shall know more anon. Send in some help—
our master's ill o' the sudden. Send some help!

　　　　　　　　　　　　　　(*Exit* SERVANT.

Wilf. 'Twere best to raise him, Sir.

Fitz. Soft, who comes here?

Enter HELEN

Helen. Where is he? Ill! and on the ground! Oh, Mor-
　　timer!
h, Heaven! my Mortimer. O, raise him.—Gently.
peak to me, love. He cannot!

Mort. Helen—'Twas I that———
　　　　　(*he struggles to speak, but appears unable to utter.*)

Helen. Oh, he's convulsed!

Fitz. Say nothing. We must lead him to his chamber.
eseech you to say nothing! Come, good lady.

　　　　　(FITZHARDING *and* HELEN *lead* MORTIMER *out.*)

Enter BARBARA, *on the opposite side*

Barb. O, Wilford! I have flown to you! You are innocent.
-The whole house now has it, you are innocent. Thank
eaven! Speak; tell me—How—how was it, dear, dear
Vilford?

Wilf. I cannot tell you now, Barbara. Another time: But
is so.—I cannot speak now.—

Barb. Nor I, scarce, for joy. See! hither come your fel-
ws, to greet you. I am so happy!

Enter SERVANTS, *&c. &c. &c.*

Servants. Joy! Wilford!

Wilf. Peace, peace, I pray you. Our master is taken ill:
o ill, my fellows, that I fear me, he stands in much danger.

That you rejoice in my acquittal, I perceive, and thank you. Sir Edward's brother will explain further to you: I cannot. But believe this:—Heaven, to whose eye the dark movements of guilt are manifest, will ever watch over, and succour the innocent, in their extremity. Clamour not now your congratulations to me, I entreat you: Rather, let the slow, still voice of gratitude be lifted up to Providence, for that care she ever bestows upon those deserving her protection!

FINALE

Where Gratitude shall breathe the note,
    To white-robed Mercy's throne,
Bid the mild strain on æther float,
    A soft and dulcet tone.

Sweet, sweet and clear the accents raise,
While mellow flutes shall swell the song of praise.
        Melody! Melody!
    A soft and dulcet melody!

Where fever droops his burning head;
Where sick men languish on their bed;
        Around let ev'ry accent be,
            Harmony! Harmony!
        A soft and dulcet harmony!

THE END

PRINTED IN GREAT BRITAIN
AT THE UNIVERSITY PRESS, OXFORD
BY VIVIAN RIDLER
PRINTER TO THE UNIVERSITY